FINANCIAL

PEACE OF MIND

FROM THE WORD

Biblical Guidance in Daily Doses...

Stan Hutchinson

Volume I

FINANCIAL PEACE OF MIND FROM THE WORD

Copyright © by Stan Hutchinson
Published by: BISCA Publishing
                149 Ashford Park
                Macon GA   31210

Cover design: Leyna Marie

First Printing: 2014
Printed in the United States of America

ISBN-13: 978-0615976952 (BISCA Publishing)
ISBN-10: 0615976956

Shepherd Care Orphanage
Eku, Delta State, Nigeria
West Africa

Dedicated to the orphans and widows at Shepherd Care Orphanage from whom I have learned to appreciate the wealth with which God has blessed those of us in the United States of America.

Also, to Chaplain Richard Obarorakpor and his wife, Funke, who originally had the vision for Shepherd Care Orphanage. For all the unselfish service that you have rendered, the untold sacrifices that you have made, and a faith in God that is contagious to those around you, **THANK YOU!**

All revenues (100%) derived from the sales of *Financial PEACE of MIND from the WORD* will go for the support and maintenance of the ministry of Shepherd Care Orphanage and Bender International Shepherd Care Academy, the school currently under construction on the orphanage grounds. As Chaplain Richard is fond of saying,

"To God Be the Glory!"

Financial PEACE of MIND from the WORD is a well written guide for not only today's Christians, but for anyone who wants to learn about true financial security in a tumultuous world.
Dr. Howard Wasdin
New York Times bestselling author of *SEAL Team Six-Memoirs of an Elite Navy SEAL Sniper*

Financial PEACE of MIND from the WORD is chock-full of much-needed daily doses of spiritual and financial wisdom designed to sharpen your mind and quicken your soul. Stan, make no mistake, you've knocked it out of the park with this invaluable tool of balanced, biblical stewardship for the Body of Christ!
Todd L. Shuler
Internationally known management consultant & speaker
Amazon bestselling author of *The Well-Watered Life: Experiencing God's Goodness in the Desert Places of Your Life.*

Financial PEACE of MIND from the WORD is a daily reminder that our treasure is connected to our heart. These devotions challenge us to view finances through the lens of scripture, and give an accurate picture of what it means to be a biblical steward. This is a great resource for anyone who wants an accurate perspective on stewardship.
Dr. Lee Sheppard
Senior Pastor
Mabel White Baptist Church, Macon GA

Stan really hits the mark; he combines timeless Biblical principles with current and easy to understand examples of how to live in God's financial freedom. If we could muster the courage to follow this plan nationally, we would truly be the "Land of the Free."
U.S. Rep. Kristi Noem S.D.

Financial PEACE of MIND from the WORD is an excellent study in spiritual truth regarding our finances. Chock-full of relevant stories, it combines biblical insight and practical application with your own opportunity for personal reflection. If you are looking for an easy-to-digest daily guide to get you on track toward victorious financial living or simply keep you focused on what you are already doing right, this is the book for you.
Julie Hadden,
As seen on *The Biggest Loser*,
Author of *Fat Chance*

Since having received Stan's *Financial PEACE of MIND from the WORD*, I have taken to read it daily. Although I personally have shepherded my friends, family and clients with biblical counsel for over 25 years I am finding fresh new insights into God's word for Biblical Life and Financial Stewardship. In the end, it's not what God wants *from* us, it's what He wants *for* us and Stan helps us see this in his writings!

Jerry Black
President, Legacy Planning Group, Inc.
Suwanee, GA

One of the strategies of the enemy is to plague you with financial handicap in order to arrest your potential. Resist by taking on the Armor of Warfare against him. When you read through these "daily nuggets" with diligence, Stan Hutchinson, powerfully - but carefully, shows how to open the mind of your spirit to the philosophies of handling finances God's way based on Biblical truths. These daily devotions, written under the in-depth revelation of God's Word, offer you a "definition" of financial freedom that teaches you to build your life on God's financial principles so that you can completely trust God to guide and provide for you all the days of your life.

Chaplain Richard Obarorakpor
Pastor, Hospital Chaplain, President & CEO of Shepherd Care International Ministries in Eku, Delta State, Nigeria, Africa.

My first introduction to Stan Hutchinson was when he was a Sunday school teacher in a department I led. I found him to be a true "man of the Word." Later, after I took a pastorate, Stan again came into my life when he made me aware of Financial Peace University®. As a certified instructor Stan convinced me of my congregation's need for this information. When I heard Stan was doing some writing I knew it was going to have his passions in the forefront. Sure enough *Financial PEACE of MIND from the WORD* is all about the Word and the peace it brings when its principles are applied. This is a must-read book to keep close by so the truths contained within can be applied daily.

Dr. Norm Yukers
Senior Pastor
Pine Forest Baptist Church, Macon GA

Having known Stan Hutchinson for over 10 years, I know of no finer man. He has an unquenchable desire to see others live according to God's Word. Likewise, Stan desires to teach people what the Bible says about money, talents, and obedience. His latest work, *Financial PEACE of MIND from the WORD*, is the product of years of intense Bible study that couples scripture with lessons Stan learned living real life. Stan's book is "must reading" for anyone who can use some fiscal assistance and direction, practical application with all-things financial, or for those who need affirmation that they are doing things financially and biblically correct. I hope you enjoy Stan's work as much as I have.

Joe S. McDaniel
Pastor and author of *31206: The Boys of Willingham High*

Four words best describe Stan Hutchinson, "A man of integrity!" This book is a MUST for anyone's library!

Rev. Glynn Grantham
Retired A/G minister
Warner Robins, GA

Stan Hutchinson mines God's Word to compile into one book, *Financial PEACE of MIND from the WORD*, daily reminders that encourage and convict us. He drills down with precision to the heart of modern day idolatry, the love of money, with biblical admonitions that challenge and remind us of that vanity. This book, ingested daily, like a baby aspirin, is good for our heart toward God.

Sonny Perdue
Governor, State of Georgia (2003-2011)

ACKNOWLEDGMENTS

Each of our lives is a composite of people who have impacted us plus the experiences we have undergone, both good and bad. As I have grown older, I find myself looking back and assessing some of those impacts. While the list can get lengthy rather quickly, a few relationships stand out as benchmarks.

Three of those benchmarks appear at the top of my list as mentors that have definitely and permanently shaped my life. We all need mentors in our lives. I was fortunate to have three parties that influenced me in my early years. Additionally, I have had the good fortune of maintaining friendship with each of these for decades:

- B.H. Claxton: my high school agriculture teacher spoke wisdom into my life when I was but a teenage in need of direction. Thank you, Mr. Claxton, for being a friend for more than 50 years.

- Fred & Odell Windham: I always thought there was nothing you could not do, and to this day, I am not sure that I was wrong. Thank you for wisdom and direction throughout my life.

- Lee (deceased) & Martha Black: although we did not know it at the time, you mentored the importance of "family" as the fundamental structure for success. I shall always be thankful for your investing yourselves into my life.

- Marci Hutchinson: thank you for being an understanding spouse who shows respect, even when I do not deserve it - for the encouragement to keep writing, though, in my mind, I am not a writer (God must have a sense of humor).

- Linda Kile: for being a friend of a magnitude that most never experience. Thank you for proofing manuscripts and giving me invaluable feedback.

- Nancy Dumas: for being YOU! You are always there to assist with whatever is needed. Thank you for your assistance in helping make this project to come full circle.

- Jo Ann Josey: for igniting the spark needed by pushing me off dead center to make this project happen.

FOREWORD

"Common sense ain't common," Will Rogers quipped, but all of us would agree that he had far more of it than most. He had some wonderful and humorous insights on money like, *"Too many people spend money they haven't earned to buy things they don't want to impress people that they don't like."* I know people like that who have bought things and then never even taken them out of the box. These possessions just sit in the basement or on a closet shelf collecting dust.

Will Rogers also spoke about laying aside money for a rainy day, *"The time to save is now. When a dog gets a bone, he doesn't go out and make a down payment on a bigger bone. He buries the one he's got."* He reminded people that, *"The quickest way to double your money is to fold it in half and put it in your back pocket."*

I wish Will Rogers had said much more about money in his folksy, humorous way because people sure need it. Money issues are one of the most common contributors to divorce. As a physician, I've seen financial problems lead to incredible stress, hypertension, heart attacks, strokes, death and even suicide. Almost every time, the problem was not that the person couldn't make enough money, but simply that they were so terrible managing what they had. They spent too much. They took on too much debt. They made foolish investment risks. They built a house they couldn't afford to pay the mortgage on. They laid nothing aside for emergencies or in case they lost their job. Thus, they ended up paying an enormous price for their foolishness, both psychologically and physically. It affected their relationships with their friends, their family and, for some, it bankrupted their soul.

We all need more common sense and you will find it in *Financial PEACE of MIND from the WORD*. One reason you can learn from this book is because it is based on what God, the author of common sense, inspired the authors of the Bible to write. God's Word is full of sound advice on money issues because God knows how important this issue is in the lives of His children. Unfortunately, most of His children can't quote one verse about money, and if they even know one, they misquote it and say, *"Money is the root of all evil."* The Bible actually says, "The <u>love</u> of money is the root of all evil" (**1 Timothy 6:10**, KJV).

The second reason you can learn from this devotional is that financial issues are a chronic disease for almost all who suffer this malaise. There is no magic pill or quick "read this book" solution. We have to first change our understanding of how to handle money and then we have to change the habits that developed from our deformed worldview of finances. Bad money thinking and bad money behaviors are chronic problems that require ongoing, long-term treatment.

Until now, there hasn't been any good medicine to give. That is where Stan Hutchinson has broken new ground with a daily devotional book on financial issues. You and I will both benefit from a year of daily doses of God's principles on money to cure the disease that plagues us. You won't believe what fifteen minutes of reading and reflecting on God's teaching will do for you!

Lastly, your daily dose of common sense will be given to you in a wonderful palatable format. This medicine tastes good. Why? Because this devotional book was not written by a so-called financial expert with multiple degrees who heads a national organization. It was written by someone just like you and me, someone who learned to apply God's principles in the school of hard knocks.

Stan was not born with a silver spoon in his mouth. He began working at the young age of ten because he came from a very poor family with eight children. He had to find his own money to go to college and earn his engineering degree. He saved, planned ahead and invested well simply by following God's good advice. Friends and even people he didn't know personally noticed his peace of mind and good money management habits. They began asking for down to earth advice on money management or about how to get out of the money mess they were already in.

Stan explains God's principles and illustrates them with stories and analogies that make them come alive. In a folksy way, he unfolds truth, changes individuals' worldviews, and teaches good money handling habits. As a result, your life will change, your stress will be lessened, your relationships will improve, and you will have financial peace of mind.

This book is just what the doctor ordered. There is no doubt that reading this book about money is the best investment you can make!

David Stevens, MD, MA (Ethics)
CEO – Christian Medical & Dental Associations

INTRODUCTION

Money may very well be the most misunderstood commodity in the history of mankind. Although it is not the most important thing in life, it is so significant that nothing can take its place. In view of its importance, one would think that great effort would be expended by everyone to gain the utmost knowledge about money and its far reaching impact upon our lives. Sadly, this is not the case. We live in a culture filled with myths about money. These myths have been represented as truth so often that practically everyone has bought into lifestyles that lead to confusion, controversy, discontentment, stress, home disruption, and for many, financial ruin.

Money, while being a necessity, must be viewed and kept in its proper perspective. Although many people attempt to attain peace of mind by majoring upon the acquisition of wealth, they ultimately wind up in a state of emptiness and disillusionment. There are four essentials that must be interwoven in order for one to experience real peace and contentment. Family relationships, money, time, along with applied biblical guidance work together to give true peace of mind. Note the cover of this book portrays these fours elements. Attention must be devoted to all of these if one expects to experience real contentment and peace.

Almost everyone agrees that the Bible contains great advice about life, from improving your marriage to getting along with your boss at work. But does the Bible really say much about money? Does it really give us practical advice that we can apply to our own lives in today's world?

The Good News is YES! Absolutely! The Bible is as relevant and helpful today as when it was written. The Bible actually says much more about wealth, money and possessions than most of us are willing to hear. Did you know financial issues are mentioned in the Bible over 2,200 times? God must be pretty serious about this subject to talk about it that much.

In fact, Jesus says in **Luke 16:11**, *"So if you have not been trustworthy in handling worldly wealth, who will trust you with true riches?"* It appears from this verse that God uses money as a "test" of our management and stewardship skills before entrusting us with spiritual things (the true riches).

This initiative takes a different scripture on a daily basis that deals with money, riches, possessions or finances and considers what God has told us in His Word and how it relates to us today. There is more written in the Bible about this topic than anything else. Jesus repeatedly used the topics of money and possessions in His teaching ministry. He apparently knew the importance of money and yet in this modern age, we continually sidestep the subject. It is due time that we consider what God has to say about managing money!

It is my hope that you will be challenged by these daily doses from the Bible and the thoughts that I present from a layman's viewpoint. I do not ask or expect you to endorse my exposition without question. My aim is to entice you to study God's Word for yourself and allow the Holy Spirit to speak to you on the important subjects dealing with money.

People do not change their opinions and beliefs overnight. It takes convincing evidence over a long period of time to experience real change. I challenge you to stick with this study for the course of a year. If you do, I am certain that you will discover that much, if not most, of the teaching on this subject by our schools, businesses, society, and even the church does not align with the Bible. Commit to for an entire year and I will assure you that your beliefs and attitudes about money will change.

This is the first of two volumes. It covers the first 6 months of the year. Volume II will be released shortly and will cover 1 July through 31 December. Invite a friend to walk this journey alongside you. Open your mind and heart and allow the Holy Spirit to speak His message to you!

Let the journey begin...

The rich rule over the poor,

and the borrower is slave to the lender.

Proverbs 22:7 (NIV)

☐

JANUARY 1

Proverbs 21:25 *The desire of the lazy man kills him, For his hands refuse to labor.*

Over the course of the past year, I read several books about the younger generation commonly referred to as "millennials." To say the least, the younger generation processes information differently than those of us who are over the hill. Therefore in an effort to more fully understand the thinking process of the younger generation, I stepped out into this reading endeavor. In my mind, I have come to one undeniable conclusion: the millennials are exactly what we have brought them up and trained them to be ...nothing more, nothing less!

When we look back and reflect, it is our nature first and foremost to justify our preferences and habits as a baseline by which we measure all others. Example: the millennials are not as responsible as my generation. We apply this rationale to the secular as well as spiritual areas of life. To assume that today's generation is the same as that of 20-30 years ago would be grossly incorrect. Let me hasten to add that there are always exceptions; I speak in generalizations. The younger generation is much different than when I was their age. I started my married life when I was only 20 years of age. To clarify however, when I took on the responsibility of a family at age 20, I already had 10 years of working experience. From age 10, I worked and provided all spending money, clothes, entertainment and dating expenses, car, insurance, gas, and even all college tuition. I came from a family of eight children. Our parents fed us and gave us a place to live. That was all they could afford. Beyond that, it was up to us to fend for ourselves. We learned the work-reward principle early in life. In most cases, that is not true in today's culture.

If you are blessed to have young children living at home, the beginning of a new year is a great time to reflect upon scriptures relating to work and labor. As previously stated, the millennials are exactly what we parents have trained them to be. In fact, the same can be said about every generation regardless of what they may be called. The generation into which your children fall will ultimately be exactly what you train them to be. In other words, any given generation is not to be blamed nor credited for what they have become; the credit or blame, as the case may be, goes to the generation of the parents, those who actually did the training. That's a scary thought isn't it?

Now is a good time to get back to the basics of scripture in training our young people the value of work ...yes physical labor. I am not proposing child sweat shops, but parents have the responsibility to teach their children the value of labor. Here are just a few scriptures relating to the subject:

- **Proverbs 10:16** *"The labor of the righteous leads to life, The wages of the wicked to sin."*
- **Proverbs 12:24** *"The hand of the diligent will rule, But the lazy man will be put to forced labor."*
- **Proverbs 13:11** *"Wealth gained by dishonesty will be diminished, But he who gathers by labor will increase."*
- **Proverbs 14:23** *"In all labor there is profit, But idle chatter leads only to poverty."*
- **1 Corinthians 3:8** *"Now he who plants and he who waters are one, and each one will receive his own reward according to his own labor."*
- **Ephesians 4:28** *"Let him who stole steal no longer, but rather let him labor, working with his hands what is good, that he may have something to give him who has need."*

These are but a few scriptures on the subject of labor. As already stated, the next generation is going to be exactly what we train them to be. Oh, by the way, here is one for your comfort: **Matthew 11:28** *"Come to Me, all you who labor and are heavy laden, and I will give you rest."*

Reflections...

JANUARY 2

Proverbs 14:4 *Where no oxen are, the trough is clean; But much increase comes by the strength of an ox.*

As we have just come through another Christmas, you no doubt heard the story of the birth of Jesus in a stable. Unfortunately there are few today who have actually had the opportunity of performing chores in the stables. At the best of times, stables are messy, if you know what I mean. In other words, livestock are not housebroken, so when nature calls, they answer. At the not-so-good times, stables are deplorable. During rainy seasons, you can find yourself knee-deep in what you would prefer not to think about.

Proverbs 14:4 presents a word picture of a much nicer than usual stable. I fear that due to the lack of stable experience of most readers, the full meaning about which the writer was speaking may not be fully appreciated and, possibly, may even be lost. If there is no ox in the stable, then the trough and the entire stable is much cleaner. It is less problematic to those who may have weak stomachs.

If we have a choice, we will usually choose the stable with the clean trough, the one that has less foul odor and more clear walking space. We don't like to be bothered with the uncouth environment and stench resulting from the presence of oxen. However, we need to look a little deeper into this situation. The fact that the trough and stable are clean is evidence that oxen are not present. But if there are no oxen present, then there is no capacity to accomplish work since the oxen of that day was the horsepower-producing force by which crops were produced, timbers were moved and heavy loads were carried from one point to another. Without the oxen, no appreciable work was going to occur.

This word picture is still pertinent today. There are going to be some headaches and some foul odors when we are in the trenches of life. We are going to make some real blunders and yes, even some bad investments. Everything we touch does not turn to gold. Every deal we make is not going to be a bell-ringer. Every job we start is not going to be joyfully successful. But, we have to keep doing what it takes to get the job done and be successful. If you choose the stable with the clean trough, you will have a little cleaner area to occupy and you will not have to put up with the stench; however, you can know that from the get-go, your fate is doomed. By choosing the more comfortable environment, you have no opportunity for the increase from the strength of the ox. Instead of taking the easy path, choose persistence, perseverance and hard work for which there is no substitute!

Reflections...

□

JANUARY 3

Proverbs 22:22-23 *Do not rob the poor because he is poor, Nor oppress the afflicted at the gate; (23) For the Lord will plead their cause, And plunder the soul of those who plunder them.*

May 22, 2011 was a day that will long be remembered by many people, but more especially by the survivors of the most deadly tornado to hit our country in 60 years. Joplin, Missouri was almost wiped off the face of the map as the twister swept through the city of 50,000 with no regard to those in its path. At least 116 people died within the few moments of destruction and devastation.

It has been said that in times like these, the best and the worst come out in people. This was true in Joplin as it has been in almost every other disaster site. Good people with good intentions rallied to the aid of the suffering survivors in Joplin. However, simultaneously, GREED entered. Scam artists with the sole purpose of taking advantage of those most vulnerable began almost immediately to hit upon their victims. Price gouging scoundrels entered the city that was in shambles and charged exorbitant prices for menial chores that good-willed people were donating for free. So-called repairmen and carpenters hit the ground running to take advantage of those who had lost so much and were still in shock. There were even some from other parts of the country who set up phony charities and collected money that they represented would go toward alleviating the pain of those suffering loss. However, all monies collected went into the pockets of these scumbags.

Apparently there has always been that select part of humanity among us whose primary purpose in life was to take advantage of the poor and suffering. Such is noted here in **Proverbs 22:22** as well as other scriptures. We see the same scenario replayed in almost every disaster. We see greedy varmints targeting our aged population. We see self-serving individuals taking advantage of those who are sick. These are some of the lowest of the scum when their primary aim is to

6

inflict additional pain and suffering in order to rake in profit for themselves.

This scripture gives some insight about the attitude of God towards such perpetrators. The wrath of the Lord is riled at such unconscionable actions. It is clear that God is highly displeased with the act of taking advantage of the poor and suffering. We should therefore do all that is within our power to come to the aid of the poor and suffering. In **Luke 12:15**, Jesus said, *"Beware, and be on your guard against every form of greed;"* It certainly is a sobering thought of having the Lord plundering the soul of those who plunder them!

Reflections...

☐

JANUARY 4

Proverbs 26:27 *Whoever digs a pit will fall into it, And he who rolls a stone will have it roll back on him.*

Marketing is an integral part of our capitalistic economy. In fact, marketing occupies a high priority in the retail industry. In very simplistic terms, the primary objective of marketing is to convince you that your NEED for a product is greater than your discipline to hold onto your money. In other words, the goal of marketing is to get money out of your pocket and into the hands of the retailer.

This is done by using very appealing tactics. At times marketing creates an urge to purchase that is so great that we feel we cannot live without their gadget. The new cars with their leathery smell hypnotize us. Devoid of rational discretion, we fall into the trap. I counseled with a person in the past that was taken by such marketing tactics. This particular person was one that would normally be considered above the reaches of marketing schemes. With a background in accounting, one would think that he would have crunched the numbers before committing to a debt large enough to be mistaken for Stone Mountain. Yet it happened...a very intelligent individual made some very irrational decisions. As he discussed his dilemma, he lamented over the situation he had created.

All too often this scenario is replayed. Someone who is otherwise considered a rational individual creates a large debt by making purchases that far overextend his ability to repay. When such a situation is created, it is like a set trap awaiting its prey. Suddenly and usually without warning, he falls into the pit of debt that he has dug. In his own mind, he was man-handling the large stone of debt when all of a sudden, the momentum shifted and the debt stone rolled back on him.

My friend was in a *pickle* of a mess. Even though he was approaching retirement age, he had placed his lifelong savings at risk because a marketing scheme had painted an irresistible picture. Throughout the book of Proverbs, we are instructed to "get wisdom and understanding." If we get godly wisdom, then we will not be swayed by the marketing schemes that attempt to convince us to mortgage our futures in exchange for momentary pleasure. **Proverbs 16:16** *"How much better it is to get wisdom than gold! And to get understanding is to be chosen above silver."*

There are always consequences to face when we violate the wisdom of God's Word. Debt is much like a deep pit. It is easy to fall into, but very difficult to climb out. Lest we be naïve, let us be mindful, *"Whoever digs a pit will fall into it, And he who rolls a stone will have it roll back on him."*

Reflections...

JANUARY 5

Ecclesiastes 5:10 *Whoever loves money never has money enough; whoever loves wealth is never satisfied with his income. This too is meaningless.*

The Book of Ecclesiastes gives us a snippet of the reality of life. In essence, no matter what you have or do not have in this life on earth, all is vanity. We are going to die and leave everything. Fred Rose and Hank Williams wrote a song in 1952 called, *"I'll Never Get Out Of This World Alive!"*

Even though we hear these truths about life in this world, we still have a difficult time letting go of money and the "stuff" that money buys. When we have money, we discover that we desire more. Regardless of the amount that we have, we always crave more. The current state of our economy is a prime example of this truth. As we saw the housing bubble burst, the immediate question that was on everyone's lips was, "How did this happen?" In light of this scripture, it is not difficult to understand that in the majority of these crises, there was a desire for "more." Affordable housing with a payment that fits into the budget was no longer enough; there was an overriding desire for a bigger, better house that carried much larger payments.

We see individuals who sacrifice their families with the excuse that they "need" to concentrate on excelling in their jobs and climbing the corporate ladder. They need to get the next bonus; they need to get the next salary level. They need to get the next promotion. Again when the love of money is the driver, the current level is never sufficient; they always want more.

So what is the answer to all this nonsense? The answer is simple. The Bible teaches that we should not love money. Money never satisfies. It is necessary to exist, but regardless of the amount we have, if we love money, there is always a desire for more. When we love money, we are easily led into paths that we normally would not choose. When we love money, we make choices we normally would not make. When we love money, we catch ourselves doing things we normally would not do.

10

The Bible gives warning about this very situation: **1 Timothy 6:10** *"For the love of money is a root of all kinds of evil. Some people, eager for money, have wandered from the faith and pierced themselves with many griefs."*

Don't allow yourself to get caught up in the love of money. It only leads to trouble. It is disastrous to families. Money never satisfies. Money is only temporary. The love of money is vanity. Remember, *"Whoever loves money never has money enough; whoever loves wealth is never satisfied with his income. This too is meaningless."*

Reflections...

JANUARY 6

Romans 12:6-8 *Having then gifts differing according to the grace that is given to us, let us use them: if <u>prophecy</u>, let us prophesy in proportion to our faith; (7) or <u>ministry</u>, let us use it in our ministering; he who <u>teaches</u>, in teaching; (8) he who <u>exhorts</u>, in exhortation; he who <u>gives</u>, with liberality; he who <u>leads</u>, with diligence; he who shows <u>mercy</u>, with cheerfulness.* (emphasis added)

Most of us have heard countless sermons on the gifts that God gives within the body of the Christ. There are numerous discussions concerning the giftedness of individuals and many times the laity is encouraged to take inventory in order to determine the areas in which God has gifted them. There are numbers of evaluations one can go through to confirm his areas of giftedness. Going through a giftedness evaluation can be an arduous task, but one that needs to be done.

God has placed certain gifts in the church body so that the church can perform the mission to which it has been called. It is no mystery that there needs to be fulfillment in areas such as proclaiming the Word, ministering to needs within the body, teaching the Word in small groups, and encouraging those within the assembly of believers. We need leadership for guidance of the body and we need those gifted in mercy to help us along without condemnation when we get off track. We, no doubt, have heard the need for all these gifts discussed many times. However, the one gift on which most remain silent is the gift of "giving." There are probably many who have never heard any teaching or preaching on the gift of giving. "Wonder why that is the case?" you may be asking. Well, I'm glad you asked that question.

In my humble opinion, I believe one reason why there is so little teaching, preaching and discussion on this gift is because it brings guilt upon most of us. We quickly realize that we may not be fulfilling that to which God has called us. It is threatening to us since we find security in our wealth. If we became generous givers, that means we may have to trust God ...what a novel idea! I don't claim to know what difficulty you may have with this area of giftedness. I can only speak from my personal struggles.

In preparation for my participation in the recent mission trip to Nigeria, God led me to read a number of books. Books like *The Hole in Our Gospel* (Richard Sterns) and *Fields of the Fatherless* (Tom Davis) as well as *Radical* (David Platt) began to eat away at my pride. When I learned the statistics about the *Jesus Film Project* (Campus Crusade), I was challenged. On average, one soul comes to Christ for each dollar that is contributed to that project. I suppose it would be appropriate to ask, "How many souls did you have for lunch today?" We live in the most blessed nation on the face of the earth. Yet, the spiritual gift of generous giving is seldom found in churches. Many believe that God has raised up America so His Word would go forth to the poor, lost and dying world. Yet, we have spent beyond our means to the point that the average family cannot even pay what they owe, let alone think about becoming a generous giver. So where does this leave us? If we take God's Word to heart, it will lead us where God is calling us. There should be generous givers in all churches, just as there are ministers and teachers. It is time that each of us prayerfully takes the necessary steps to determine his area of giftedness. When we do, there is little doubt that we will discover that God has called many to be generous givers. How about you? Has God called you to the GIFT of GIVING?

Reflections...

JANUARY 7

Luke 18:23-24 *When he heard this, he became very sad, because he was a man of great wealth. (24) Jesus looked at him and said, "How hard it is for the rich to enter the kingdom of God!"*

When was the last time you knew of someone who was sad because he had a lot of money? Sounds odd, right? Yet, when we get down to the nitty-gritty, this man that confronted Jesus experienced sadness because of his attachment to his great wealth. The message Jesus delivered gripped his heart; still, he chose to place his trust in his wealth. Regardless of the level of wealth one possesses, true happiness and contentment are found only in trusting Jesus.

According to research done by the Barna Group, Christians today are basically indistinguishable from non-Christians in almost all areas of life. Christians are caught up in the economic frenzy of "keeping up with the Joneses" just like everyone who is not a Christian. Christians experience basically the same financial hardships that are exacerbated by hyper-consumerism just like non-Christians. Christians are caught in the rat race of trying to accumulate wealth just like non-Christians. When we stop and analyze, this can become quite confusing.

Jesus had previously taught that it is impossible for man to dedicate himself to wealth and serve God too [**Luke 16:13** *"No servant can serve two masters; for either he will hate the one and love the other, or else he will be devoted to one and despise the other. You cannot serve God and wealth."* (NASB)]. If you read just another verse, you will note that the Pharisees LOVED money and that is exactly what Jesus was addressing. Any time we get to the point that we "love" money, we have crossed the line. When one loves money, money controls that individual. That individual cannot place his allegiance and faith in God, because his affections are directed to money.

God is a jealous God. He will not share the #1 position with anyone or anything. It is God or nothing! The rich ruler was sad because his love was focused on his money. He was unwilling to sacrifice the position money held in his life and focus on Jesus instead. Was he drawn to Jesus and His message? Absolutely! Yet, he was not willing to make the sacrifice required to place Jesus first in his life. Many face the same crisis today. If we place our love on money or possessions, then we cannot be a part of the family of God. Jesus said we cannot do both. We will be just like the rich ruler ...we will go away sad.

In this story, this man was rich. Ironically, one does not have to be rich to fall into this trap. The amount of money is incidental to the act of misplaced devotion. Understand, there were characters in the Bible who were very rich and yet, they were also very godly. The difference was simply that their faith, allegiance and trust were not in the money they possessed; they were in God that they served. This rich ruler was not willing to give up the grip that money had upon his life; therefore, his wealth absolutely was what made him very sad!

Reflections...

□

JANUARY 8

1 Chronicles 29:11 *Yours, O Lord, is the greatness, The power and the glory, The victory and the majesty; For all that is in heaven and in earth is Yours; Yours is the kingdom, O Lord, And You are exalted as head over all.*

How great is God? You may be asking, "What kind of question is that?" It appears the author in this verse was grasping in an attempt to put into words his version of an answer to that question. Words of the magnitude of power, glory, victory and majesty still fall short in a full description of the greatness of God.

He goes further in making the proclamation that all that is in heaven and earth belongs to God. He is exalted as head of all; "all" goes beyond what our minds can conceive. However, "all," you will note, does include everything that is within the earth. Once we have drilled down to this level, we can begin to get a grasp, an appreciation, a recognition of one little compartment of the awesomeness of God.

As humans, we sometimes have difficulty relating to what we call qualities. Qualities like power, glory, victory and majesty usually cannot be measured quantitatively. We recognize their existence, but have difficulty relating to them. On the other hand, we can relate to tangible matter. We can understand when the Bible states that God owns EVERYTHING in the earth. Granted, most of us may not like it, but we do have the ability to comprehend the statement. We have now drilled down from a **grasp** to an **understanding**.

At this point, we are now responsible for our acceptance or rejection of the fact (as proclaimed by the authoritative Word of God) that God does in fact own everything in the earth. If we do accept and acknowledge God's ownership of all, we must concurrently accept and acknowledge that we own NOTHING.

Our next drill down point comes in the form of a question. "If I own nothing, then what is my responsibility concerning all that is in my possession?" That is a very perceptive question on your part! The

16

answer to this question is found in **Matthew 25:14-30**. No doubt, we are all familiar with the parable of the talents. In simple language, God entrusts varying portions of His stuff into the care of each of us. EVERYTHING in our possession is owned by God, not us. Our responsibility is to manage God's stuff in a manner that pleases Him, just as Jesus taught in the parable of the talents.

We have now drilled down to the level where you and I live everyday life. The question that each of us faces day in and day out is, "Am I managing God's stuff in a manner that pleases Him?" It is a daunting question! It is an intimating question! It is a continuous question! It is a question to which each of us will be held accountable!

Reflections...

JANUARY 9

Proverbs 27:24 *For riches are not forever, Nor does a crown endure to all generations.*

In today's culture, much attention is given to riches and wealth. With numerous media available today, news about the rich and famous grabs our attention at the drop of a hat. We become mesmerized with news about one of the elite, regardless of the validity or reliability of its source. In fact, tabloids thrive at the expense of the gullible by constantly throwing out tidbits of information about those who have great wealth.

John D. Rockefeller died at the age of 98 in the year 1937. At the time of his death, he was proclaimed to be the richest man in the world. We would probably refer to him as the Bill Gates of his day. A news reporter whose duty it was to assemble the obituary, asked the chief aide of Rockefeller, "How much did Mr. Rockefeller leave behind?" to which the aide simply replied, "All of it!" When the richest man of his generation was overtaken by death, he was on common ground with every pauper who had gone before him. We are just like Mr. Rockefeller; we are going to leave everything behind. We are not going to take any of our accumulated wealth with us when death calls.

One of the icons of the computer and gadget age, Steve Jobs, lost his fight with cancer after having attained a lofty position as one of the greatest innovators of the modern electronics age. When asked about his opinion on the success of Bill Gates, he replied, "Being the richest man in the cemetery doesn't matter to me." Unfortunately, many get caught in the race of trying to be just that, the richest man in the cemetery. How ridiculous is that?

Many of us live our lives as if we really believe that money is eternal. We dedicate the major portion of our allotted time not to the pursuit of God, but to the pursuit of wealth. Money is only temporary. It is not reliable. Many times money disappears even though we have a tight grip on it. Money can buy entertainment, but not contentment. If we can learn and live the biblical perspective and truth about money, we will simplify our lives tremendously.   Money and riches are NOT forever!

Reflections...

JANUARY 10

Luke 18:12 *I fast twice a week; I give tithes of all that I possess.*

We sometimes forget that Jesus faced a lot of controversy during His ministry on earth. Believe it or not, the main source of that controversy was the religious groups. I have often wondered what would happen if Jesus were to come into our churches today. What would happen if He stood and taught an unorthodox message to self-righteous church members? No doubt, there would be an abundance of controversy generated.

The setting in this portion of Luke is one such instance. Jesus tells the story of the self-righteous Pharisee as he stood praying in public. He was not just praying in public, more specifically, he prayed to be HEARD by the public. He boasted of his own goodness and criticized those who were unlike him. He exhibited a braggadocios spirit while basically elevating himself above others.

This Pharisee specifically bragged about his tithing. Let's look more closely at this braggadocious attitude of boasting about one's giving. Jesus condemned this Pharisee: *"For whoever exalts himself will be humbled, and he who humbles himself will be exalted."* **...Luke 14:11** Jesus addressed the issue of giving for the purpose of being seen. **Matthew 6:1...** *"Take heed that you do not do your charitable deeds before men, to be seen by them. Otherwise you have no reward from your Father in heaven."* It becomes very clear that giving to God has more far reaching implications than just putting money into an offering plate. Giving is an issue of the heart of man. It is not about the amount one gives; rather, it is about the motivation of giving. Jesus goes on to say that one should not draw attention to himself when doing charitable deeds. He does not stop there. If one is guilty of drawing attention of others in order to gain their praise, then their praise is the only reward he will ever receive: *"...Assuredly, I say to you, they have their reward."* **...Matthew 6:2**. There is no reward in eternity for giving that is motivated by a self-serving spirit. So, if you have ever been guilty of giving in order to be seen and complimented by those around you, enjoy it. Their praise is the only reward that you will ever receive.

How about your giving? Do you give to God out of a heart of love and obedience, or do you give to be recognized by others and patted on the back? Are you motivated by atta-boys, or is your giving a personal act of worship to God? The Bible instructs us to tithe and give offerings. Let's make sure that our giving is pure in the sight of God. Let your giving be from a heart of love and obedience to God, not to be seen by men!

Reflections...

□

JANUARY 11

Luke 16:1-2 *He also said to His disciples: "There was a certain rich man who had a steward, and an accusation was brought to him that this man was wasting his goods. (2) So he called him and said to him, 'What is this I hear about you? Give an account of your stewardship, for you can no longer be steward.'"*

As young boys growing up on a small farm in South Georgia, my brother and I were required to work for almost as far back as I can remember. Regardless of your age, there was always a job to match your stature. During spring planting, we had the job of "dipping fertilizer" and filling the planters with seed corn. I realize that there are few who relate to the term "dipping fertilizer." Basically, it involved keeping the fertilizer hoppers on the planters filled with fertilizer when our dad came to the end of the rows where he had us stationed. Once the fertilizer and seed hoppers on the planting rig were filled, Dad would navigate another round of planting. While he was on the journey to the opposite end of the field and then on the return trip, my brother and I had plenty of time on our hands to do some wrestling and generally getting into things we should have left undisturbed.

Even though I don't remember all the details, it was one of those times that in the midst of our tussling, we somehow managed to spill almost a whole bag of fertilizer (100 lbs,) plus a bag of seed corn (56 lbs.). Fertilizer was expensive, but seed corn was out of sight; it was beyond expensive! We were able to pick up and recover only a small portion of both of these precious commodities. We had to come up with a plan and do it quickly; Dad had already turned around at the opposite end of the field and was headed back our way. Wouldn't you know it, I had a brilliant idea. We could simply cover all the remaining spilled fertilizer and seed with the loose soil in the freshly plowed field and no one would ever be the wiser. Like a cat on a hot tin roof, we dashed around scattered all the evidence and then carefully, but very quickly, covered up all our mess and declared to each other that even though it was a close call, we had beaten the wrap. ...or so we thought! About a week later all the corn seed that we had covered with loose warm soil sprouted and shot out of the ground like a big bass that had just bitten into a double treble hook breaking the surface of a still lake. It was unreal! All our mess that we so meticulously covered was exposed. The moral of that story is very simple: you can cover your mess for only so long and then the truth is going to be revealed. Needless to say, my brother and I had a lot of explaining to do ...we had to give account for what we had done.

The same is true with how we manage the money and possessions that God gives to us. We will be required to give account for our stewardship. We are stewards of God's possessions. We are commissioned to manage faithfully. If we are not good stewards, we can cover our mess only so long. We will have to give account of all our actions and the job that we do. Jesus taught that more will be given to those who are faithful and manage well. Conversely, for those who manage foolishly, what we have will be taken away. *"For whoever has, to him more will be given; but whoever does not have, even what he has will be taken away from him."* ...**Mark 4:25**

Reflections...

_____

_____

_____

_____

_____

_____

_____

_____

_____

☐

JANUARY 12

Luke 16:10 *He who is faithful in what is least is faithful also in much; and he who is unjust in what is least is unjust also in much.*

If you get engaged in a conversation, before two minutes have passed the conversation will probably have crossed the path of money. Usually there is an expression about wanting or needing more money.

Isn't it amazing that we live in the country with the most wealth in all the history of mankind and still we want more? We live in the largest and most comfortable homes of any place in the world, but they are not good enough. Our country has some of the most extravagant infrastructure known to man, but we still desire more and better. As a whole, the citizens of our country have the most technologically advanced electronics, but that is not good enough.

Whatever happened to being content with what you have? The Apostle Paul gave us some good advice in this area: **Philippians 4:11** *"...for I have learned in whatever state I am, to be content:"* Of course, Paul was content not because of his material possessions, but because he was faithful to God. Faithfulness to God brings one contentment whereas love for money and possessions only leaves us wanting more. Our faithfulness to God is reflected in the way we manage God's possessions. Since God is the owner of everything (**1 Corinthians 10:26** *"the earth is the Lord's, and all its fullness."*), then our faithfulness is reflected by how we manage money. If we are faithful in a little, then God can trust us to manage well with greater amounts. Conversely, if we are unfaithful with little, we will also be unfaithful with much. Our constant desire for more is usually generated by our self-consumptive lifestyles resulting in our being unfaithful to the principles of money management contained in the Bible. If our management of money is consistent with biblical principles, we will have the contentment about which Paul spoke.

Our attitude towards money and possessions is directly related to our faithfulness to godly principles. Let's do a financial management checkup. Instead of constantly wanting more, and more, and more, let's concentrate upon being faithful with what God has already given us. If we are faithful with little, then He can trust us to be faithful with much.

Reflections...

_____

_____

_____

_____

_____

_____

_____

_____

_____

_____

_____

_____

_____

_____

_____

_____

_____

□

JANUARY 13

Luke 16:12 *And if you have not been faithful in what is another man's, who will give you what is your own?*

Much of my working career was spent traveling. Many times, I traveled by air to destinations. Once there, I rented cars for local transportation during my time in the area. That meant eating all meals out, sleeping in hotels every night and basically living out of the suitcase. Over the long haul, week in and week out, this got to be a very tiring lifestyle. One can fully appreciate the challenges of a job of constant travel only if he has experienced it.

One thing that a job of traveling offers is the opportunity to take good care of things that are not your own, or abuse them as the case may be. Through the years, there were numerous opportunities to observe my coworkers' attitudes toward taking care of someone else's property. Some were comical, some were not, but all were revealing. Many years ago, one such coworker was extremely meticulous with the care of his company furnished car. In fact, he took such good care of his company cars that there was always a waiting list of names of those wanting to purchase his cars once they were turned back in and available for sale. Harold was very faithful with what belonged to someone else.

Of course, this was not always the case. There were some who would never clean the construction site mud from their feet before getting into a rental car. Their attitude was, "That's what I pay rent for." There was one who was fond of stomping the brakes, locking all tires down, and skidding to a stop from 60mph while screaming at the top of his voice, "Brake Check!" ...and then, there was one who, when at restaurants that provided real cloth napkins, would always (without fail) blow his nose on the napkin at the end of the meal. That gave me a disdain for restaurant cloth napkins to this very day!

Whether you have ever given it much thought or not, the manner in which you care for property that belongs to someone else is very important. In fact, it is a really big deal. Our behavior in this regard displays outwardly the degree of our responsibility and also our character. Jesus set the stage on this one. If you are not faithful to care for that which belongs to others, then who is going to give you something for your own? Since God owns everything anyway (**1 Corinthians 10:26**), He gives us what He knows we can handle. If we, by our actions, are good stewards, He gives more into our care. If we manage well what belongs to someone else, (God in this case), then He will give more: **Matthew 13:12** *"For whoever has, to him more will be given, and he will have abundance; but whoever does not have, even what he has will be taken away from him."*

Reflections...

JANUARY 14

Joshua 1:7 *Only be strong and very courageous, that you may observe to do according to all the law which Moses My servant commanded you; do not turn from it to the right hand or to the left, that you may prosper wherever you go.*

The Bible gives instruction in a number of locations to be strong and courageous. This encouragement applies to several different areas of life. What exactly does it mean to be strong and courageous? First of all, we have a choice. We can choose to follow this advice and be strong and courageous or we can choose not to take a stand. Secondly, in everyday language, it means to stand against the opposition. Standing strong and courageous is the opposite of going along with the tide.

Many years ago, when I was much younger, a group of friends and coworkers decided to travel down to the coast and seine for shrimp. At that particular time of the year, the shrimp were supposedly swimming up river with the inbound current caused by high tide. The plan was to seine the river just before it emptied into the Atlantic Ocean. It sounded like a good plan; that is, until we actually launched out into the deep, as it were, and commenced the laborious task of trying to pull the seine against the incoming tide. We discovered that although we were exerting all the energy we could muster, we made little to no forward progress. The force created by literally hundreds of thousands of gallons per minute of water passing through our seine was greater than our combined effort in an attempt to move in the opposite direction. Therefore, the Newtonian law of force once again prevailed. We did find, however, that we could go "with the tide" with ease. In fact, we could really cover a large territory by going with the tide. But we also discovered that going with the tide produced no harvest of shrimp. The shrimp were moving at the same speed and direction as our seine, therefore they were not caught in the net.

So it was in the life of Joshua. Going along with the crowd (tide) would not produce the harvest that God had prepared for him. Thus, he was instructed to be strong and very courageous. The only way that our seining for shrimp would have been successful was for us to be strong

28

and very courageous and prevail against the tide. God assured Joshua that he would be rewarded for his valiant efforts of following the law that Moses has laid and not varying to the right or the left. In short, he would prosper.

The same is true with us today. If we will follow the principles given in God's Word concerning money, we will prosper. Does that mean that we are guaranteed a certain return on investment? No. It does mean, however, that by following God's principles, we will be better off than not following His principles. There are many ways in which we benefit. Sound financial decisions, peace of mind, security in Him, and contentment are but a few of these benefits. Don't attempt to put God in a box and limit the form of how He may cause us to prosper. He will bless us if we are strong and courageous in observing His principles – not turning to the right or left.

Reflections...

JANUARY 15

2 Corinthians 8:2 *that in a great trial of affliction the abundance of their joy and their deep poverty abounded in the riches of their liberality.*

We who identify ourselves as Christians are really a motley crowd. Have you ever noticed how long it takes us to find something about which to complain? There is an old saying that describes the time: "about two jerks of a sheep's tail." Now, I don't know exactly how long it takes to jerk a sheep's tail twice, but I have a feeling that it is not very long. And that is how long it takes Christians to complain ...not very long.

I have stated that Christians should be the happiest people on the face of the earth. ...happy not because of a lack of difficulty and turmoil in our lives, but happy simply because we know who holds our future.

Christians especially like to complain about their poverty. Listen and you will hear comments like, "If I just had more money, then I would pay tithes," or, "I wish I had a better paying job so I could buy a house in a better section of town," or, "That preacher constantly preaches on giving just because he knows I am not giving anything." The list could go on and on. I am sure you get the idea.

The Macedonians about which Paul was writing in **2 Corinthians 8** were Christians who probably would have been justified if they would have chosen to complain. But they didn't! Instead, they gave large offerings even though they were extremely poor. They did not make excuses by saying "if I only had this," or "if I had that." Their generous giving amazed even Paul.

Note, there are three attributes given about these generous givers:
- They were in a great trial of affliction
- They had an abundance of joy
- They were plagued with deep poverty

That is amazing when you stop and think about it; they were experiencing great trials of affliction and found themselves living in deep poverty, yet they had an abundance of joy. How could this be? They had plenty about which to complain, yet they possessed a contagious joy. They were happy! Their secret was simply that they were givers. In fact, they were not just ordinary givers, they were cheerful givers as Paul noted in **2 Corinthians 9:7** " *...for God loves a cheerful giver."*

Instead of being Christians who complain about the status quo, let us learn this lesson from the poor, destitute Macedonians: when we give cheerfully, we will experience an abundance of joy.

Reflections...

JANUARY 16

1 Corinthians 4:2 *Moreover it is required in stewards that one be found faithful.*

The term "steward" is an old English word. It simply means one who manages the affairs of someone else. A steward is not an owner; rather, he manages what belongs to the owner. A steward is responsible to the owner for the manner in which he manages. He must answer for his actions or failure to act as the case may be.

The previous verse states that we are servants of Christ and stewards of the mysteries of God. One of those mysteries that we have difficulty understanding and accepting is the fact that God is owner of everything **(Psalms 24:1; 1 Corinthians 10:26)**. That means that the truck that I call mine really is not mine; it belongs to God. The house in which we live is not really our house; it belongs to God. The 401K is not really mine; it also belongs to God. My bank account is not really mine; it belongs to God. God owns it all!

If we can ever get the truth of this mystery into our spirit, then we begin to develop an appreciation for the opportunity of being a steward of God. The steward has the inside track to the owner. He is able to consult with the owner when in doubt or when a question of direction arises. A steward can tap into the wisdom of the owner to insure that he is managing correctly. These are but a few of the advantages of holding the position of steward.

On the flip side, a steward also has a responsibility to the owner. In fact, he has an awesome responsibility to the owner. The steward is ultimately responsible to the owner for every management decision that he makes ...good and bad! It is the responsibility of the steward to make sure that all management practices are in alignment with the philosophy of the owner and never violates the owner's values. You might say that the steward has to be in tune with the owner in order to know how to properly manage. The result of bad management is something to be feared. The result of good management is the reward of approval and favor of the owner.

Since God owns everything and we own nothing, everything we possess has been entrusted into our care for us to manage. It befalls our responsibility to manage in a manner that is pleasing to the owner (God). Not only is it in our best interest, *"Moreover it is required in stewards that one be found faithful!"*

Reflections...

☐

JANUARY 17

1 Corinthians 16:1-2 *Now concerning the collection for the saints, as I have given orders to the churches of Galatia, so you must do also: (2) On the first day of the week let each one of you lay something aside, storing up as he may prosper, that there be no collections when I come.*

The Apostle Paul addressed the issue of giving as he wrote to the Corinthian Christians. Note that he referred to the fact that he had previously given the same instruction to the churches of Galatia. The inference here is that the message applies to all Christians regardless of the place you live or the time you live. So, we can conclude that this message applies to us today.

There are several points in verse 2 that are foundational to New Testament Christian giving. Let's take a look at these since they form the backbone of our giving to God. First, he said *"on the first day of the week."* We are to give in a sequential and consistent manner. Our giving is a continuous activity. Some Christians say they give when they feel **led** to give. Paul takes the "feeling" element out of the equation. God has given us a plan, so we have to look no further. We just need to obey. Secondly, he addresses the question of who is required to give. "Each one" of you, meaning everyone who labels themselves as Christian, is required to give. This should serve as a wake-up call to many church members since the Barna Group research reveals that in evangelical churches, almost 50% give little-to-nothing. Again, we do not have to pray about this; God's Word has already spoken. Thirdly, we are required to give based on the amount of our increase ..."*as he may prosper.*" Those who make a lot are required to give a lot; those who make little are required to give little.

The plan that God has given, if followed by all Christians, would more than fund all the ministries of every local assembly of believers. In fact, if everyone followed God's instructions, church leadership would be looking for additional ministry opportunities. Some churches would have problems spending that much money! It is going to be a dreadful day when we stand before God to give account for our giving, or lack

34

thereof, if we are among those who fail in this commandment. God loves a cheerful giver. Put yourself in a position to be the recipient of God's love. Give as He has instructed!

Reflections...

☐

JANUARY 18

Matthew 20:10-11 *When those who were hired first saw that, they assumed they would get far more. But they got the same, each of them one dollar. (11) Taking the dollar, they groused angrily to the manager,* (MSG)

The parable of the Laborers in the Vineyard is one of the more perplexing that Jesus used in His teaching. This one flies in the face of our western culture and more specifically American Capitalism. Most are familiar with the story; however, it would still serve us well to go back and re-read the entire parable in **Matthew 20:1-16**.

The owner of the vineyard hired workers to labor in his vineyard. As he was pressed to get all the work done, he went back and hired additional workers. In fact, as the day progressed, he hired workers on five different occasions: early morning, 9:00 am, 12:00 pm, 3:00 pm and 5:00 pm. He promised all workers that he would pay them a "fair wage." At the end of the day, the owner summoned his foreman and instructed him to pay the workers beginning with those hired last. Every man was paid the same amount of money regardless of the number of hours he had worked. Needless to say, this went over like a lead balloon. Those workers who were hired first and who worked the greatest number of hours were irate. They felt like they should have been paid much more than those who worked only one hour. Admittedly, at first glance, this does not seem fair.

There are several lessons contained in this parable. Let's take a look at just a few. First, the owner of the vineyard promised every man that he would be paid a "fair wage." The owner did not violate that contract. Those who were hired first and started to work early in the day had agreed upon the wage for which they would work. They were paid that agreed wage. The problem was encountered when the owner showed mercy to those who worked fewer hours by paying them a very generous wage. It is important to remember that the owner did not violate his contract with the first hires.

36

There is another lesson here about confidentiality of salaries. The sharing of how much everyone makes on the job usually brings about discontentment, especially to those on the lower end of the scale.

Yet another lesson is the fact that the owner had the right to do as he pleased. It was his money with which he was paying wages. As long as he did not violate his agreement with others, he had the right to show mercy and bless some as it pleased him. So it is with money and possessions that may find refuge under the umbrella of our care. Some of us have little and some have a lot. Since God is the owner, He can choose to give to us as it pleases Him. We can work hard and we should, but it is God who gives all that we have. It is not our great talents that produce wealth; He is the one who enables us to get wealth. **Deuteronomy 8:18** *"And you shall remember the Lord your God, for it is He who gives you power to get wealth..."*

Reflections...

JANUARY 19

Proverbs 10:4 *He who has a slack hand becomes poor, But the hand of the diligent makes rich.*

No doubt, we all read the story of the *Tortoise and the Hare* when we were children. It would probably help adults today to go back and read (and study) the book again. Of course, in the story the tortoise and the hare were involved in a race. The hare, being much faster than the tortoise, literally lay down on the job in the middle of the race. His reasoning was that he was so much faster than the tortoise that the tortoise could not possibly be a contender in the race. So, the hare lay down and took a nap.

The tortoise, as slow as he was, kept on track and on pace. He was not sidetracked by those observing the race, even with all their cheering. He kept his focus and kept moving forward. My 3 year old grandson used to love this story. There was one of the repeating sentences that he especially loved and would take over and repeat that very meaningful line that contains a tremendous principle: "I may be slow, but I am steady." Of course, the tortoise passed the hare that was sleeping and went on to win the race. This is a great story with a great meaning.

In fact, this story basically goes hand-in-hand with **Proverbs 10:4**. This should serve as a work ethic model in the workplace, especially for followers of Christ. We may be like the tortoise in the story. We may not have the most talent and we may not have all the opportunities that others have. But, if we will continue to do our best with diligence, our hard work will pay off in the end. Conversely, if we become enamored with our abilities and talents as the hare did, we are inviting failure. If we become slack and start taking our job for granted, we are headed for the poor house.

This verse encourages us to stay focused on what we are doing, keep priorities in order and maintain diligence. These are the things that will take us to success. Let us remember that those who have slack hands become poor, but the hand of the diligent make rich!

Reflections...

⬜

JANUARY 20

Proverbs 11:24 *There is one who scatters, yet increases more; And there is one who withholds more than is right, But it leads to poverty.*

M any Christians have a distorted view on the subject of money and money management. Some discuss eagerly the "evils" of money and yet they work overtime in an effort to get more money. What kind of deal is that? Some talk about those evil rich people while working themselves into a frenzy trying to keep up with the Joneses. With all the talk about how money will take good people down into the cesspool of degradation, I have never seen even one of these "self proclaimed" saints give away all their money in order to distance themselves from the same evils they quickly condemn. So what's up with this issue of Christians and money?

I'm glad you asked that question! The answer is really pretty simple. It's all about mindset, or attitude, if you will. Our mindset about money screams loudly in the form of our outward behavior. If we hoard money, we are quick to condemn everyone around us when it comes to finances. An attitude of hoarding is evidenced by a clinched fist holding tightly every single dollar that comes into our possession. The opposite of hoarding is generosity. When we hoard money, we manage with a clinched fist; when we give generously, we manage with an open hand. Our attitude expresses who we consider the real owner of the money to be. When I acknowledge that God is the owner and that I am constantly managing His money, I tend to manage differently than when I have the attitude that I am the owner.

Recognizing that God is the owner allows one to exercise the faith of managing with an open hand, not a clinched fist. With an open hand, some of the money may leave and be scattered. There may be an occasion to help someone who is in need. A widow, orphan or single mom may have a financial need that can be met by some of God's money being scattered from one's hand and distributed to the needs of others. Managing with an open hand is the opposite of hoarding. God loves generosity. He loves a cheerful giver.

So, when there is temptation to clinch tightly the hand that holds the money, remind yourself of the real owner. Recognize that you have two choices: manage with a clinched fist or an open hand. The NIV states **Proverbs 11:24** plainly: *"One man gives freely, yet gains even more; another withholds unduly, but comes to poverty."*

Reflections...

JANUARY 21

Proverbs 20:4 *The lazy man will not plow because of winter; He will beg during harvest and have nothing.*

Laziness has a way of robbing us of what God has designed us to be. There are so many times in our lives that we catch ourselves compromising by choosing the status quo rather than accepting a challenge before us that may change things forever. On numerous occasions, those opportunities that we so casually forego may be the key not just to survival but to changing the balance of our lives. Yet, opportunities go uninterrupted and undisturbed. If we are not careful, we will find that each time we allow one of those opportunities to drift by us, we set a pattern that is more easily followed the next time an opportunity comes our way.

Behavioral conditioning is a constant occurrence in each of our lives. Sadly, an apathetic attitude can become more than an occasional occurrence. This pattern can become a behavioral trait that the Bible refers to as "laziness." Apathy is a first cousin to laziness. Our constant failure to act upon opportunities will eventually set the pattern for the balance of our lives.

This message is very clear. It is not difficult to understand. A lazy man who fails to till his land will arrive at harvest time with no harvest. He is void of yield as a direct result of his failure to perform the required work necessary to produce a harvest. What is the net result? That lazy man who refused to work when others were laboring now resorts to begging because he has no food for survival. He begs for sustenance. Basically, he has a self-imposed mentality of entitlement. He now looks to others to take care of his needs not because of natural and uncontrollable misfortune, but directly because of his laziness.

In our nation, there is an increase of the entitlement mentality. Don't misunderstand, I know there are those who genuinely have the needs. I am not referring to the legitimate needy. However, there are growing numbers of those on welfare who are well able to work, but choose rather to seek handouts. Laziness has become a lifestyle for them.

Entitlement cries out, "It is your duty to take care of me while I do nothing." It is a pitiful and even shameful condition. Let us be diligent always to take advantage of opportunities we are presented while remembering: *"The lazy man will not plow because of winter; He will beg during harvest and have nothing."*

Reflections...

JANUARY 22

Philippians 4:6 *Be anxious for nothing, but in everything by prayer and supplication, with thanksgiving, let your requests be made known to God;*

There are many things in life that may cause anxiousness. What exactly does it mean to be "anxious?" The dictionary gives a long list of synonyms which include: uneasy, concerned, worried, troubled, upset, careful, wired, nervous, disturbed, distressed, uncomfortable, tense, fearful, unsettled, restless, neurotic, agitated, taut, disquieted, apprehensive, edgy, watchful, jittery. This is quite a list of words that are basically interchangeable with the word anxious.

While this verse does not explicitly or exclusively deal with the subject of money, it certainly is applicable. Take a close look at the synonyms again. Practically every one of them can be used to describe a person's state of mind when faced with adverse monetary issues.s Think back for a moment to the beginning of the great recession of 2008. If you happened to have had an investment portfolio in the stock market, you probably can vividly relate to each of these descriptive terms. If you are "upside down" in a car loan, you can no doubt choose a few of these words to describe your state of mind. If you are "under water" on you home mortgage, you know all too well the "knot in the stomach" feeling for which you may choose several of the terms to describe your mental and emotional state.

Financial problems can produce anxiety "big time!" Not only do we personally experience these sensations, we are likely to transfer them to those with whom we are closely associated, namely our family members. We begin to see the snowball effect beginning to take its toll and if not checked has the potential to cause a financial avalanche.

There is relief from these emotions that appear uncontrollable. The first step is to come to the realization that we are not the owners of the investment portfolios, or the cars, or the homes. When we acknowledge that we are not owners, but only managers, we can let go of the anxiety brought about by money problems that are beyond our control. As Dr. David Jeremiah has amply stated, when the investment portfolio is spiraling downward, we can pray, "God, you know, you are the owner of the 401-k; you might want to take a look at it because it has not been doing too well lately." When we acknowledge God's ownership, it becomes much easier to *"Be anxious for nothing..."*

Reflections...

_____

_____

_____

_____

_____

_____

_____

_____

_____

_____

_____

_____

_____

_____

_____

_____

_____

_____

JANUARY 23

Luke 12:47-48 *And that servant who knew his master's will, and did not prepare himself or do according to his will, shall be beaten with many stripes.* *(48)* *But he who did not know, yet committed things deserving of stripes, shall be beaten with few. For everyone to whom much is given, from him much will be required; and to whom much has been committed, of him they will ask the more.*

Citizens of the United States enjoy one of the most advanced cultures known to man. We have poverty in our country, but certainly not on a scale of other countries. If it were possible to create a prosperity index that was a function of per capita income and opportunity, there is little doubt that America would rank top in the world. The "opportunity quotient" (that's what I would call it) simply means that a person born in the U.S. will have a greater opportunity to attain a high standard of living than anywhere else in the world.

Although one has almost unlimited opportunity to excel and do practically anything he desires, we see growing numbers choosing mediocrity. In many universities, less privileged foreign students come into our country and soar to excellence. Could it be that we have grown numb to the existence of opportunity? Have we been so conditioned by the constant presence of opportunity that it no longer makes an impression upon us? Have we become acclimated to the status quo and content to choose mediocrity over excellence?

We have forgotten to teach our younger generation that along with every opportunity, there exists a corresponding responsibility. Responsibility has been forgotten. We live in the land of plenty and home of the brave (yeah, I know it is really land of the free). We forget that it was not of our own volition that we were born in these United States of America. We all have had numerous opportunities thrust in our direction our entire lives. We enjoy a standard of living that is second to none in the world today. What we overlook, however, is the fact that along with our prosperity, we have greater responsibilities

46

than those who enjoy less. Jesus himself taught that we will have to give account for how we managed the prosperity that we have enjoyed.

What are you doing with the opportunities and prosperity with which you have been blessed? Jesus said, *"For everyone to whom much is given, from him much will be required."* Are you using everything that you have in a manner that will vindicate you when you give account?

Reflections...

_____

_____

_____

_____

_____

_____

_____

_____

_____

_____

_____

_____

_____

_____

_____

_____

JANUARY 24

Proverbs 6:9-11 *How long will you slumber, O sluggard? When will you rise from your sleep? (10) A little sleep, a little slumber, A little folding of the hands to sleep - (11) So shall your poverty come on you like a prowler, And your need like an armed man.*

Vacation, holidays and retirement are important items on the agenda of most workers. One's view of time off work varies. Some look to time off as an opportunity to rest the weary bones and muscles. Another may view time off exactly opposite; he may see an opportunity to cram in additional activities that cannot be handled during a normal work schedule. Yet another may absolutely cherish time off as exactly that ...time to do nothing ...not rest up ...not catch up on extra chores ...just while away the time with nothing to show except the mark on the calendar indicating the passing of another day.

And of course, there are those who have nothing but time off! They never go to work. In fact, some work harder to distance themselves from work than they would have to work if they actually had a job. There are those whose main goal in life is to have lunch interrupt their night's sleep followed by an afternoon nap and then early to bed by nightfall.

The Proverbs speak often on the subject of work and frequently about diligence. The reality of a slothful behavioral pattern is stated in verse 10: *poverty* will sneak up on you like a prowler. The question cries out in this passage: *"How long will you slumber, O sluggard?"* When will you awaken and come to your senses? What will it take to motivate you to fulfill the purpose for which God put you here on earth? Yes, these verses carry a spiritual connotation. Are we, as Christians, found guilty of a little sleep, a little slumber, a little folding of the hands to sleep ...just going through our days never really seeking God's plans and purposes for our lives? Are we guilty of sleepwalking through our days and never really developing a personal and active relationship with God through Jesus Christ?

48

There are many questions here. But go back and look at this passage. The main impetus is the question, *"How long will you slumber, O sluggard?"* It is a question that each of us will have to address for ourselves. Just as the literal interpretation declares that our continual slothfulness results in poverty overtaking us, so it is with our spiritual lives. Let us be challenged and awaken our spiritual lives to the plans God has for us, knowing that if we don't, spiritual poverty will overtake us like a prowler.

Reflections...

JANUARY 25

Proverbs 25:28 *Whoever has no rule over his own spirit Is like a city broken down, without walls.*

Discipline is a word that makes most of us shudder. If someone says they like discipline, we think they must undoubtedly have a serious problem; they are kind of weird. When we get down to the nitty-gritty of life, most of us really do not like discipline. However, the irony is that we DO like what discipline produces.

We need discipline in different areas of our lives including, but not limited to, spiritual, physical (exercise and eating habits) and certainly the financial. It is amazing that we sometimes concentrate only on one area while allowing another area to go untended completely. Professional athletes, for example, subject themselves to grueling physical conditioning in order to achieve the necessary physical stamina required to excel in their sport. They exercise a disciplinary regimen that most of us would consider cruel and unjust punishment. Yet with all their physical discipline, the majority ignores financial discipline completely. *Sports Illustrated* has reported that of all professional football players in the National Football League, 78% file bankruptcy or are in serious financial trouble within 2 years of their leaving the sport. In 2009, the minimum entry level salary of NFL players was $310,000 annually. The average career of a NFL player is only 3 ½ years. Void of great emphasis on financial discipline from the beginning, these individuals face a tremendous threat of economic pressure. Sadly, many end up in bankruptcy.

Success in one area of life but void of discipline in other areas of life spells doom and often leads to one's downfall. When one enjoys success in a specific area of life, he often concludes that he is good in all areas of life. That is a dangerous path to travel. Jim Rohn stated it well: "Affirmation without discipline is the beginning of delusion." If we do not maintain rule and control over ourselves, then we are susceptible to serious problems that lead to embarrassment and pain. It does not matter how much money one makes; discipline over spending must always exist. William Feather stated, "If we do not discipline ourselves the world will do it for us," and how true that is.

It makes no difference whether we make $30,000 or $300,000 a year, we all must exercise financial discipline. Although we make discipline out to be an enemy, in the end, discipline is our friend. It is the ingredient we must have for an enriched and rewarding life. **Hebrews 12:11** *"No discipline seems pleasant at the time, but painful. Later on, however, it produces a harvest of righteousness and peace for those who have been trained by it."*

Reflections...

◻

JANUARY 26

Proverbs 22:9 *He who has a generous eye will be blessed, For he gives of his bread to the poor.*

Approximately 99.99999999% of all Christians insert one petition into all prayers that are uttered from their lips. If you concentrate really, really, really hard, you may be able to guess the phrase to which I refer. It goes something like this: "Lord bless me..." Without hesitation and without apology, we continuously pray for the Lord's blessings. In addition, I might add, we pray for the Lord's blessing without any forethought. It just comes to us naturally.

Here is something at which we should step back and possibly take a look. When I pray, "Lord, bless me," then I become the focal point of the prayer. Basically, it's all about me. There is much in the Bible that directs us to give honor and praise to God when we pray. We are to lift Him up and glorify Him. We are to speak of His goodness. God inhabits the praise of his people (**Psalms 22:3**). Regrettably, we usually tailor our prayers to fit nicely around our needs and desires. While there is nothing inherently wrong with seeking God's favor, maybe we need to get our eyes off the apples on the ground and look up into the trees that produce them and from where they have fallen. Maybe God has already given us direction as how to receive His blessings, even before we ask. Maybe He has already made provision to shower blessings upon us, but we have failed to heed His directions. Is there any possibility of this being the case?

"He who has a generous eye will be blessed." God has already made the provision to bless us even before we pray about it. He has told us what we need to do. In **Malachi 3:10**, we are directed to bring the tithes into the storehouse. Here again, the foundation was laid onto which the blessing of God will flow. After we follow His directions, then see: *"If I will not open for you the windows of heaven And pour out for you such blessing That there will not be room enough to receive it."*

We are guilty sometimes of asking God for something that He has already provided. There comes a time when instead of repetitious prayer, we just need to DO what God has already told us. Giving is a part of being a believer in Christ...a BIG part. We are blessed when we give to the poor. This really is not rocket science. God loves a cheerful and generous giver. It is time for growing and maturing Christians to have a generous eye...an eye to give. As Christians, we need to mature and develop that generosity for which God has already equipped us. *"But a generous man devises generous things, And by generosity he shall stand."* ... **Isaiah 32:8**

Do you desire God's blessings? Then follow His directions!

Reflections...

☐

JANUARY 27

Matthew 6:19-20 *Do not lay up for yourselves treasures on earth, where moth and rust destroy and where thieves break in and steal; (20) but lay up for yourselves treasures in heaven, where neither moth nor rust destroys and where thieves do not break in and steal*

Many Christians in our country have heard numerous sermons preached using these verses as the primary text. It is somewhat a paradox when we are told that we are not to lay up treasure on the one hand and then we are told that we should be prudent and plan for the future by saving. So which is right?

The answer lies in one's mindset. The book of Proverbs is filled with admonitions to us about being diligent with money. Matthew gives us fair warning about allowing money to become a god to us. Therein lies the great danger. Note that verse 19 gives the specific reason for piling up treasure ...*"for yourselves."*

There is always uncertainty when one is attempting to amass wealth. There are thieves that will steal, there are market fluctuations that will eat away gains, and there are business failures that will crash one's investment into the ground. In reality, there are no guarantees in this world. There are no fool-proof investments. Everything is temporary. That is the point that the writer was making here. In this life, everything is uncertain and is going to fail. We are going to give up all the treasures that we gather. However, he then contrasts the vulnerability of investments in this life with the certainty of investing our treasures in things with eternal values (treasures in heaven).

The shortfall of this discussion is that few ministers follow through and tell us "how" we can actually lay up treasures in heaven. We are never given the details of how to accomplish this. Here in simple terms is what you have been awaiting. Here is the bottom line of how to lay up treasures in heaven: invest your money in things that have eternal value. If we search the Bible for things with eternal value, we will find there are two specific things mentioned in scripture. One is God's

54

words: *"Heaven and earth will pass away, but My words will by no means pass away."* **Matthew 24:35; Mark 13:31; Luke 21:33.** Secondly, the soul of man is eternal: *"And these will go away into everlasting punishment, but the righteous into eternal life."* ... **Matthew 25:46.**

So, when we invest our treasure in the Word of God and souls of men, we are literally laying up treasure in heaven. We are investing in things that have eternal value. Why take on the risk of guaranteed loss by laying up treasures on earth when we can have eternal rewards by laying up our treasures in heaven?

Reflections...

JANUARY 28

1 Chronicles 29:9 *The people rejoiced at the willing response of their leaders, for they had given freely and wholeheartedly to the LORD. David the king also rejoiced greatly.*

Flip Flippen stated, "No organization can rise above the constraints of its leadership." It is always refreshing to see leaders who do what they are supposed to do ...*lead*! Leaders are positioned to go before, to blaze the trail, to be in the forefront. Many want to be called leaders, but not everyone is willing to pay the price to be a leader. If you think you are a leader, turn around and look to see who is following. If no one if following, you are not a leader; you're just out for a walk!

In his book *Good to Great,* Jim Collins says that there are very few really great leaders among us. Why? Because very few are willing to pay the price that true leaders have to pay. Bill Hybels describes the price of leadership quite amply in his book *Descending to Greatness.* Real leaders pave the way by serving those whom they are leading. They possess a servant's heart. A true leader would never conceive the idea of "sending" where he has not already gone and is willing to go again.

In **1 Chronicles 29**, King David showed the real, genuine characteristics of leadership. In preparation for the building of the Temple, he led the way with generous giving far beyond any requirements. In addition to the giving from the position of his office, he gave generously of his personal treasure. As he led the way in giving, he challenged those under his command: *"Now, who is willing to consecrate himself today to the LORD?"* (verse 5). His leadership did not go unnoticed by those in authoritative roles serving under his command. All the leaders of families, officers of tribes, commanders of the thousands and commanders of the hundreds followed the leadership of King David in giving.

In addition to the fact that all the leaders participated, the really unique characteristic was the joy with which they all gave. They REJOICED as they gave. They were having a good time. I once had a pastor who would make the statement as the offering plates were being passed, "Give until it hurts and then keep giving until it feels good!" There is something to be said about his theory.

We have a tremendous example on giving in this chapter. Let it serve as our instruction to giving. Let us learn the joy of giving. And if it hurts when you start giving, keep giving until it feels good!

Reflections...

JANUARY 29

Acts 11:28-29 *One of them named Agabus stood up and began to indicate by the Spirit that there would certainly be a great famine all over the world. And this took place in the reign of Claudius. (29) And in the proportion that any of the disciples had means, each of them determined to send a contribution for the relief of the brethren living in Judea.*

In today's Christian culture, most churches and parachurch organizations are having problems meeting their budgets. Contributions are down and it is seemingly becoming harder and harder to convince members to follow biblical principles in giving. Almost all giving is done in a reactive manner; that is, people give to meet the budget or to help with relief after a disaster, or maybe to assist some family that has experienced excessive misfortune.

Some people have a wrong attitude about giving. Instead of releasing their gift, they want to maintain control and dictate exactly how and for what it will be used. A lot could be said about this, but that is another discussion for another day.

These verses in **Acts 11** depict a situation that would be considered extreme in today's culture. It appears that Agabus gave a prophesy through the anointing of the Holy Spirit about an oncoming famine across the Roman world. Don't miss this now, the famine is still out into the future; it has not yet occurred. Upon hearing this prediction of famine that was about to happen, the disciples committed to give to help relieve the effects of the famine that was yet to come. It is interesting to note that their giving was "proportional." They basically gave a percentage of what they had, not just an offering. It appears that their commitment was established and pronounced prior to the famine. In every sense of the word, their giving qualified as proactive giving. They literally committed to give before the need existed.

What would motivate them to do such a thing? One can only conclude that they did so because of their respect for the prophetic words spoken through the Holy Spirit and their love for God. Their hearts had

58

to be clean in order to be attentive to the Spirit. The bottom line is that their giving was a matter of the heart. It is no different with us today. Our giving, or lack thereof, is a reflection of the condition of our hearts. God's Word has given us direction in the area of giving. There is no question concerning the clarity of its instruction. The question that arises is simply, "What is the condition of our hearts?" As it was in this case with the disciples, so it is with each of us: our giving is a matter of the heart. We can make all kinds of excuses and attempt to rationalize our shortfall of giving. All will appear as empty words in the ear of God because He knows our hearts!

Reflections...

JANUARY 30

1 Corinthians 13:3 *And though I bestow all my goods to feed the poor, and though I give my body to be burned, but have not love, it profits me nothing.*

This verse may throw some for a loop. We talk a lot about giving because the Bible talks a lot about giving. We are not just encouraged to give; we are commanded to give. Further, not only are we commanded to give, we are commanded to give generously.

And then, along comes this verse saying that there is a potential that we can give literally everything we have, and it may count for naught. What kind of deal is that?!!! Plain and simple, we are to give out of a heart of love. In reality, when our giving is done properly, it is actually a byproduct of love. One of the most elementary verses in the entire Bible, and at the same time one of the most profound, is **1 John 4:8** – *"...God is Love."* When we give out of a heart of love, it is an expression of love. Furthermore, when we give out of a heart of love, we are more like God our Heavenly Father, for He *is* love.

Paul wrote about the giving of the churches of Macedonia. In **2 Corinthians 8**, Paul describes these very poor people who gave far beyond their means. It is quite intimidating to read all that Paul had to say about these saints (I use that term literally). They were enthusiastic just to have the opportunity to give. In Paul's words, they were *"imploring us with much urgency to accept their gift."* Now that is GIVING. How did this come to be? Paul stated, *"They first gave themselves to the Lord."*

Have you ever looked for an opportunity to give? I am afraid that many of us do just the opposite; we look for reasons not to give. Again, we can see plainly that giving is far more than a financial issue. It is a matter of one's heart.

Yes, we should give. We should give liberally. We should give out of a heart of love. But let us get our priorities in order. In order for our giving to be what God intends, let us first give ourselves to the Lord! Then our giving will be motivated by love.

Reflections...

◻

JANUARY 31

Deuteronomy 10:14 *Indeed heaven and the highest heavens belong to the Lord your God, also the earth with all that is in it.*

We have all heard it and we have all said it: God owns everything. This is yet another verse in the Bible proclaiming that truth. Even though we see it, we hear it and we say it, the question begs, do we really believe it? I submit to you that most of us do not.

I would say just look around, but in lieu of that I will say look into a mirror and take inventory. Most of us spend 40+ hours per week working. Some (me included) go years working, not an average of 40 hours, but closer to 70 hours per week. For what? We rationalize by repeating the politically correct answer...to provide for our families. However, we are quick to overlook the new car every 3-4 years, the house that is twice as large as we really need, not to mention the expensive wardrobe and, oh yes, the bass boat, 4-wheeler, guns and ... and ... and ... We attempt to justify our work as providing for our families when, in fact, we are piling up stuff in our rented storage units since our garages are already full.

Then we go to church (once in a while) and bemoan our inability to pay tithes and give offerings to God because life is rough and we are barely getting by. After all, we have already acknowledged that God owns everything. So, He really doesn't need the minuscule amount that we can give (probably loose change from the front pocket). Sadly, this scenario is not really extreme; instead, it is a rather common occurrence.

Getting back to the original thought, if we really believed that God owns everything, our attention and endless effort to acquire more stuff would be refocused on Him. "Stuff" would no longer hold a position of preeminence in our daily lives. If we really believed that God owns everything we would never dream of indebting ourselves to the point that we could not give as He has instructed us to give. If we really believed that God owns everything we would love Him instead of loving our "stuff."

We must awaken to reality. We are here in this life for only a short time. At the end of our time, we will relinquish ownership of all the stuff in our possession. Actually, we do not really own it anyway ...it is just in our possession. Go back to the mirror. Ask yourself a few questions. Do you really believe that God owns everything? If so, maybe it is time that you and I both start acting like we believe it!

Reflections...

FEBRUARY 1

Malachi 3:9 *You are cursed with a curse, For you have robbed Me, Even this whole nation.*

Malachi gave God's message to Israel after they had returned to their country from decades of captivity. When they were held captives, they were humbled. However, once they regained their freedom, in a very short period of time, they fell back into the same old routine... business as usual. They became self-centered, thinking only of what they could gain for themselves. They started to default in their giving to the support of ministry. They kept the best for themselves and gave the leftovers to God. These leftovers came in the form of crippled animals for sacrifice rather than the best, the unblemished as required.

Does this sound familiar? Does this resemble the pattern of a host of professing Christians in our current culture? There are many Christians today who give nothing at all. Without question, they will give account to God for their lack of stewardship. There are those who give, but only the leftovers. If they have money left after everything else has been attended, then God gets a tip. It goes without saying that these givers are spasmodic in their giving. Let's face the truth; if your giving is from what is left over, you are putting God at the end of the line rather than the head.

God, speaking through Malachi, was not restrained in expressing His displeasure about this situation. He spoke to the nation as a whole since the above described attitude was prevalent across the country, pretty much as it is today across the church. A curse was pronounced upon the nation of Israel because of its self-centeredness in lieu of honoring God. God made no bones about it; He stated outright that they were thieves guilty of robbing God. That is a serious charge! However, in reality, it was more than a charge; it was fact. God cursed the nation as a whole because of the prevailing attitude toward giving.

Do we in the church today think that God will give us a free pass? Do we think that we somehow rank higher and have God's favor shining down upon us like the hot July sun? Do we really think that we are any different than the Israelites? If we consider our nation today, we begin to get a glimpse of what God was talking about when He pronounced a curse upon Israel. Please understand, I am not a doomster. But we need to awaken and renew our commitment to follow God's principles in our giving. We very well may stand in danger of becoming a "cursed" nation just as Israel in this account.

Reflections...

FEBRUARY 2

Proverbs 3:1-2 *My son, do not forget my teaching, but keep my commands in your heart, (2) for they will prolong your life many years and bring you prosperity.* (NIV)

Have you ever thought about the lengths that some of us go to reach certain goals that we deem important? Understand from the beginning that I have nothing against a strict regimen of discipline to accomplish goals. In fact, that strict discipline is the very thing that provides the means for accomplishment of goals. But aside from that, we sometimes miss the mark in laying out the plan to reach our desired position.

Just this week as I drove to a certain location, I was reminiscing in what a great job I had done in finding the shortest route to my destination. And to that point, it was, in fact, shorter than the original route that I had in mind...by several miles and much less traffic with which to do battle. After I had made this trip a couple of times, I made the mistake of viewing the point of origin and destination on an internet map. Wow, was I shocked! I discovered another route that would cut off about 40% of the miles that I had thought was the shortcut.

That's the way life is. We think we have the very best answer (and sometimes we think we have ALL the answers) only to find out later that there is a better way. We are apt to focus only on what we assume is the solution to our challenge rather than investigating the different possible solutions and then choosing the best. This is especially true when handling money and finances. We like to believe that we have the best management techniques, make the best investment choices, get the best buys and save the most. Yet in all our glory (self proclaimed, of course) we miss the mark many times. We should view these couple of verses in **Proverbs 3** as being profound. They do proclaim a profound message. If we will remember the teachings in God's Word and keep His commandments, not only will our lives be extended, but we will fare much better financially than leaning to our own understanding. Just three verses down we are told to lean not on our own understanding but acknowledge Him and He will make our paths straight.

Many times we pray for God to intervene in our financial matters so that we may prosper. We go so far as to pray for God to perform miracles in order that we will prosper. Here is one for the record. God has already revealed in His Word the instructions for us to follow in managing our finances. He has given us all the information we need to manage successfully. Our problem is that we, for the most part, simply have not followed God's plans financially. Many of us are still traveling our self-proclaimed best route, but it is not God's route. His Word gives many principles to which we have thumbed our noses while praying for God's blessings. What is needed in our finances is not a miracle from God but rather obedience from us. Instead of begging God to see things our way, bless our plans and send us miracles, it is time that we look to His instructions and follow His plan. *"Behold, to obey is better than sacrifice,"* ...**1 Samuel 15:22**. We just need to understand that when we *"do not forget His teachings, but keep His commands in our hearts, they will prolong our lives many years and bring us prosperity."*

Reflections...

_____

_____

_____

_____

_____

_____

_____

_____

FEBRUARY 3

Luke 19:8 *Then Zacchaeus stood and said to the Lord, "Look, Lord, I give half of my goods to the poor; and if I have taken anything from anyone by false accusation, I restore fourfold."*

From childhood, most of us have heard the story of Zacchaeus and have sung the song about the "wee little man." As children, some of us even used this story as our defense when we got into trouble for climbing trees which was against the rules for young lads (not that the rules were deterrents to such activity). We could quote the story in order to justify our "biblical" behavior. I can't say that I remember that defense as having any redeeming effects though.

The account of Zacchaeus gives an example of a person whose life was literally transformed once he had a personal encounter with Jesus. We don't hear very much about changed lives anymore. Because of his vocation and subsequent activities as a tax collector, Zacchaeus was a despised individual. In our colloquial vernacular, we would probably call him the "scum" of the earth. As a footnote to us Christians, Jesus befriended Zacchaeus and chose to spend time with him. That one will set most of us back into our seats! But because Jesus called Zacchaeus out and became his friend, an astonishing and new individual was born. To put it mildly, there was a profound change in the life of Zacchaeus.

Immediately, the focal point of the life of Zacchaeus changed from one of making money by scheming and cheating activities to one of giving to the poor. To those from whom he had extorted money, he vowed to repay. That was serious sincerity. I'm not sure what you would call this, but when I was growing up as a young Christian many years ago there was a word used to describe this activity after a life-changing experience of coming to know Jesus Christ ...RESTITUTION. It is a word that you seldom hear anymore. I'm not sure why, other than maybe it is no longer politically correct. Note that Zacchaeus was willing to repay not only the amount that he swindled; he repaid it multiplied by four.

There are some Christians who are in need of revisiting the story of Zacchaeus. There may be some wrongs committed in our past that need to be righted. I recall more than 30 years ago when I was running a small business, a teenager whose dad was one of our customers, came in and wanted to talk with me. His subject of conversation was very much to the point. He said that on occasions, he had been guilty of stealing soft drinks from our break room and that he was there to make restitution. He continued to tell me that he had a personal experience with Jesus Christ. He felt strongly the need to go to those he had wronged and make apologies and restitution wherever possible.

Again, this is seldom seen and taught anymore. More of us need the spirit of the renewed Zacchaeus because we certainly have had the spirit of the old Zacchaeus at some point in our past!

Reflections...

FEBRUARY 4

Luke 22:5 *And they were glad, and agreed to give him money.*

What would you do for money? To what extent would you sacrifice your morals for the almighty dollar? To what lengths would you go to gain money at the threat of tarnishing your integrity? Where do you place more value, your character or wealth? These are questions with which we all come face to face at one time or another. We live in a culture that force these temptations upon us as we walk down the road of life.

Judas Iscariot was confronted with similar questions. When confronted with the choice of being a faithful disciple of Jesus or acquiring wealth, he chose the money. Of course, we all know the story of his betrayal of Jesus which led to unfathomable torture and ultimately his physical death. Following his deplorable act, Judas came to his senses and regretted his decision. His attempt to "undo" his evil choice culminated in a deeper and darker despair that finally drove Judas to suicide.

We are quick to condemn Judas for his choice. Yet, are we not doing the same thing when we openly and deliberately choose monetary gods rather than being a faithful follower of Jesus? We allow our jobs to absorb time that could be given to carry out God's call of the great commission. We take money that could be used to minister relief in the forms of food and shelter to widows but selfishly purchase toys that we do not need. Rather than giving to feed and clothe the poor, we opt to buy automobiles at excessive prices on the premise that we "need" a new car. Yes, choices confront us daily. Many times we choose to feed our own self-centered desires rather than hear the voice of the Holy Spirit speak through God's Word.

Some justify their self perpetuating devices for gain like not reporting income to the federal government by saying that the government wastes too much money. Many think nothing of cheating on taxes by

70

asking for payment in cash so there is no paper trail to link their side job income to the Internal Revenue Service.

Again, the question in the beginning was, "What would you do for money?" Usually there is someone close by who is glad to help you make the wrong choices that ultimately destroy your testimony. Similarly, there were those who were glad and agreed to pay Judas money once he made the choice to betray Jesus. The enemy is always within a stone's throw and waiting eagerly to assist us in making choices concerning money that will violate our morals, breach our integrity and deface our character. Don't be a Judas Iscariot. Choose a life of faithfulness and be an uncompromising follower of Christ!

Reflections...

☐

FEBRUARY 5

Matthew 14:17-18 *And they said to Him, "We have here only five loaves and two fish." (18) He said, "Bring them here to Me."*

What would be your reaction if Jesus spoke to you asking the question, "How much do you have?" That question would probably be somewhat troubling to most of us. However, it would probably knock your socks off if He followed up by saying, "Bring it all to Me." Yet, that is exactly what he told the disciples in this account according to Matthew. To make the incident more disquieting, the lad who actually owned the objects that were the point of discussion was not even in the conversation. The disciples were speaking about the lad's lunch. As a side note, we have no record that they had obtained his permission to offer his lunch to Jesus.

This is one of the greatest examples of giving in the New Testament, not unlike the widow who gave all she possessed (**Mark 12:41-44**). The lad gave all he had and expected nothing in return. The fact that he was expected nothing in return may be of greater significance than the fact that he gave all he had. This is the essence of true giving.

Of course, in this familiar story, Jesus blessed the five loaves and two fish and then gave the food into the hands of the disciples. They were charged with distributing it to the five thousand men plus women and children. I am afraid that I would have had a real problem with this. As an engineer, my nature would have caused me to methodically divide the servings into equal parts. I can visualize myself attempting to divide a loaf of bread into a thousand pieces or divide one of the two fish into five thousand pieces. To say that the pieces would have been small would have been a gross understatement. But for sure, the disciples did not approach their task with my engineering mentality. What a sight it was for them to pull and break a piece of bread with no resulting void or depletion. After the thousands were fed and "filled," the leftovers were gathered together. It took twelve baskets to hold the leftovers...more than what Jesus began with!

72

There are several perspectives by which this great miracle can be viewed. Not the least of these is the fact that when we give unselfishly to Jesus with a pure heart and without personal motives of receiving back, He can bless the gift and cause it to go farther than we can even comprehend. The blessings of God are beyond our mental capacity. With that being said, would it not be wise for us to give with a pure heart and without any ulterior motives of receiving back and then watch to see what God will do?

Reflections...

FEBRUARY 6

Luke 12:15 *And He said to them, "Take heed and beware of covetousness, for one's life does not consist in the abundance of the things he possesses."*

In America, we work hard to acquire possessions. Of course, there are many countries in the world where individuals are not allowed to own anything of value. In comparison, Americans have a greater propensity to be lured onto the path of acquiring "stuff." And, we do a good job of it. During one of my very first financial counseling encounters, I went to the home of the client for our appointment. As I was preparing to leave their home, they ushered me out the back door through the garage. There, in what was supposed to be the storage place for their cars, were so many "toys" that I had trouble walking the path to the outside doorway. From 4-wheelers to motorbikes, to bicycles, to exercise equipment to whatever your mind could imagine, it was all present and piled in heaps. They had enough stuff to stock their own Academy Sports store! (That is stretching the truth, at least a little.) I hope you caught the purpose of my visit in the home ...personal financial counseling. They could not pay their bills!

Our culture teaches us to get more stuff so we will be happy. Yet, more stuff only creates an appetite for more stuff, and thus the vicious cycle begins to spin out of control until one day there is not enough money to make monthly payments on all the acquisitions. In this culture, keeping up with the Joneses is no longer acceptable; we must now stay ahead of the Joneses. I recently ran into a situation where a relatively young couple was in bankruptcy, yet they were still driving expensive cars - her BMW and his Mercedes - with both working very menial jobs. In many instances, our culture takes us in an opposite direction from the financial teachings of the Bible.

As followers of Christ, we need to come to the understanding that we are not called to impress our peers with our stuff. We are to honor God and that is especially true in the area of financial matters. From cover to cover, the Bible expounds financial commands and guidelines for managing money. Yet as a whole, we turn deaf ears and blind eyes to its counsel.

Regardless of how much stuff we have and the extent to which we have gone to acquire our stuff, it adds nothing to life. Our mountains of possessions will eventually disappear, either prior to our death or at our death. We will take none of it with us. If we admit the truth, our stuff actually takes away our life. Thus once again, the words of Jesus shout loudly to us, *"Take heed and beware of covetousness, for one's life does not consist in the abundance of the things he possesses."*

Reflections...

□

FEBRUARY 7

Leviticus 27:30 *And all the tithe of the land, whether of the seed of the land or of the fruit of the tree, is the Lord's. It is holy to the Lord.*

Numerous times throughout the Bible, instruction is given concerning the tithe. The tithe is defined as one-tenth of one's increase, plain and simple. Oftentimes it is also referred to as "first fruits." Although Moses incorporated tithing into the law, it was a practice centuries before. In the New Testament, Jesus talked about tithing and basically referred to it as a starting point of giving, a minimum if you will.

This verse in Leviticus makes a couple of resounding statements: *"the tithe is the Lord's. It is holy to the Lord."* That should make us sit up and take note. Tithing is an act of worship. It is recognition that God is really God. Throughout both the Old and New Testaments, it would be inconceivable to come to worship God without a gift (sacrifice). Historically, giving has been more a part of worship than singing praises and preaching. It was very common to build an altar and offer a sacrifice (offering) as an act of worship to the Lord.

Yet with all its significance, our generation chooses to downplay the importance of following biblical instruction of presenting our tithes to the Lord. In our current economic state, multitudes of Christians have been sold a bill of goods (or stated more correctly, a bill of debt). Many are to the point that they cannot mathematically bring 10% of their income to God and pay their bills too. They have encumbered themselves with debt primarily for nonessentials. They have enslaved themselves to the lender (**Proverbs 22:7**).

In the process of counseling with couples experiencing financial difficulties, I have repeatedly heard comments like, "We would like to be able to pay tithes and give offerings, but we just don't have anything left over after we pay the bills." That statement is true; the principle is false. It is false simply because the priorities are inverted. Nowhere does the Bible tell us to give God what we have left over. Conversely, we are to give the first fruit. Before any bills are paid, before we buy groceries, and certainly before we spend money on pleasure items, we are instructed to give to God. Some say that it is just too tempting to spend the tithe money and therefore none remains for giving. Here is a solution that removes ALL TEMPTATION of using tithe and offering monies to buy stuff or pay bills. Here is a guaranteed, fool-proof method of ensuring that you will never again fall into the trap of spending the tithe and offering money on other things. Are you ready??? Pay the tithe and give the offering FIRST. Consequently, the object of temptation is not available. Give the first fruit FIRST! Remember, *"The tithe is the Lord's. It is holy to the Lord."*

Reflections...

FEBRUARY 8

Matthew 25:15 *And to one he gave five talents, to another two, and to another one, to each according to his own ability; and immediately he went on a journey.*

A lot of people feel pressured when someone else has more than they have. There are endless family arguments, many times escalating to lawsuits, over estates and inheritances. On the job, one employee becomes disgruntled when he discovers that a coworker's wages are higher than his. This same discontentment is fuel to the fire in the allurement of "keeping up with the Joneses." What we have is never good enough if someone else has more.

It would serve us well to read and study carefully this verse. First, the three servants were not given equal amounts. In our modern culture, this would bring on screams of discrimination. Secondly, the amount given was based on each individual's ability. ...SHOCKING!!! I can just hear the third servant pitching a tantrum, kicking and screaming at the top of his lungs, "Life is not fair!" If this is your attitude, then wake up and smell the roses ...LIFE IS NOT FAIR!

The mindset in America is "bigger is always better." However, the truth is, it really does not matter. In this parable that Jesus used in his teaching, the amount each person received was completely irrelevant. The point Jesus made was that each of us is responsible for what we do with what is entrusted into our care. It makes no difference whether it is a small amount or a large amount. But first, we need to come to grips with the fact that we are each different and are given different amounts. We need to get over the fact that our friend may be given more. We should take our eyes off what is given to our friends and keep our eyes on what has been given to us. The amount given to each of us is linked to our ability to manage.

We are rewarded by how well we actually manage our talents. Note that the servant who was given only one talent dug a hole and hid it. He did not use the talent or allow it to grow. As a result of his slothfulness (laziness), the one talent he had was taken from him and

78

given to the one who was originally given five. As unfair as our current culture would label this incident, it is representative of God's justice.

We should recognize from the get-go that we are treated as individuals. God gives each of us different amounts to manage based on our abilities, not the democratic process. We are responsible for what we actually do with our talents. Each of us will be required to give account for our actions (or lack thereof). We will be rewarded (or scolded and deprived) as a result of our actions.

Reflections...

FEBRUARY 9

1 Timothy 6:17 *Command those who are rich in this present age not to be haughty, nor to trust in uncertain riches but in the living God, who gives us richly all things to enjoy.*

There exists much confusion in our culture today about wealth and riches. Of course, that perplexity is not limited just to our generation; it has been around for centuries. Consider the confusion issue in the form of a question: "Do you love riches or the One who owns the riches?"

Unfortunately, many love the riches. Not only do people love riches, they do it with an arrogant attitude. With a proud and snooty disposition, individuals are quick to turn their noses on modesty and opt to their ritzy lifestyles. They fill their lives with activities that reflect the object of their love ...wealth. Their main concern and underlying guide for everything is the profitability and accumulation of more wealth. Don't misunderstand. One does not have to have a lot of money to fall into this lifestyle. In fact, most do not. It is a mindset that drives one's actions and dictates motives. Self gratification is at the top of the priority list. Enjoy and make the most of life; you only go around once, so enjoy it while you can. You know the routine; you see it every day.

In Paul's writing to Timothy, he is very forthright in his instruction. He sounds a warning about attitudes and keeping priorities in proper perspective. Riches and wealth are uncertain. They will take wings and fly away. Materialism and worldly wealth cannot be trusted.

But, we are not left stranded. We should put our trust in God and God alone. He is dependable. He is the same yesterday, today and forever (**Hebrews 13:8**). Not only that, he is the One who owns all the riches. Do you prefer an account in the bank, or would you rather have the whole bank? God is much more than our finite minds can comprehend. Why settle for a few measly dollars when we can go to Him and *experience* Him? Regardless of the dollar amount that you may assign, whether it is a thousand, a million, or one hundred million dollars, the

80

riches are still uncertain when compared to the faithful God who gives us richly all things to enjoy!

Reflections...

☐

FEBRUARY 10

1 Timothy 6:10(b) *...Some people, eager for money, have wandered from the faith and pierced themselves with many griefs.* (NIV)

The story is told of a dedicated Christian businessman who was very successful. In a few short years his business escalated as did his salary. One day in a serious conversation with his pastor, he confessed that he was experiencing a problem with tithing. As he related to his pastor, "When I made $50,000, I had no problem giving $5,000 to God. But my salary is now up to $500,000 and there is just no way that I can tithe on that much money. I mean, that is a lot of money." He then asked the pastor if he would pray that God would help him come to the point where he could once again have peace with tithing. At that request, the pastor immediately asked if he could pray right then. As he prayed he said, "Lord, my brother is having a problem tithing on his large salary. Therefore, I pray that you would reduce it back to $50,000 so that he can again have peace with tithing."

Unfortunately, some of us react in a similar manner when God blesses us. Instead of increasing the percentage that we give to God we do just the opposite and reduce it. When we are struggling financially, we often focus more intently on God. We know that He is our source and therefore, we are dependent upon Him. However, as our financial position improves, if we are not careful and intentional, our focus will move from God and become fixated on money. Money has purchase power and therefore, at our will, we begin looking to money as our source of survival rather than to God. When our focus is on money, our typical behavior is to drift and wander away from God.

This process of wandering is subtle and can occur even without our knowing it is taking place. Slowly, one small step at a time, we place our dependence upon the power of money to supply our needs rather than looking to God. We allow things to come between us and God; our once intimate relationship eventually becomes a distant relationship. We no longer have time to pray and seldom find time to read the Bible. Church activities become secondary to activities of pleasure and self gratification. We have drifted away from the faith and are no longer fulfilling God's purpose for our lives. After a while, we do not look to God at all. We have allowed money to replace God in our lives. In this state, many disasters lie ahead and we find that we are on a collision course with discontentment and the allusions that life without God brings.

It is noteworthy that money does NOT cause us to wander away. We CHOOSE that course of action. We make that choice ourselves and yes, it is a choice. Let us pray that God will always keep us humble and that we will maintain the correct perspective of money lest we allow it to replace God in our lives.

Reflections...

☐

FEBRUARY 11

2 Corinthians 9:7(a) *So let each one give as he purposes in his heart, not grudgingly or of necessity...*

When we analyze this verse, it can become troubling. Why? Most giving and collections are conducted in churches in America as a matter of "necessity." Up front, lest this whole discussion be dismissed due to naivety, let it be clear. Church leadership is forced to revert to measures in collections of offerings that would not be necessary if church members practiced giving as taught in the Bible. Consider specifically the teachings of this particular verse.

The Apostle Paul gives leeway to the individual here. He assumes that it is his or her solemn responsibility to plan ahead when considering the matter of giving. Giving should not be an impromptu activity as is the practice in many congregations. One should not sit in church and be swayed by a convincing sermonette and then consequently make a decision of the amount that he gives for a particular offering. Yet, we all have probably done exactly that. Paul is teaching that we should be so engaged with the ministry of the church that we make giving not only a serious matter of prayer, but also a matter of planning. Now there is an idea ...plan ahead what you will give.

When we get "in tune" with God, He will direct us to His plan. If we are living and "giving" in His plan, we do not rely upon impulse to strike us and frivolously make decisions about giving. Giving with a plan brings satisfaction and contentment. Note that Paul calls it "purposing in our hearts." What more can you say; planned giving has purpose. It allows us time to review and scrutinize the motive as well as the amount of giving. Suppose we are having a moment of selfishness and "inward" thinking. Planned giving provides an opportunity for the Holy Spirit to change us and then help us conform to His will.

Last, but certainly not least, if the church as a whole followed these guidelines of giving, there would never be a need for church leadership to rally the body in "necessity giving." The need for fund raising campaigns and special project collections would not exist. There

84

would never be need for a plea for budget giving because everyone's giving would be driven by obedience and not from necessity. It is unfortunate that a large part of giving in the church today falls into the category of necessity giving.

How do you approach giving? Is it planned with a purpose of heart? Is it done freely and cheerfully, or grudgingly? Is it done out of love and obedience, or out of necessity?

Reflections...

⬜

FEBRUARY 12

Hebrews 7:1-2 *For this Melchizedek, king of Salem, priest of the Most High God, who met Abraham returning from the slaughter of the kings and blessed him, (2) to whom also Abraham gave a tenth part of all, first being translated "king of righteousness," and then also king of Salem, meaning "king of peace."*

The story quoted here in Hebrews is taken from Genesis 14. This is the first recorded occurrence of the giving of a tenth to the ministry of God. Note that this first instance of tithing was several hundred years prior to the Law of Moses. Some today refute the practice of giving a tenth on the basis that is was Old Testament law. While Moses did, in fact, incorporate the requirement of giving the first fruit, the tithe, into the Law, it existed long before. Likewise, it is noteworthy that the account of Abraham giving the tithe to the priest Melchizedek is recounted in the New Testament. It has residual importance in the New Testament as well as the Old Testament.

What motivated Abraham to take such a drastic step as to give a tenth to the priest of God? Was a precedent set previously that Abraham followed? One cannot be absolutely certain since it is not specifically mentioned in scripture. However, there are observable patterns in scripture. We know the tithe belongs to the Lord (**Leviticus 27:30**). God set a part aside for Himself. Malachi also strongly supports this in Chapter 3 in his discourse concerning men robbing God of tithes and offerings.

From the beginning, God has always set aside a portion for Himself. In **Genesis 2**, God reserved a portion of which man was not allowed to partake. Man was given permission to eat and enjoy all the trees in the garden except one, the tree of knowledge of good and evil. We all know how that went down. Death was the result when man disobeyed God's command and took what God had reserved for Himself. There were monumental consequences for the disobedience in the form of the curse of death.

The spoils from Joshua's first battle in the conquest of Canaan at the City of Jericho were reserved by God for the specific purpose of going into the treasury of God (**Joshua 6:19**). These were the "first fruits" that God demanded. Yet again, there was intrusion by man into God's portion. Achan was overcome by temptation of the riches and stole some of the spoils resulting in serious consequences for man's disobedience. Thirty-six men lost their lives as a direct result. Man took the portion God set aside for Himself and the result was a curse of death.

Malachi 3, likewise, pronounced a curse upon the nation of Israel because they were robbing God of tithes and offerings. Do you see the pattern of God's expression of displeasure when men disobeyed Him by taking the portion that He set aside for Himself? The pattern is clear. Obedience to God's commands in handling the first fruits brings blessings. Disobedience to God concerning His portion brings about a curse. There is no doubt that Abraham was led by the Spirit of God to give a tenth to the priest, Melchizedek. In view of his obedience, as well as the other incidents of disobedience, Abraham set a good example for us to follow!

Reflections...

☐

FEBRUARY 13

Hebrews 13:6 *So we say with confidence, "The Lord is my helper; I will not be afraid. What can mere mortals do to me?"* (NIV)

In today's economy many are finding themselves in the midst of economic disaster. The message was driven home by the headlines recently in the local Macon newspaper, *The Telegraph*. The lead article on the front page outlined a recent study comparing personal financial security. It revealed that residents of our home state of Georgia are at the very bottom of the list when compared to all states in the nation. Home foreclosures are at an all-time high and are predicted to continue to climb even higher in this current year. Due to cut-backs and business closures, many are losing their jobs. Since most are living on the financial edge, as this recent article revealed, they are thrown instantly into financial turmoil.

Where do we turn when confronted with such drastic economic conditions? Who has answers to these problems? Some ask if, in fact, answers even exist. **Hebrews 13:6** gives us the key to the direction we should focus when confronted with these seemingly insurmountable difficulties. Our confidence of help is in the Lord. Not only is He our source of help, we refute that man can ultimately have dominion over us…"What can man do to me?"

If we look back one verse (**Hebrews 13:5**), we find the cause of many getting themselves into financial difficulties. This verse commands that we, *"Keep your lives free from the love of money and be content with what you have."* Not all financial woes come about in the manner, but certainly, great numbers do. When money is our main focus, it becomes the love of our lives: then, by default, God cannot be Lord of our lives (*"You cannot serve both God and Money"*…**Matthew 6:24**). When we focus on money as the answer to all our problems, we look to money as our source and not to God. If we look to money as a way to get whatever we desire, then God is no longer our provider. In short, if we do not guard ourselves from the love of money, then money literally becomes our god.

We are instructed to be content with what we have. No amount of money brings contentment. Only God brings contentment. Also in verse 5, we have the promise that God is always with us; He will never leave us nor forsake us. Some additional, really good news is that He is our helper. With that knowledge we can proclaim with confidence to ourselves and to those around us, *"The Lord is my helper; I will not be afraid. What can man do to me?"*

Reflections...

FEBRUARY 14

James 5:*4 Indeed the wages of the laborers who mowed your fields, which you kept back by fraud, cry out; and the cries of the reapers have reached the ears of the Lord of Sabaoth.*

Hopefully you have never been defrauded of wages for which you worked hard, but many have. A member of our family was in the home construction business. On more than one occasion he was defrauded by shysters acting as general contractors. Their scheme was to contract a job, sublet the work out to others, receive payment from the owner and pocket all the money, never paying those who actually did the work. This scenario is frequently repeated in the construction business as well as other industries. Such behavior causes undue harm on hard-working, good-willed and trusting people. Although it is no consolation, it has been that way through the ages.

Thieves always have a plan to get away undetected and never get caught. Swindlers think they are more intelligent than everyone else and that their plan is beyond the comprehension of even the smartest people around them. Cheaters are of the mindset that if they can get by without being caught, then they have won. Isn't it strange that the oppressor and aggressor always put themselves above everyone else?

However, a thief's scheming ways will not always prevail. Usually thieves are caught. Swindlers, while underestimating the intelligence of their victims and overestimating their own, make fatal mistakes that lead to capture. Cheaters ...well sometimes they just cheat the wrong person and are brought to justice by a slap of reality up side the head. Regrettably, all thieves, swindlers and cheaters are not caught in their schemes to defraud others. Sometimes they go for years and seemingly, justice is not served.

Take heart; God knows even the intent of the heart and thoughts of the mind (**Psalms 94:11**). He knows us better than we know ourselves. He hears the cries and prayers of those who have been defrauded. Nothing is hidden or unknown to God. While thieves, swindlers and cheaters may think they have beaten the system, know that it is only for a period of time. Their crimes do indeed cry out and reach the ears of the Lord. He is the ultimate judge.

This should serve as a reminder to all of us that God is God (duh! ...where have we been?). The crimes of the unjust reach out to the ears of God. Likewise, He knows all our thoughts and deeds. Let us be encouraged because we serve the omniscient God who, in His time, will serve justice!

Reflections...

☐

FEBRUARY 15

Proverbs 12:24 *The hand of the diligent will rule, but the slack hand will be put to forced labor.*

Have you ever wondered why it is that one person works diligently and even feverishly to do a good job while another is content to do only what it takes to get by? Many times a similar situation occurs on a job when these two described workers are literally working side-by-side. When the remuneration (also known as pay check) is the same, there exists a situation for friction to occur. This scenario plays out in almost every job level of every industry. Most of us have either been the victim or have seen it happen. The common response is that it is not fair. If one works harder and more diligently, then he should be compensated accordingly.

We can reflect back on the life of Joseph in the Old Testament. He encountered an unending series of "unfair" situations in which he came out holding the short end of the stick. However, we know the end of his story. God used all of these "unfair" events to mold and make Joseph into the person He needed to fill a very special position later in his life.

This verse in Proverbs gives us a very similar hope. Many times it seems that no attention is given to the one who works tirelessly with diligence. However, we are given the hope that eventually *"the hand of the diligent will rule."* Conversely, the slack hand of the goof-off will eventually become his own downfall. It may take time, but, on a daily basis, the slothful person is gradually determining his own destiny.

So, when you are fulfilling your call with diligence, take heart in knowing from God's Word, in due time, your diligent work will be rewarded. There will be a time of reaping that will come as a result of your diligent service. Be patient, maintain the right attitude and rest in the promise that *"The hand of the diligent will rule, but the slack hand will be put to forced labor. "*

Reflections...

FEBRUARY 16

Proverbs 17:16 *Of what use is money in the hand of a fool, since he has no desire to get wisdom?* (NET)

No matter where you grew up, there probably were some things with which you occasionally came into contact that were dangerous. It may have been animals, certain activities, or maybe even certain people. For me, the most dangerous critters were rattlesnakes. Growing up on a farm meant that we had to work in the fields and many times there were high grass and weeds that made ideal cover for the chilling, hair-raising diamondbacks. Occasionally, someone in the neighborhood would kill a rattler and then came the rituals. One, I remember in particular, was to place a dead 5-6 footer in the back of the pickup truck and then drive over to where a friend was working. You jump out of the truck, raise the hood on your truck and call out to your neighbor to hurry and hand you the stick from the back of the truck. Of course, you can imagine what happened when he ran over to grab a stick and there lay a huge rattler.

You may not have had rattlesnakes in your background, but no doubt there was something that struck a note of fear, especially if it caught you by surprise.

This Proverb gives us one of those "rattlesnake" situations. As innocent as it may seem and as common as it may be, money in the hand of a fool is a "rattlesnake" situation. It is dangerous for a foolish person to have money and have no desire to seek wisdom. Maybe this sheds light on some of the problems that we currently have in North America. It is a fact that the United States has been blessed with a great amount of wealth when compared to other nations in the world. Yet with those blessings of wealth, we have failed to seek wisdom thereby creating a danger to our society. If we look down just a few more verses, we see again the urgency of seeking godly wisdom: *"A discerning man keeps wisdom in view, but a fool's eyes wander to the ends of the earth."* ... **Proverbs 17:24** (NIV)

We can literally write this in a mathematical formula:

"Money + a Fool – Wisdom = Danger"

In particular, parents should pay attention. If you are planning to leave an inheritance of money to your children, teach them to seek godly wisdom. One of the greatest curses you can place upon your children is to give them money without teaching them godly principles of handling money. You would never knowingly give your child a rattlesnake: *"Which of you, if his son asks for bread, will give him a stone? Or if he asks for a fish, will give him a snake?"* ...**Matthew 7:9-10**.

Don't curse your children, teach them to get wisdom!

Reflections...

☐

FEBRUARY 17

Proverbs 21:20 *There is desirable treasure, And oil in the dwelling of the wise, But a foolish man squanders it.*

The relationship of wisdom and money is one of the main themes of the Proverbs. In many instances, the Proverbs stress that money without wisdom is folly. Also, as the case is in this particular verse, the consequence of handling money without wisdom is unveiled. One would think, with all the instruction from Proverbs, followers of Christ would take this as a very serious point. And yet, that is not the case. Many times we see what we might consider smart Christians fall into the traps of money and do stupid things. They make bad decisions that bring untold hardship upon themselves and their families.

The question begs, why would smart believers not seek godly wisdom with which to manage money that God has given? Maybe it is ignorance; maybe it is too complicated; or maybe no one has ever told them that the presence of money requires wisdom. Simple arguments can readily dispel each of these excuses. James gives us a procedure so simple that even a cave man could do it: *"If any of you lacks wisdom, let him ask of God, who gives to all liberally and without reproach, and it will be given to him."* ... **James 1:5**. All we have to do is ask and our Father is willing to give us wisdom. Then, what is the cause of this problem?

After counseling with many people and observing many more, I am convinced that the main reason many do not seek godly wisdom with which to manage money is that they are afraid that God will give them godly wisdom with which to manage money! If that sounds somewhat redundant, it was done on purpose. Some do not want God to interfere with their plans mainly because those plans are self-serving. They are afraid that God might direct them to use money to help someone in need, or care for a widow, or assist in caring for orphans, or any other number of worthwhile, godly causes. There are some who prefer country club membership over foreign country relief. There are some who prefer special care inside the church walls rather than helping to put up church walls in a country where people have no church in which to worship. There are some who prefer a new jet ski rather than hopping a jet to the other side of the world and taking the gospel to someone who may otherwise never hear about Jesus.

Yes, some are afraid that if they ask for wisdom with which to handle money, God will interrupt their plans. Thus, the truth of the Word prevails: *"There is desirable treasure, And oil in the dwelling of the wise, But a foolish man squanders it."*

Reflections...

FINANCIAL PEACE OF MIND FROM THE WORD

□

FEBRUARY 18

Proverbs 15:17 *Better is a dinner of herbs where love is, Than a fatted calf with hatred.*

I remember hearing my grandfather tell about experiences his family encountered during the years of the Great Depression. Being in his early thirties, it could be said that he was in the prime of his life with a young family made up of his bride and six children with the seventh coming along in the midst of the troublesome time. He was a farmer which gave him advantages not afforded those who did not have the means to grow food. Even so, he told of times when the family would gather for meals that consisted of a couple items ...cooked, dried beans and turnip greens. Meat was a delicacy that they rarely enjoyed. As Granddad told the stories, I could visualize the family gathered at the large table for their one-course meal ...beans. For variation, the next meal would probably be turnip greens. If, per chance, you just had to have dessert, you could eat some more beans. If you wanted an appetizer, you guessed it ...you had a choice of beans or turnip greens. The one unique detail that he always emphasized was that the beans would rattle when they were dipped onto the plates. Apparently, the dried, hardened beans were not easily softened with cooking.

However, the one thing the family always did have in the absence of an abundance of food was, as Grandpa put it, a whole bunch of love. Family life back then was much different than today. Since no "electronic" entertainment existed, each family was responsible for creating their own. Thus was born within my granddad a unique ability to write and sing Christian music, a trait that was handed down to several of his children and still exists today into the third and fourth generations.

Turnip greens (herbs) and beans were common in that household, but those simple foodstuffs were sprinkled with a generous portion of love. Seldom, if ever, did they have T-bone steak or filet mignon. When they were able to raise a cow, it was sold at market to provide money with which to purchase the few precious necessities such as salt, sugar, flour, etc. But they discovered that happiness and contentment did not

98

require meals of steak (fatted calf). In our culture today, we see a common scene play out time after time. Families have an abundance of wealth and possessions, but these are also accompanied with hatred and discontent. Especially prevalent in the lives of the high-profile, high society, Hollywood types is an abundance of wealth. However, these are frequently accompanied with hatred and anxiety producing unfulfilled lives.

If you reach a point in life where your meals consist of beans and turnip greens and you cannot understand why you don't have filet mignon, before you draw conclusions, stop and consider: *"Better is a dinner of herbs where love is, Than a fatted calf with hatred."*

Reflections...

FEBRUARY 19

Matthew 6:13 *And do not lead us into temptation, But deliver us from the evil one. For Yours is the kingdom and the power and the glory forever. Amen.*

Most of us approach this life as if we were in control, as if we literally controlled the universe. News alert! We don't! In fact, our own activity is about all that we can control. At times, we make choices that put us in the right place so that God can shower us with His blessings, but let's recognize it for what it is ...God blessing us. We can work diligently and see the benefits, but according to Proverbs, that is God rewarding us for our diligence (**Proverbs 10:4** *"He who has a slack hand becomes poor, But the hand of the diligent makes rich."*).

It is incumbent upon us that we first recognize that God is in control of everything. Nothing catches God by surprise. The following verse is so comprehensive: *"Yours O Lord is the greatness and the power and the glory and the victory and the majesty."* ...**1 Chronicles 29:11**. Those are not only broad, descriptive words, but they are indeed powerful descriptive terms of the greatness of our God.

Following the recognition that God controls everything, it follows closely that He owns everything; it is His kingdom, not ours. All the heavens and all the earth belong to God. Everything that I have and everything that you have belongs to God. It is humbling to come to the point of admission that I own nothing; God is the owner of everything I claim as mine. We Christians are learning to say the right things. We can spout out quickly that God is owner of everything. The question is not, "Do we know the politically correct answer?" The real question is, "Do our actions reflect that God owns everything?"

Then, the real test comes. Do we recognize and acknowledge that God has dominion over everything? He is the one who sends the storms and He is the one who calms the storms. He is the one who causes crops to grow and produce a harvest and He is the one that is in control when crops fail. He is the one who brings a new life into this world and He is the one who told us that it is appointed that we shall die. He is the one that gives us the good days and He is the same one that gives us some bad days (**Ecclesiastes 7:14**). **Ecclesiastes 3** tells us about the seasons of God. In all the good and bad, God is in control.

Life becomes meaningful when we come to grips with these points. Lest we think that we are in control, that building wealth is going to give us the power to be happy and content, that we control what our future holds, let us go back to the basics where Jesus taught us to pray: *"And do not lead us into temptation, But deliver us from the evil one. For Yours is the kingdom and the power and the glory forever. Amen."*

Reflections...

FEBRUARY 20

2 Corinthians 9:7(b) *...for God loves a cheerful giver.*

There are several different types of givers mentioned in the New Testament. Have you ever asked yourself what kind of giver you are? From time to time, it is healthy for us to assess our position on important matters to see where we are and also to see if we need to make changes. While this list of types of givers specifically mentioned in the New Testament is probably not exhaustive, it does provide a measure so that we can evaluate our position. Let's look at these:

Legalistic givers – **Luke 18:12** & **Matthew 23:23**: Both these scriptures reference the Pharisees who were bound in legalism in much of what they did and their giving was no exception. They put their giving as a matter of public exhibition so that everyone could see and give them a pat on the back. Their giving certainly was not done from the heart.

Sparing givers – The Apostle Paul referenced these in **2 Corinthians 9:6**. Sparing givers are meager givers. They give enough to say that they are givers: no more, no less. Like the legalistic givers, their giving is not from the heart, but more from a guilt complex.

Non-givers – **Luke 12:15-31**: The story is told of the rich farmer whose crops produce bountifully to the point that he did not have enough storage space. Greedily he went about making plans to create additional storage space which would allow him to hoard everything instead of giving a portion away. While this sad scenario plays out in this particular instance with a rich person, it is also prevalent in those who are not rich. The amount of wealth a person possesses has little to do with whether or not he is a giver. Non-givers are like the Dead Sea. It has tributaries running into it, but nothing running out. There is no life in the Dead Sea. Its water is polluted and has the stench of decay.

Grudging givers – **2 Corinthians 9:7**: Paul again talks about those who do participate in giving, but it is well known that their giving is not done with a willing spirit. Sometimes referred to as stingy givers, these give more or less out of necessity because they would feel badly if they

102

did not give at all. In essence, they give to soothe their conscience. Their giving is in minuscule portions.

Generous/Liberal givers – **Romans 12:18; 2 Corinthians 8:2**; the early church in Acts 4: Generous giving is not measured in dollar amounts. Generous giving is actually not measured by what is given but rather by what is left after giving. Paul described the giving of the Macedonians as *"a great ordeal of affliction their abundance of joy and their deep poverty overflowed in the wealth of their liberality."* ...**2 Corinthians 8:2**. The Macedonians gave out of their poverty with great liberality. The early church described in the Book of Acts, Chapter 4 gave with no regard of their personal needs or desires. Many of them sold everything they owned and gave the proceeds to the church to meet the needs of others.

Cheerful givers – **2 Corinthians 9:7(b)** *"...for God loves a cheerful giver."* All born-again believers and followers of Christ should fall into this category, even if we do not reach the previous category of generous givers. The root meaning here is happy or hilarious givers. The opportunity should make us happy enough to laugh out loud.

Greatest Giver – **John 3:16**: While we cannot approach this category of giving, it is our responsibility and duty to acknowledge that God is the greatest giver. He alone occupies this position.

While God is the Greatest Giver, let us remember that we are made in His image and therefore when we are born-again, we should have His nature and be **great** givers!

Reflections...

FEBRUARY 21

Proverbs 22:4 *The reward of humility and the fear of the LORD Are riches, honor and life.* (NASB)

Our culture today really does not teach us to be humble and in no way does it teach us to show *"fear of the Lord."* As a matter of fact, the news media will go to any length to avoid any mention of the name of God, Jesus or Christ. They act like a death-threatening allergic reaction is going to capture them in its clutches and squeeze out their life. It is safe to say that the news media in general abhors any verbal expression about God, Jesus or Christ.

Showing humility and the fear of the Lord does not mean that one is going to be accepted in our society. In fact, most of the time, the opposite is true. National Football League star, Tim Tebow, has faced untold ridicule at the hands of the news media. Others of notoriety have assumed a staunch stand for God have faced similar mockery.

However, in the midst of all the noise raised by the media, there is an underlying respect for people who live out a life of humility and fear of the Lord. Tim Tebow is probably the most respected football player in recent history, not because he invented the "tebowing" kneel with one knee on the ground and one fist curled into the forehead, but because his private life is filled with activities that honor God (...doer of the word ...**James 1:22**).

Does this mean that we will automatically become rich if we show humility and the fear of the Lord? In dollars and cents ...no! In blessings of contentment and riches in eternity ...yes! Eternity is what matters. This life is but a flash in the pan. To have material wealth in this life is meaningless. This world's wealth brings only anxiety, worry and discontentment if not used to honor God.

So, when we are assessing the things that really matter, let's look to that which really has eternal value: *"The reward of humility and the fear of the LORD Are riches, honor and life."*

Reflections...

FEBRUARY 22

James 1:11 *For no sooner has the sun risen with a burning heat than it withers the grass; its flower falls, and its beautiful appearance perishes. So the rich man also will fade away in his pursuits.*

In my opinion, there are few things as beautiful as fresh-opening red roses. There is just something about the coloration of the petals that exemplifies God's magnificence. As the rose bud begins to open, it is as though everything around it stands still in awe of its majesty. So it is with most flowers. Within God's creation of flowers lies an unmatched splendor that is without reproducibility (*"Consider the lilies, how they grow: they neither toil nor spin; and yet I say to you, even Solomon in all his glory was not arrayed like one of these."* ... **Luke 12:27**).

There is, however, another characteristic that we must recognize as a fact of nature. As beautiful as they are, the longevity of flowers is somewhat short at best. Cut flowers, with which so many of us are familiar, display their grandeur for only a few short days, even with the best of care. Live flowers are very susceptible to the elements of weather. Many will wilt quickly under the pressure of hot, direct burning sunlight. We have come to know that the lifespan of the beauty of flowers is somewhat diminutive at best. So we learn to enjoy them while we can; then, we have to clean up the mess!

A person who pursues riches as his life's purpose is analogous to a flower. They are flashy and draw attention in their prime. People around them are enamored with their flamboyance. Just think for a moment about some of the TV shows that exist now or in the past that highlight the rich and famous. In fact, that very name, *The Lifestyles of the Rich and Famous* for years drew viewers like buzzards to road-kill. *Entertainment Tonight* parades the gaudiness of the rich while many of us sit on the edge of our sofas drooling. While the rich draw our attention, we fail to see the Paul Harvey of the story (...rest of the story!).

Scripture tells us that the pursuits of the rich are like the flower that wilts under the burning sun. Although they do demand attention, it is short-lived. It may catch our attention to the point of being contagious, but its glimmer will fade fast. The bottom line is that this world's riches are only temporary, as is the beauty of the flower. Don't place your hope in temporal riches: *"But seek the kingdom of God, and all these things shall be added to you."* ... **Luke 12:31**

Reflections...

☐

FEBRUARY 23

Philemon 1:18-19 *But if he has wronged you or owes anything, put that on my account. (19) I, Paul, am writing with my own hand. I will repay - not to mention to you that you owe me even your own self besides.*

The Book of Philemon is Paul's letter to Philemon greeting him and asking a favor of him. Onesimus was Philemon's escaped slave who had come to the saving grace of Christ through the ministry of Paul. It is strongly believed that Philemon also was a convert of Paul. Paul pleaded that Philemon would accept Onesimus back as more than a slave; he requested that Onesimus be accepted as a brother in Christ.

It is one thing that we go to bat for a new convert as a matter of assisting him to find and settle into a new life. However, it is going the extra mile to do what Paul did by standing good for any indebtedness that may be outstanding as a result of Onesimus running away from his master. We do not know if there possibly may have been some thievery involved in this escape, but certainly that possibility existed. Without wavering, Paul declared that he would make good anything that Onesimus owed Philemon.

Paul did not make his proposition a matter of command, but rather as a plea to a fellow brother in the faith. He did slide one under the door on Philemon by stating *"not to mention to you that you owe me even your own self besides."* This situation has a similar flavor to the parable of the unforgiving slave that Jesus taught in **Matthew 18:21-35**. Though we do not know the debt owed by Philemon, Paul reminded him that he too should forgive Onesimus, just as he was forgiven.

As followers of Christ, we should have the mindset to which Paul referred. God has forgiven us much. It is therefore incumbent upon us that we stand ready to forgive those who are indebted to us. Then, also, we should be ready to take it to the next level as Paul did and personally stand good financially for those who need our assistance. We are not going to take any of our wealth with us when we leave this world. The only thing that really counts is what we can do with it while it is in our possession here in this life. As Paul showed, stepping up and helping others is one of the best things we can do with what God has entrusted into our care (*"...Assuredly, I say to you, inasmuch as you did it to one of the least of these My brethren, you did it to Me."* ... **Matthew 25:40**).

Reflections...

☐

FEBRUARY 24

Deuteronomy 8:17 *then you say in your heart, 'My power and the might of my hand have gained me this wealth.'*

When things are going according to our plans, we all have a tendency to sit back and compliment ourselves on a job well done. When things are not going according to our plans, we all have a tendency to look for someone to blame. In short, we are quick to accept the credit when there are good results and then not accept the responsibility when results are not so good. This just seems to be human nature. It is just another example of our sin nature. It was present in the very first two individuals who walked upon the face of the earth. When Adam and Eve were confronted by God after they had violated God's strict ordinance not to eat of the fruit of the tree of knowledge of good and evil, they both scurried from accepting the responsibility of their actions. Eve's reply to God was, *"The serpent deceived me, and I ate."* ...**Genesis 3:13**. She blamed the serpent. Adam's reply to God was *"The woman whom You gave to be with me, she gave me of the tree, and I ate."* ...**Genesis 3:12**. Adam blamed both Eve and God.

Human behavior has not changed down through the centuries. Even small children will play the blame game. And to the other end of the spectrum, we are quick to take credit for a good job. We beam ear to ear when we hear flattering remarks. Watch a parent glow when his child excels. When compliments are given, watch everyone rush to the front of the line to make sure they receive their "proper recognition."

If we have done well with finances, it is our nature to elaborate, sometimes endlessly, upon the minute details of how we have been able to reach our accomplishment. Quite often, you may hear about the good investment choices, the long hard hours worked, the smart choices and the frugal lifestyles for which "I" was responsible. In success, we become plagued with the "I-tis syndrome." It is all about "I, Me and My."

110

Earlier in life, the term "self-made" man was one to which I ascribed and held in high esteem. However, as I later learned, I can accomplish nothing except with the power of God. There are no self-made men. It is God who gives the power to obtain wealth (**Deuteronomy 8:18**) as well as all other accomplishments. I must at all times be cognizant that God enables me. I can do nothing within myself. I must always know that if I allow, my old nature will walk me down this same old self-righteous path: *"then you say in your heart, 'My power and the might of my hand have gained me this wealth.'"*

Reflections...

FEBRUARY 25

Haggai 1:6-7 *"You have sown much, and bring in little; You eat, but do not have enough; You drink, but you are not filled with drink; You clothe yourselves, but no one is warm; And he who earns wages, Earns wages to put into a bag with holes."* *(7) Thus says the Lord of hosts: "Consider your ways!"*

At the time of this scripture, the Lord's house lay in ruins while the people concerned themselves only with their selfish motives. They built houses for themselves. However, at the same time, the consensus of the people was that it was not time to build the Lord's house. In other words, it was more important to them that they attend to their own desires than to attend to the things of God. God spoke asking, *"Is it time for you yourselves to dwell in your paneled houses, and this temple to lie in ruins?"* ...**Haggai 1:4**.

This seems as though it could have happened this very day. God has told us to go out and to build His kingdom (**Matthew 28:18-20**). Yet, our reaction is much the same as the people in the day of Haggai: *"The time has not come, the time that the Lord's house should be built."* ...**Haggai 1:2**. We become all wrapped up in our pursuit of wealth and accomplishments and tell the Lord to wait.

You may take offense and question whether or not this is true. Think with me for a moment. If you have ever attempted to get people involved in ministry, you know very well how difficult it is to recruit workers who are willing to roll up their sleeves and get to the task at hand. I know of an attempt to enlist help in ministry that required only a couple hours a month. One of the more popular responses offered to the request was "I don't have time." I say more popular simply because that response kept coming up. Although I have no way of knowing, I wonder how many hours these same people spend in front of the TV on a daily basis, yet they do not have time to assist in the building of the Kingdom of God. Yes, they were saying, *"The time has not come, the time that the Lord's house should be built."*

Our self-centered culture has produced a generation that is completely wrapped up in self gratification. In our ambivalence, we have mass discontentment. The end result is opposite what we set out to achieve. We work long hours, but get further behind. We eat in abundance even to the point of gluttony, but our hunger is not satisfied. We drink, but remain thirsty. We have closets full of clothes, but nothing to wear. We earn more money than any time in our lives, but we cannot pay the bills. Does this sound familiar? As God spoke through Haggai, He has a word for us: *"Consider your ways!"*

Reflections...

FEBRUARY 26

Proverbs 23:17-18 *Do not let your heart envy sinners, But be zealous for the fear of the Lord all the day; (18) For surely there is a hereafter, And your hope will not be cut off.*

One of the most startling statistics from the Barna Group is that there are basically no differences in the attitudes and goals of Christians and non-believers. In practically every major area in which research has been done, there are little to no distinguishing differences in the two groups. Is something wrong here? Shouldn't followers of Christ be different from non-believers? We are told in Romans that we should not conform to this world (**Romans 12:2**). That sounds like there should be something that distinguishes us from the world. Both **Titus 2:14** and **1 Peter 2:9** speak about a "peculiar" people, one that is special to God. So how is it that according to modern scientific research, we are not different?

I suppose there are a number of explanations to rationalize where we are. We could probably come up with excuses in an attempt to explain our position. However, the facts speak; in fact, they speak loudly! It is evident that followers of Christ have allowed their hearts to become envious of sinners as stated in **Proverbs 23:17**. We have bought into the idea that we should have elaborate lifestyles just like "everyone" else. Regardless of whether we can afford it or not, we want everything that everyone else has. We rationalize our wants by our selfish reasoning that we "deserve" to have things since we are Christians. How naïve we are!

It is my humble opinion that the enemy has basically neutralized the witness of modern-day Christianity by leading us blindly down the road of materialism that has landed the majority of born-again Christians in debt up to their eyeballs. Because Christians have allowed themselves to become enslaved by debt (**Proverbs 22:7**), we cannot answer the call when the Holy Spirit speaks to us and calls us to participate in specific ministries within the church. Recently I was talking with an esteemed friend who shared his experience of being able to spontaneously step up and make a significant monetary

114

contribution to meet a need of a new church plant. He was able to do that because of one reason: he was debt-free. On the flip side, about the same time in another church, there was a specific need and the membership struggled and eventually failed to meet the need. Why? Many of their members were struggling and being crushed with debt. Debt makes us slaves. It removes us from God's availability list.

The enemy likes nothing better than to neutralize your testimony. He can successfully accomplish that if you allow your heart to envy sinners and fall into the debt trap. This phenomenon has occurred to many Christians across our nation. God's Word gives us directions to prevent our becoming victims. Do not be conformed to this world; do not allow your hearts to become envious of sinners.

To the contrary, *"... be zealous for the fear of the Lord all the day; For surely there is a hereafter, And your hope will not be cut off."*

Reflections...

☐

FEBRUARY 27

Ecclesiastes 6:2 *A man to whom God has given riches and wealth and honor, so that he lacks nothing for himself of all he desires; yet God does not give him power to eat of it, but a foreigner consumes it. This is vanity, and it is an evil affliction.*

There are people around us every day who seemingly have everything, and yet, they are unhappy. Hollywood sends out this message on a daily basis and we "common" people never receive it. We are still enamored with the lifestyles of the rich and famous. Something inside tells us that if we can just make more money, gain more wealth, or attain a certain status in society, then we will be happy.

God is giving us a message. Happiness and contentment are not found in the riches, wealth or social status. Even though we may be the recipient of God's blessings of riches and wealth, those things that God gives us will not bring us the fulfillment that God has reserved for Himself.

I challenge you to listen to conversation of those around you. When we are young, we are constantly talking about what position at work will make us happy, what position in the social realm will bring fulfillment, which country club will help us attain business acceptance, which investment will help us reach our financial goals, etc, etc, etc... Then, as we get older, all we talk about is the "good ole days" of the past, how good it "used to be," if we could just go back to_____. What is going on here? We are either looking forward for happiness and contentment or we are looking back. But somehow, we never seem to find it. It is as though we have leaped over it somewhere in the course of life. Simply put, if we are not careful, we will find ourselves attempting to measure happiness and contentment with "events and things" that occur in our lives. "Events and things" do not bring happiness and contentment. A personal relationship with God does!

116

When God gives us riches, wealth and honor, our response should be to look to Him, not only to give Him thanks, but also to give us fulfillment. Unfortunately, we are too often like the fat hog that never looks up to see from where the acorns fall. We look for the material blessing of God to find happiness rather than looking to God Himself. God has designed His plan so that we are not fulfilled with material things. Even though He blesses us with riches, wealth and honor, He does not allow us to "eat" those things and receive fulfillment. We will leave all those things behind when this life is over. Someone else (foreigners) will come along and consume them. If we look to riches, wealth and honor for fulfillment in life, the wise man Solomon has given us some good advice: *"This is vanity, and it is an evil affliction."*

Reflections...

FEBRUARY 28

John 12:3 *Then Mary took a pound of very costly oil of spikenard, anointed the feet of Jesus, and wiped His feet with her hair. And the house was filled with the fragrance of the oil.*

When was the last time that you were criticized because of the amount that you gave to God? Let's clarify that...when was the last time others criticized you because you gave such a large amount to God? For most of us, the only criticism that we have received is due to the fact that we gave so little.

Mary set an example for us. She was completely absorbed, if you will, in the act of giving to Jesus. She did not stop and pinch the pennies to be sure she was not going to over give. She did not watch others sitting nearby to gain their approval. She did not call a budget committee meeting to make sure that the amount of her gift was plausible and would fit into her budget. No, she was absorbed with the very presence of Jesus as she went about the worshipful duty of pouring the expensive oil over the feet of her Savior, massaging it into His feet and then proceeding to wipe His feet with her hair.

Do you think she was concerned with who was watching? Do you think for a minute that she was saying that maybe no one would notice? Hardly! The fragrance of the oil filled the house. Everyone around was well aware of her gift. She did not concern herself with what others thought. She gave her gift in openness; everyone could see exactly what was happening. That was quite different from our giving these days. The attitude of Christians today is that all giving should be done under cover so that no one will ever know about the gift. While it is true that we should never give in order to receive the praise of men, there are numerous occasions in the Bible that support and encourage open giving while everyone is watching. Giving is not a matter of who is watching; rather, it is a matter of the motives of the heart of the giver.

118

Mary was sharply criticized because she gave a very expensive gift to Jesus. Judas, who is described a couple of verses down as being a thief, quickly raised his voice in opposition (consider the source). Judas was operating at full-steam in a spirit of greed while Mary was moved by the Holy Spirit to show her love for her Savior. She proved her love with her generous giving.

Let each of us pray that our giving to God will be with the same unique dedication and love shown by Mary. Wouldn't it be great if we began to have complaints within our churches about the sizeable gifts that we are giving!

Reflections...

□

MARCH 1

1 Timothy 5:3 *Take care of widows who are destitute.* (MSG)

The 5th chapter of 1 Timothy is all about taking care of relatives (family) and goes even further to cover those in the church who also are in need. The emphasis is on one's immediate family and the widows.

Taking care of those in need is humane. We read through these passages and say, sure, that's the thing to do; it is the "right" thing to do. However, when the plates are passed, for some reason we have short arms; our monetary means fall short of the plate and hit directly into the bottommost parts of our pockets, forever to remain.

All of us can manufacture arguments for why we do not come to the rescue of destitute widows. Most of us have probably made those arguments at one time or another. However, all the arguments in the world do not negate what the Word has to say. As the church (body of believers) and as individuals, we should take the instruction from the Bible literally and *"Take care of widows who are destitute."*

Yes, there are conditions given in the chapter by which our actions are to be guided. Most of us never get close enough with our actions to be concerned with those conditions. Most churches are more concerned with the planning of the next outing or entertainment extravaganza than devising a plan for taking care of widows and orphans.

James also addressed this issue: *"Pure and undefiled religion before God and the Father is this: to visit orphans and widows in their trouble, and to keep oneself unspotted from the world."* ... **James 1:27**. Maybe it is time for us as individuals and as churches to reassess our motives and actions. Are we motivated to "do our own thing" or do we seek to be obedient and do the will of our Father? That is a fair question for each of us ...think about it!

Biblical Guidance in Daily Doses . . .

Reflections...

121

MARCH 2

Malachi 3:5 *"And I will come near you for judgment; I will be a swift witness Against sorcerers, Against adulterers, Against perjurers, Against those who exploit wage earners and widows and orphans, And against those who turn away an alien - Because they do not fear Me," Says the Lord of hosts.* (NASB)

There is one thing that modern-day Christians do not want to talk about or hear: judgment. This is not a popular subject. This has not always been the case. If we go back in time for approximately 40 years, there was a lot of preaching, teaching and talk about God's judgment. There was an awareness of right and wrong based upon the Bible. Even though we do not like to hear the "negative" side, the Bible does, on occasion, proclaim God's judgment on certain violations of God's law. **Malachi 3:5** is one such proclamation.

It is particularly interesting to note the violations specifically named in this verse. The reference to those who exploit wage earners, widows and orphans catches the eye. These sins are probably the most subtle of all listed. These are the ones that go unnoticed in the community, unless you are the one being violated. Even though they are not in the limelight, they may, in fact, occur more often than the others that are listed. We have become anesthetized to the point that we pay little to no attention when these violations are present.

To exploit a wage earner is nothing less than robbery. There is a price to be paid for a violation of this nature. Turning a deaf ear and blind eye to widows and orphans while driving our BMW's to our vacation beach townhouses do have consequences. Many of us will spend more money on gasoline just driving to and from our vacations than is required to care for an orphan for an ENTIRE YEAR!

Why do we ignore that which is so obvious? How is it that we have no concern for the very people to whom Jesus gave most of His time during His earthly ministry? How is it that we do not get alarmed even though these violators are grouped right there with what we classify as

122

the "really bad" sinners, namely fortune tellers, adulterers, liars under oath, and those who discriminate against people who are different? We seemingly turn our heads and continue with business as usual. There is a reason why we do these things with no conscience. That reason is stated in the last of this verse: *'"Because they do not fear Me," Says the Lord of hosts.'*

We can thumb our noses at these violations which translates into thumbing our noses at God. Our actions do not go unnoticed. God has declared, *"And I will come near you for judgment; I will be a swift witness against you."*

Reflections...

_____

_____

_____

_____

_____

_____

_____

_____

_____

_____

_____

_____

_____

☐

MARCH 3

Ecclesiastes 7:11 *Wisdom is good with an inheritance, And profitable to those who see the sun.*

Throughout the Proverbs, we read time and again about the importance of getting wisdom. In fact, wisdom, knowledge, understanding, and money are mentioned from the beginning to the end of the Proverbs. In this verse, note how two of those are coupled. Money (inheritance) needs the guidance of wisdom in order to accomplish its full purpose. Money without wisdom is dangerous. We read an account of this in the New Testament in the incident of the prodigal who took his inheritance with the absence of wisdom (**Luke 15:11-32**). The entire inheritance was squandered in riotous and wasteful living. We have seen similar scenarios play out within our lifetimes, especially when one comes into a sizeable amount of money quickly. Everyone can probably relate a story of someone they have known who has blown their inheritance in short order in the absence of wisdom.

There is an underlying truism in this verse that we need to capture. It deals with the responsibility of parents who plan to leave their children an inheritance ...and doesn't that include most of us? Parents have a moral and godly responsibility to teach their children how to manage money. One of the worst things we could possibly do to harm our children is to leave them an inheritance without teaching them good money management skills. Not training them to manage money is like pronouncing doom upon them.

Most of us can quote **Proverbs 22:6** *"Train up a child in the way he should go and when he is old, he will not depart from it."* The very next verse proclaims the chilling results of bad money management: *"The rich rule over the poor and the borrower is servant to the lender."* Maybe, just maybe, these two verses contain a message to parents!

Has there been a deficiency of training your children in the area of money and finance? As you are formulating your estate plan, whatever you do, don't overlook the importance of their training. No parent wants to willingly give a sentence of destruction to his children. While you still have time, train your children how to use wisdom to manage their inheritance.

Reflections...

MARCH 4

Ecclesiastes 5:11 When goods increase, They increase who eat them; So what profit have the owners Except to see them with their eyes?

We live in a culture that is a perpetual cheerleader, always cheering us on to more and more, bigger and bigger, faster and faster, and the gerbil keeps running on the wheel but never getting anywhere. To exist in our business culture, one must always be driving for more; there is no such thing as maintaining the status quo. There is never any time to just be content with a "good" business. We must constantly keep "ramping it up" to bigger and better things. In our business culture, to just maintain in essence means you are dying.

Our personal lives follow the pattern of our businesses. We are constantly trying to cram more and more into our schedules. As we are doing so, we are opening ourselves up for first-class burnout. We see it happening around us all the time. We even see it happening in the church. In fact, ministry ranks near the top of all professions/vocations experiencing burnout.

As followers of Christ, we need to chill for a moment, take a few deep breaths and consider the words of the wise man Solomon. When we experience an increase in goods (income), we experience more cares (expenses) to take away the luster (net gain) of the increase. In layman's terms, an increase in business brings with it an increase in the expenses required to generate that increase. Net gain is very little to nothing. In realistic terms, the gerbil is just running a little faster to get to the same destination to which he was previously headed ...nowhere!

We can work ourselves into a frenzy – to the point of over exertion – and the net gain may be negligible. All that we gain is the satisfaction of saying that we have increased our business but not our profits. In our personal lives, we can increase our activities, but wind up with a lower quality of life.

Be careful. Don't allow the drive for an increase in money to land you on an endless gerbil wheel. Don't allow activities in your personal life to rob you of enjoyment of life. As Solomon states, "this too is vanity!"

Reflections...

□

MARCH 5

Proverbs 15:6 In the house of the righteous there is much treasure, But in the revenue of the wicked is trouble.

By its very nature, the house of the righteous is filled with treasure. The righteous are rich beyond the wealth of this world. Again, by its very nature, the house of the righteous is rich with contentment and happiness that this world's money cannot buy.

I am reminded of a family that I once knew who would be considered poor by the world's standard. In fact, they would have qualified for a box seat at the low end of poverty. They had approximately three times the national average of 2.3 children. However, their children were different; they were well-mannered and intelligent. It did not seem that they went lacking for anything in particular. In fact, they did quite well, thank you! No, they did not have all the modern technological gadgets that most of us have, but then again, they did not need them. They thoroughly enjoyed the quaint, simpler things of life. In my opinion, their house was filled with much treasure.

There was another similar example that I witnessed first-hand on our recent mission trip to Nigeria. The orphans at Shepherd Care Orphanage numbered approximately 50. They had no possessions to claim as their own; yet the simple lifestyle as they all gathered together was one reflecting a house filled with much treasure.

These two examples are drastically different from many households in our country and even in our own neighborhoods (maybe our own house!). Many households are filled with trouble, bickering, fighting, scheming, and sometimes prolonged anxiety and discontentment. So what made these two examples above different? They were filled with God's righteousness. His love penetrated not the walls of the house, but the innermost parts of the hearts of those residing in the houses. Money may make one wealthy by worldly standards, but only God's love and righteousness make one truly RICH!

Reflections...

MARCH 6

Deuteronomy 28:12 *The Lord will open to you His good treasure, the heavens, to give the rain to your land in its season, and to bless all the work of your hand. You shall lend to many nations, but you shall not borrow.*

As Christians, we always are looking for "blessings" from the Lord. However, don't allow yourself to become derailed when you do not receive those blessings on your unique timetable. There are numerous scriptures that inform us that serving God does not automatically bring with it a life of bliss. **Ecclesiastes 7:14** is one of those scriptures that will all but destroy the theology of some as we are not always promised those good days for which we constantly yearn. When we have the good days of prosperity, we should enjoy them; however, when the "not-so-good" days come, we remember that God is still God and that he allows for those days also.

When God blesses us, we should be diligent in managing the bounty of His blessings. Our culture is diametrically opposite this rationale. We live in a culture that is engrossed with hyper-consumerism. If we have it, we spend it; if we don't have it, we borrow and spend anyway. We think nothing of signing our lives away by way of debt in exchange for more stuff that we don't need. It is as though our culture teaches us exactly opposite what God's Word teaches about money. As in this verse, when we are blessed, we are in a position to lend to others and not have to borrow. In following God's Word, we will be the head and not the tail.

However, the choice is ours. We can follow the financial principles of the Bible and allow God to work through us to reach others; conversely, we can choose to follow our culture and consume the blessing from God in our own hyper-consumptive lifestyles becoming the tail, the one who is always borrowing. By so doing, we will live our lives in slavery as **Proverbs 22:7** so vividly points out.

Let's not allow consumerism to rob us of the opportunity of fulfilling the promises of God for our lives. Constantly borrowing is a downward road that leads to poverty. Don't fall for the beck and call of our culture. Manage God's blessings to His glory!

Reflections...

MARCH 7

Leviticus 27:30 *And all the tithe of the land, whether of the seed of the land or of the fruit of the tree, is the Lord's. It is holy to the Lord.*

It's a good place to start! Did you ever wonder why throughout the Bible there is the pattern of giving a tenth (10%) to the Lord? The tithe, or one-tenth, is found all through the scriptures. The first record in scripture of giving a tithe is **Genesis 14**. Who told Abraham that he should give a tenth? Next we have Jacob in **Genesis 28**. How did he come up with the idea of giving a tenth? Maybe it was from Grandpa Abraham; could have been. Maybe they remembered that God reserved a certain portion for Himself in the Garden of Eden and that inspired them to give 10% of their possessions. Or, maybe God just spoke to both and said this is a good place to start giving. We really do not know how they arrived at the amount.

We do know, however, that Jacob did this willingly and without reservation after he had a personal encounter with the Lord God. God more or less recounted the covenant He had made with his grandfather Abraham. Jacob had to make a choice as to whether he was going to follow God or go his own way. Of course, we know the outcome of this decision. Jacob opened his heart to God. It is interesting to note that he also opened his treasure to God.

When we have an encounter with God, we also have to make some decisions. We have to make a decision as to whether we are going to follow God or go our own way. If we choose to become a follower of God (not just a fan), then, just as Jacob, we will assume a genuine sense of responsibility. A decision to become a follower after an encounter with God is more than just giving God a nod of acknowledgment. A decision to become a follower results in a changed life with changed behavior. One aspect of behavior that changes is that we are willing to give our treasure to God. If we give our heart to God, it follows that we are going to become givers (*"For where you treasure is, there your heart will be also."* ...**Luke 12:34**). As we become more like God, we will become givers, as did Jacob.

132

So back to the original thought ...the 10%. As we have already stated, this amount is consistent throughout the Bible. This verse in Leviticus states, *"The tithe of all the land is the Lord's."* Though the argument can readily be made that greater amounts were given at specific times, we can rest assured that 10% is a good place to start!

Reflections...

MARCH 8

Matthew 6:33 *But seek first the kingdom of God and His righteousness, and all these things shall be added to you.*

What do you want out of life? Is this a really serious question or do you view it as flippant? Whether or not we stop and come face-to-face with the question, we are inevitably charting our own personal answers by the way we approach our day-to-day lives.

Most of us, if we are honest with ourselves, would come up with some somber answers if we were taking a test and were required to write down our answers. One of our main problems is that even though we sincerely desire some meaningful and worthwhile things, we find ourselves putting them out into the future and resolving that "one day" we will get serious about those goals. However, right now it is more important that we get the additional degree, so we can land the sought-after job, so we can make more money, so we can buy more stuff that we really don't need, so that we can become overly burdened by the demands of those unneeded things consuming our limited time, so that we can fit into our socioeconomic class in society, so that we can be unhappy and very discontent! So goes the *Days of our Lives.*

What is really important in life? Jesus boiled it down for us if we could just wipe the bug stains off our windshield of life and see the real worth of life. He said *"You shall love the Lord your God with all your heart, with all your soul, and with all your mind ...You shall love your neighbor as yourself."* ...**Matthew 22:37-39**. But wait a minute! What do loving God and our neighbor have to do with seeking the kingdom of God first? Glad you asked the question...

The question begs as to how do we serve God? With what activities do we involve ourselves in fulfilling the commandment to seek first the kingdom of God? First of all we can probably eliminate about 98.37% of what most of us find ourselves doing day after day. Most of our activities are either acts of self pleasure or preparation for a self-fulfilling future. You might say, "It's all about me!" Serving God is NOT all about ourselves. Serving God is about serving others. Look at the life of Jesus. His life is our example of what it means to seek first the kingdom of God. Basically, it means to love the Lord God with all our hearts, with all our souls, and with all our minds followed closely by loving our neighbors as much as we love ourselves.

This does not mean that we give up gainful employment and dedicate ourselves to live in a monastery. It simply means that our gainful employment serves as a tool to accomplish the things that are important ... loving God and our neighbors!

Reflections...

MARCH 9

Luke 14:18 *But they all with one accord began to make excuses. The first said to him, "I have bought a piece of ground, and I must go and see it. I ask you to have me excused."*

On several occasions, I have received advertising flyers in the mail or ventured into cyberspace via the internet looking at mountain cabins in North Georgia and North Carolina. As I drooled over the magnificent photos of the cabins in the hills with exquisite views for miles, I had no problem rationalizing the economic advantages of ownership of one of these properties. A quaint cabin stuck on a mountainside is our family's favorite vacation spot, even though we don't make this a frequent routine. There is nothing quite as relaxing as sitting in a rocking chair on the front porch with a good book while experiencing an afternoon cloudburst. The starry nights seem to produce brighter glows in the mountains.

No, I have no problem justifying an investment into a property that we could enjoy at-will and then rent out for income at all other times. Simple calculations prove my point, not only of justification, but even a sizeable profit. I'll bet that I almost have you convinced to my way of thinking! There is only one problem that chocked the wheels of my mental mountain real estate investment excursion. Prayer! Yep! When I prayed about it, I had this disturbing revelation (one that I already knew, so I suppose I cannot really call it a revelation). "Everything that I own consumes a portion of my life." That's the revelation. Regardless of what it is, every possession literally consumes a portion of life.

In this particular situation (the mountain cabin), the economics is not necessarily the problem. I can make that work both on paper and in reality. The problem is that a mountain cabin 4 hours away means that I will have to go up and check on it quite often. There will be routine maintenance that requires more of my time. The family will be taking more frequent weekend trips; that will detach me from some of the ongoing ministry activities into which God has connected me. Instead of doing what God has directed, such a venture would be self serving rather than serving God and others. Buying the mountain property would remove me from fulfilling the ministry to which I have been called.

In this scripture, Jesus taught this same lesson. When we become self-serving, we do not have time to serve Him. So, before you buy that next piece of ground (or whatever it may be), pray about it and see if it is REALLY God's will!

Reflections...

☐

MARCH 10

Mark 12:42-43 *A poor widow came and put in two small copper coins, which amount to a cent. (43) Calling His disciples to Him, He said to them, "Truly I say to you, this poor widow put in more than all the contributors to the treasury;"* (NIV)

Several years ago a friend and co-worker of mine was in Houston, TX. Both he and I traveled often to Houston during that period of time and were somewhat familiar with the traffic patterns of the fourth largest city in the U.S. However, the city had lowered its freeway speed limits the week prior to the time of this particular trip. Police were out in force in an effort to enforce the newly posted lower speed limit. You probably have already guessed the inevitable. He was pulled over for speeding even though he was in the flow of traffic – a lot of traffic. The officer coolly wrote his citation; my friend was agasp. He gathered his composure and calmly asked the officer, "Why, with all the hundreds of cars traveling at the same speed, did you pick me out of the pack? I was driving no faster than anyone else!" The officer politely answered, "I guess it's just your unlucky day. Have a good day, sir."

The officer used my friend to make a statement to others. He was an example, not by choice and certainly not willingly, but nevertheless, an example. You may have been caught in a similar situation at some time. Being made "an example" usually carries the connotation of punishment. It is not a position that we willingly choose.

In this passage in Mark, Jesus made an example of the poor widow. He called His disciples over pointing out to them what had just taken place before their very eyes. "Did you see what just happened? Did you see the amount given by that poor widow? She gave more than everyone else combined!" I can just imagine there was an excitement in His voice as He pointed out the sacrifice of the widow. She had been made an example, albeit, a GOOD example. In fact, it was not just a good example; it was one that has been used for centuries to teach sacrificial giving. Jesus caught the rarity of the moment. He made sure that it did

138

not escape not only the attention of those standing nearby, but also, the attention of hundreds of millions of those of us to follow.

What kind of example are you? Are you a good example or does your giving need improvement? Do you give or just tip? Do you give generously? Do you give sacrificially? Could Jesus use you as an example to others in the area of giving? These are questions that we each have to answer for ourselves. However, know for sure that regardless of the level to which we give, it is by no means private. Jesus is positioned and is watching! (**Mark 12:41**)

Reflections...

MARCH 11

1 Timothy 3:3 *not given to wine, not violent, not greedy for money, but gentle, not quarrelsome, not covetous;*

The Bible gives many "dos" in its directions concerning money. Of course, the most recurring is "do give." There are also a few "don'ts" to go along with the "dos." Don't be greedy for money! Don't form a love for money. Don't hoard.

In this verse, Paul outlines some of the qualifications for leaders in church affairs. Thrown right into the mix is "don't be greedy for money." Greed will take a good person hostage if not controlled. Greed will cause an otherwise rational person to make irrational decisions. Greed will cause a person to lie, cheat and steal by fueling the uncontrolled passion it creates within the drive of a person.

It is noteworthy that verse 7 states that a candidate for leadership should have a good testimony in the community. There is little doubt that a person who is driven by greed will have a reputation in the community that would not be complimentary with being a leader in church affairs. A follower of Christ is a Christian 24/7. There is no separation of the "Christian" life and the "secular" life. Whatever a professing Christian is at his very worst time on the job is exactly what he is in his finest hour in church on Sunday.

One's testimony about money in the community is an important part of his Christianity. Keep money in its right perspective, in church and in the community. Don't be given to greed, but *"...have a good testimony among those who are outside, lest he fall into reproach and the snare of the devil."* **I Timothy 3:7**

Reflections...

☐

MARCH 12

Proverbs 13:18 *Poverty and shame will come to him who disdains correction, But he who regards a rebuke will be honored.*

There is something in our human nature that fuels our fire of always wanting to be right. It really doesn't matter what area of life, we like to think that we have inside information and the upper hand. Even in areas in which we have zero expertise, if we are not careful, we will exude our vast lack of knowledge to our own detriment and embarrassment because of our ignorance.

The Bible has more to say about money than any other subject. Scriptures give us a tremendous amount of instruction on what we should do with money along with what we should not do. The Bible gives us all the information we need to be successful, faithful stewards of the treasure that God elects to entrust into our care. Yet, even with this vast reservoir of knowledge and instruction, we hear Christians requesting prayer for their "financial breakthrough." It is as though they are hunting Easter eggs and need the prayerful support of all their cheerleaders to hollow out encouragement and then BINGO, there it is! ...all bills are mysteriously forgiven, the bank account now has a surplus instead of a deficit, there is a new car sitting in the driveway, and I will live happily ever after! Right? WRONG!

This is the self-concocted theology by which some Christians attempt to live. Sorry to say, it does not align with the financial principles that God has given us in the Bible. The main problem with those of such persuasion is the fact that they are unwilling to submit to the correction of the scriptures. Rather than seeking the answers in the Word, they manufacture an easy solution – God is just going to make it all happen according to MY plans, even though I consistently ignore the principles of His Word. I have wondered why these people with such theological ideals don't do their weight loss programs the same way. I can hear the prayer requests coming in now – "Pray that I will wake up tomorrow weighing 47 pounds less than when I went to bed."

God did not give us the Bible for us to ignore and then manufacture our own plan. There are reasons He gave us so much information concerning money management. When we continue to ignore His instruction and then expect that He is going to fulfill our plan, we are showing a disdain for correction. This Proverb gives us the end result of our ignoring God's correction: *"Poverty and shame will come to him who disdains correction, But he who regards a rebuke will be honored."*

Reflections...

MARCH 13

Proverbs 13:4 *The soul of a lazy man desires, and has nothing; But the soul of the diligent shall be made rich.*

Have you ever noticed that there are some people who can tell you everything? It matters not the subject, they know it all. They have huge egos and grandiose plans on how they are going to accomplish their goals of success. They are quick to tell you why their plan is better than yours. In addition, they usually are not reserved in pointing out the flaws of your way of doing things. There is just one problem with these who have great desires: they never do anything, they are lazy!

I am reminded of one of the (very) few movies I saw as a youngster entitled *Tobacco Road*. Maybe you saw the movie or read the book. The book was published in the 1930's and the movie debuted in 1941. It had been released a number of years when I finally saw it in the '50s. Jeeter Lester was the type character described above. He was always going to do great things, but he was plagued with a problem – he was lazy. Jeeter talked a good game; he just found it difficult to deliver. One scene near the end of the movie had Jeeter sitting on the front porch of the shack in which the family lived (not that it was a lot different from my early childhood). Maw had been missing for a number of days, but Jeeter was unaffected by her disappearance. Ada, Jeeter's wife called out, "Jeeter, you need to go up into them hills and find Maw." Jeeter replied nonchalantly, "Yep, one of these days I'll get 'round tuit."

That is the way of many Christians. One of these days, they are going to get around to teaching a class, leading a small group, hosting a home cell group, supporting an orphan, lending assistance to a widow, working with the youth, visiting the nursing home, giving tithes so that ministries are funded, going on a short-term mission trip, mentoring young people, and the list goes on and on. But for the time being, they are going to sit on the front porch watching the clouds drift by. More accurately, they will sit in front of the TV while their lives drift downstream.

Many Christians talk a good game, but have nothing to show for their years of being a part of the kingdom. James admonishes us to be "doers of the word and not hearers only" (**James 1:22**). As Christians, we are commanded to be diligent and obedient. We should pattern our lives after Jesus who, at an early age, was "about the Father's business."

Yep, Jeeter, it's time to get your lazy bones off the porch, dust off your britches and get to work. There are consequences to our actions (or lack thereof) both spiritually and financially. *"The soul of a lazy man desires, and has nothing; But the soul of the diligent shall be made rich."*

Reflections...

_____

_____

_____

_____

_____

_____

_____

_____

_____

_____

_____

_____

_____

◻

MARCH 14

Leviticus 19:13 *You shall not oppress your neighbor, nor rob him. The wages of a hired man are not to remain with you all night until morning.* (NASB)

We like to think that all our neighbors are just like State Farm Insurance: "Like a good neighbor, State Farm is there." (you did hear the musical jingle, didn't you?) I have always lived by the philosophy that I will trust you until you prove to me that you cannot be trusted. While I am sure this is the best motto by which to live, it does have its drawbacks. Once in a while, there is one who comes along and confirms they cannot be trusted.

To everyone who identifies himself as a follower of God, here is special instruction. Christians are to be above board in dealings with their neighbors. There should be no oppression and no shady deals. Christians are to pay their neighbors when payment is due, not a week later, in fact not even a day later (overnight).

Christians are admonished to have straight dealings with employees. Wages are to be paid fairly and promptly. Basically, if our employees do not see Christ in us, there is a serious problem. Of all people, those who work closely with us should be the ones who know beyond any doubt the level of integrity in our lives.

What about you? Do you cut corners in your daily activities and end up slighting someone on the other end? Are you prompt in payment including that of your employees? Are you honest in reporting all details, even relating to taxes? These are just a few of the things that those around us are observing on a continual basis. Of course, the real test is what do you do when no one is observing? Are you as honest with money in solitude as you are when the CPA is watching your actions? Are you fair with everyone? Jesus reminded us that our neighbors can be anyone, even those with whom we do not associate **(Luke 12:29-37)**. Therefore, we should have straight dealing with everyone.

146

Reflections...

MARCH 15

Proverbs 14:15 *The naive believes everything, but the sensible man considers his steps.* (NASB)

T he definition of naïve is: *simple; unaffected by or absence of training; unsophisticated, guileless; characterized by a lack of sophistication and critical judgment.* To some extent, one might say that naivety is self-induced. The antidote to naivety is sensibility, informed, the use of good judgment and discretion. All of these carry an implication of "required effort" in order to eliminate one's participation in naivety. In other words, you need to use common sense when making decisions.

Recently the Bloomberg News published an article concerning state run lotteries. Of all state-run lotteries, wouldn't you know that my home state of Georgia came in as the resounding #1 winner of the "Sucker Index"! As the late P.T. Barnum (1810-1891) stated, "There's a sucker born every minute." And, I might add, it appears that a goodly share of them are born in Georgia. It is interesting to Google the term "Sucker Index." What you will get is a long list of articles, state by state, showing where each respective state rated on the most recent "Sucker Index."

The naïve person's thinking goes something like this: work hard, maintain honesty, be a good neighbor and one day when you win the lottery all your worries will be over! It would be funny if it were not so sad. Of course, gambling and the lottery is certainly not the only area in which the naivety of people shows like coffee stains on a white shirt. There is never any shortage of naïve people who rush to participate in get rich quick scams. There is an abundance of gullible and naïve individuals seemingly standing in line to be taken to the cleaners by a slick-talking used car salesman, a payday lender, or a title pawn artist. There are many looking for the next "can't miss" investment that is guaranteed to double in only one month. By the way, if this one hits you, I have a sure-fire, can't miss tip on how to safely double your money and you are guaranteed not to lose. Are you ready? Take your money and fold it in half; then put it back into your pocket (that will come to some of you later).

God's Word gives us a lot of instruction on how to manage money. Instead of trying to devise a "better" plan, we need to just follow His plan. We are instructed to work with diligence. *"The plans of the diligent lead surely to plenty, But those of everyone who is hasty, surely to poverty"* (**Proverbs 21:5**). Get rich quick does not work. Working hard, spending less than we make, saving, giving, and planning, all over a long period of time, does work. Here is a plan: be sensible and follow God's instructions! Don't be naïve; don't believe everything you hear. Couple common sense with God's plan!

Reflections...

□

MARCH 16

Numbers 5:7 *then he shall confess the sin which he has committed. He shall make restitution for his trespass in full, plus one-fifth of it, and give it to the one he has wronged.*

Restitution ...a word that we don't hear very often and almost never actually see it in action. So what is restitution? According to the dictionary:
1. reparation made by giving an equivalent or compensation for loss, damage, or injury caused; indemnification.
2. the restoration of property or rights previously taken away, conveyed, or surrendered.
3. restoration to the former or original state or position.

In the Old Testament, restitution is addressed on several occasions. In this particular case in **Numbers 5:7**, note that is was not sufficient to just restore to the original position, the perpetrator was required to add an additional 20%. We all know that was what was required in the Old Testament, but we are not bound by that law. However, there is "residual value" in much of the Old Testament Law from which we can learn and benefit.

I wonder what our country's crime statistics would look like if our court system imposed this type penalty today. If a carjacker was required to pay the value plus 20% of the Mercedes that he stole, maybe he would think twice the next time he was tempted to repeat the crime. If the thieves who broke into the neighbors home, ransacked it and stole family heirlooms were required to pay the value of the loss and damage incurred plus an additional 20%, there may be some discretion used before they attempted the next venture.

Too many times in our society, the victim loses with no restitution of his loss. In fact, many times in our current culture, the victim is made to feel like the criminal, all in the name of protecting the "rights" of the perpetrator. Criminals are driven by greed, laziness and lack of respect for others' properties with no threat of reprisal. Maybe it is time for our society to go back and pick up some of the "residual value" represented in the Old Testament. Maybe it is time that the guilty party accepts the responsibility of his actions and restores the victim's loss along with an additional 20% (don't do it again) penalty!

Reflections...

□

MARCH 17

Matthew 6:32 *For after all these things the Gentiles seek. For your heavenly Father knows that you need all these things.*

Have you ever really needed something but in the moment felt so consumed by that need that you could not see the light of day? Years ago when I was in college, I drove a Volkswagen beetle, an old Volkswagen beetle! Of course, I was so broke that I could not even pay attention, so taking the beetle to a shop for repairs was not even a consideration. When the clutch operating arm broke, I had two choices: drive the car (4-speed, straight shift) without a clutch or try to make the repairs myself. The second option was the more attractive, but then there were a couple of problems with taking that adventurous move. First, I had to come up with the money with which to purchase the needed repair parts and secondly, I had to make room in a busy schedule to tackle the unknown (at least it was to me!). So, back to the first option I go and literally drive the car with absolutely no clutch disengagement; I did this for two weeks in Athens, Georgia. I will spare you the details of how I was able to accomplish this feat, but suffice it to say that there was a definite art in negotiating the college town traffic, spotted with traffic stop lights and stop signs.

Then, the big day came to tackle the repair job. I did this in primitive style in my driveway with no mechanical equipment with which to work and almost no tools. Residential covenants in the neighborhood prohibited any work on vehicles that took overnight. That did it! Since I could not finish the job, I had to put it back together and try again on another day.

It was at that time while in conversation with a close friend that I related my dilemma to which he generously offered me the use of his shop to do the work. Although I had gone through much anxiety and inconvenience with this problem, I discovered the solution to my need was nearby all the time.

That is the way we live our lives. We do indeed have certain legitimate needs. Many times these needs completely absorb us. We tackle life's problems in our own strengths utilizing our talents and know-how. We get frustrated and disheartened as we grow weary. At times we reach the end of the day and our problem is still not solved. We put everything away knowing that we will face it again tomorrow.

Here is a nugget: Our *"heavenly Father knows that we need all these things."*

He not only knows our needs, He can supply our needs be they food, shelter, transportation, or a myriad other things. As God supplies the needs of the birds of the air, He knows our needs and will supply our needs if we will but get out of His way and trust not in our strength, but in Him.

Reflections...

MARCH 18

Proverbs 31:10 *Who can find a virtuous wife? For her worth is far above rubies.*

The girls get to take a day off. This one is for guys only!

What value do you place upon your wife? Some of you are probably asking, "What kind of question is that?" Others are commenting, "One does not value his wife in terms of dollars and cents." Still others are wishing that _____ ...oh well, that one is better left unstated. For the most of us, this is indeed an anomalous discussion in which to engage.

While we guys feel very uncomfortable participating in such a discussion that would place a dollar value on our wives, our actions oftentimes reveal the opposite. The male species is an odd lot. We find it difficult to verbalize our feelings and then do something stupid that in reality sends a message exactly opposite of what we should be communicating to our spouses. For instance, we cannot form and deliver the simple words "I love you," so instead, we offer to take her out to a really nice restaurant to suffice. And then we do it; Joe's Outdoor Burger Barn, here we come!

I am (by far) more blessed than most men. After almost 31 years of marriage, my first wife died in an automobile accident. She was a virtuous woman. I am blessed to be married to my second wife for almost 13 years now. You know what? She is a virtuous woman. Several years ago, the wife of a good friend of mine died as a result of cancer. They were married for many years. He remarried and was doing well in the new marriage. I received a card in the mail from him in which he stated: "Many men are never blessed to have a good wife. You and I have been doubly blessed; we have had two!" His comments were so true!

Some men are guilty (with their actions) of placing greater value upon money than upon their virtuous wives. They spend all their time either working for money to buy stuff or stuffing their money into wealth.

Their actions place a greater value on the *"worth of rubies"* than the value they place upon their virtuous wife. A virtuous wife makes a mediocre man shine like a bright star in a dark night. Money is important since it is our medium of exchange as we go through life. However, its value cannot hold a candle to the virtuous wife that God has put by your side. Don't allow your values to be misdirected *"For her worth is far above rubies!"*

Reflections...

MARCH 19

Proverbs 1:5 *A wise man will hear and increase learning, And a man of understanding will attain wise counsel,*

"A prudent question is one-half of wisdom." ...Francis Bacon

What is required to increase learning? A short answer is more learning, but that doesn't really address the question. Stop and think about this simple question for a moment: "What is required to increase learning?" This Proverb indicates that a wise man will learn. The implication is that more learning produces more wisdom. Note also that one of the prerequisites of learning is "hearing." In simple terms, that means that we must shut the door on the front and open the sides! We must learn (and for some, re-learn) how to listen. If we are always talking, we will never learn anything.

There is another condition required for learning that is so basic and elementary that most of us may even think it is foolish to list. In order to increase learning, we must subject ourselves to something that we do not already know. Like I said, you may think that is simple; I think it is profound! When we subject ourselves to the unknown, most of us encounter the uncomfortable emotion of fear. We reject being in this uncomfortable place of the unknown. Think about it, if we are always in a familiar environment, we will learn nothing new since we already know what is around us. In order to expand our knowledge base, we must drive ourselves from our comfort zones out into the unknown.

In order to increase learning, we must ask questions. In fact, we must ask good questions. As Francis Bacon said, a prudent question is one-half of wisdom because we have opened ourselves to the unknown and are willing to receive information with which we are not familiar.

That is the next point: we must be "willing." That means we are admitting right up front that we do not have knowledge, but it also makes the statement that we desire knowledge. We live in an apathetic culture today in our country. Many people spend more time watching TV in one week than they spend in a lifetime planning for their

156

retirement. The end result is that the vast majority of Americans reach retirement age with less than $25,000, other than the equity in their home. With the apathetic attitude of the general population, it is no wonder that so many fall for scams and "buy-now" schemes when they don't have money (and our government shows us how to do it!).

It is time for Christians to wake up. It is time for Christians to attain wise counsel. It is time for Christians to get their finances in order. It is time for Christians to get out of the bondage of debt (**Proverbs 22:7**), it is time for Christians to be different ...bottom line: it is time for Christians to wise up! *"A wise man will hear and increase learning, And a man of understanding will attain wise counsel."*

Reflections...

MARCH 20

1 Thessalonians 4:11 *that you also aspire to lead a quiet life, to mind your own business, and to work with your own hands, as we commanded you,*

There are some people who apparently feel that it is their calling in life to stir things up. They are forever causing confusion and making a scene. Hopefully, you are not one of these rabble-rousers.

1 Thessalonians 4:11 gives very precise directions about living life. Aspire to lead a quiet life, mind your own business, and work hard. It should be noted here that leading a quiet life does not mean that you go along with everything the crowd is doing. It does not mean that you compromise your principles and conform to beliefs and activities because "everybody is doing it." Rather, we are to live biblical principles and personal convictions quietly without fanfare. Our different lifestyle of convictions and principles does not demand that we draw attention to ourselves. The next phrase puts it in perspective: "mind your own business." There is an old adage that describes this pretty well: "I had rather see a sermon than hear a sermon."

The manner in which we live our lives speaks much louder than a personal mission statement that we may continually verbalize to those around us. If our actions do not reinforce our verbiage, then we are hypocrites. Our actions in life are always affecting those around us, either positively or negatively. Of course, one of those actions is our work. From the beginning, God appointed man to work (**Genesis 2:15**) Paul wrote in **2 Thessalonians 3:10**: *"Those unwilling to work will not get to eat."* **Colossians 3:23** tells us to *"work heartily as unto the Lord and not unto men."* Work is far more than providing sustenance for living. Our work ethic defines who we really are, before God and before men. Faithful work ethic is the fulfillment of the call of God upon our lives. We don't have to wait for God to strike us with a bolt of lightning to show us His will. He has appointed us to work. So, let's be about the business to which God has called us: *"... aspire to lead a quiet life, to mind your own business, and to work with your own hands."*

Reflections...

☐

MARCH 21

Romans 11:36 *For of Him and through Him and to Him are all things, to whom be glory forever. Amen.*

As we grow up in our capitalistic economy, we learn (at least some do) that if we get a good education, then we can land a good job. If we land the good job, then we can make good money. If we make good money, then we will not go lacking and we can take care of our families. We can buy all the modern conveniences that will afford us a fantastic life. We will be happy and not be weighted down with all the cares of life. After all, isn't that what life is all about? ...and so goes the story of our lives!

We grow up learning this Cinderella story and then proceed in attempting to live it out. There is a basic fallacy in this theory: "it's all about me!" It is all about what "I" want. It is about what makes "Me" happy. It is about "My" little domain and making sure that "I" have "My" way so that "I" can be happy. Do you begin to see the fallacy?

This theory by which most of us have been trained to live is not unlike the story in the Bible found in **Luke 12:16-21**. In this story, the rich farmer already had more than he needed. His crops produced in bumper proportions. In this provision of abundance, he allowed greed to take control as he hoarded what should have been used to bring glory to God. The tragic end of the story is that he died in the midst of trying to build additional storage for goods that he did not even need. In the moment of death, he immediately gave up all his possessions and all his "stuff." Everything, yes everything, instantaneously fell under the ownership of someone else. He had no control over relinquishing ownership and, for certain, he did not take any of the "stuff" with him into eternity.

So, what about the story of your life? Are you falling into step with the scenario of the rich fool? It may be time to ask the following questions:
- What is the purpose of it all?
- Why do I have what is in my possession?
- What should I be doing with all that God has given me?

160

Romans 11:36 gives us more than just insight; it gives us the "reality of life." Read carefully, study, and meditate on the content of this verse. All things are "of" God, all things are "through" God and all things are "to" God.

All things are "of" God: He is the source. All things are "through" God: He is the agency through which all things work at His command. All things are "to" God: the purpose of existence of all things is to bring honor and glory to Him, not us. Everything we have, including our bank accounts, investments, homes, automobiles ...yes everything, is "of" God, "through" God, and "to" God. All possessions are given to us to be used to bring glory and honor to Him. Let us come to the realization of this truth: *"to whom be glory forever. Amen."*

Reflections...

☐

MARCH 22

Revelation 3:17 *Because you say, "I am rich, have become wealthy, and have need of nothing" - and do not know that you are wretched, miserable, poor, blind, and naked -*

There is a very sad and disturbing story detailed in Revelation 3. It is the depiction of the status of the Church of Laodicea. It appears from all accounts that this is an accurate description of the current church across America. A few terms that could be used to portray this church might be apathetic, unconcerned, lackadaisical, indifferent, or lethargic.

From this verse it appears that one of the root causes that brought this church to its current state was the prevalence of abundance. The people stopped depending upon God and starting trusting in their money to deliver them from all kinds of needs. As a result of their trust in their wealth, they felt they no longer had a need for God. When one has no need of God, one has no time for God. When God no longer holds the position of preeminence in one's life, there no longer exists an intimate relationship. God will not play second fiddle to our riches and be on standby in the wing waiting for us to call Him only when "we" determine we need Him. He demands the position of preeminence ...all the time!

As we have stated in times past, the Bible speaks more on the subject of money than any other topic. There is a reason for that. God knew our susceptible nature when it comes to money. He knew that we quickly forget that He owns everything and that we are His stewards. Thus, He gave us a lot of instruction to lead us in the correct direction and keep us on the right path concerning wealth. However, when we choose to ignore His directions, then over a period of time we will arrive at the place of the Church of Laodicea. We will gloat about our wealth and have the attitude that we have no needs that money can't buy. At this point, money has assumed the position of god in our lives.

Check your spiritual status. What value do you place on your riches (home, automobiles, bank accounts, etc.)? Do you view yourself as being self-sufficient having need of nothing? Do you depend upon your wealth to sustain you each day and deliver you from the troubles that life throws your way? If so, then take a close look at this warning: *"Because you say, 'I am rich, have become wealthy, and have need of nothing'--and do not know that you are wretched, miserable, poor, blind, and naked--"*

Reflections...

□

MARCH 23

Acts 11:29-30 *The disciples, each according to his ability, decided to provide help for the brothers living in Judea. (30) This they did, sending their gift to the elders by Barnabas and Saul.* (NIV)

Our human nature leads us to really like things with which we agree and to think not so highly of those things which do not necessarily strike a harmonious note with our spirits. One of the scriptures that we quote very quickly is **3 John 1:2**: *"Beloved, I pray that you may prosper in all things and be in health, just as your soul prospers."* If the truth be told, we all probably have basked in a moment of our own "prosperity gospel" in quoting this verse at one time or another. But, we stop right there, never continuing to come to grips with the fullness of what the Word says in the context of why God pours out His financial blessing on us. For instance, why don't we place the same emphasis on **Acts 11:29**? It seems that we can all rally to the cause when asking for money to come to us. However, our cheers become "Ouchy" when the discussion of sending money out to help those in need is the subject at hand.

It is apparent from the scriptures that none of the disciples were rich by the standards of their day. Yet, they were not hesitant in rallying to the cause of helping their brothers living in Judea who were experiencing some very troublesome times due to famine. They were willing to step up to the task of aiding those who were suffering.

It is interesting the way verses 29 and 30 break down the process. They first decided to provide help. Now, that is important. Many of us never even get to this point. We turn our heads and will not even entertain the discussion of a need. If we are unwilling to listen to the need, then it follows that we cannot "decide" to help alleviate the need. The point is that they made the decision to help.

Verse 30 gives the substance to their decision; stated emphatically, *"This they did!"* ...and they did so by sending their gifts to the elders by Barnabas and Saul. Their action did not end with their discussion. It

164

ended with their "doing!" Too many times, we Christians talk about needs, but we fail to take action and do anything about the needs. James addressed this when he instructed us to be *"doers of the word and not hearers only"* (**James 1:22**). All of us come face-to-face with needs that warrant our attention and action. Did the thought ever cross your mind that God may be allowing these "opportunities" to cross your pathway just to see how you will react? When you see someone in need, make the decision and then do something about it!

Reflections...

MARCH 24

Romans 15:27 *It pleased them indeed, and they are their debtors. For if the Gentiles have been partakers of their spiritual things, their duty is also to minister to them in material things.*

Do you have any obligations to give monetary gifts once you have received the gospel and subsequently have become a follower of Christ? This question looms over the modern-day church as a whole. According to the actual performance within churches week after week, the feeling (as expressed by the actions of church members) of a major portion of church attendees is NO! That will probably flabbergast many. However, according to some surveys, almost 50% of evangelical church members never give anything to further the gospel of Christ.

This passage in Romans addresses this issue head-on. Church members from the very poor church at Macedonia and also from Achaia were literally thrilled to have the opportunity to give to relief efforts to assist the church at Jerusalem that was suffering as a result of famine. Get this picture: these people of Macedonia were extremely poor, yet they found a way to give and did so with great enthusiasm. Note the beginning words of verse 27: *"it pleased them indeed."* It gets better as it continues; since they had received the gospel as a result of the efforts of the church at Jerusalem, they felt that they were indebted to the Jerusalem church and that it was their duty to help alleviate the extreme needs that were being experienced by them.

Next the issue of whether of not the Gentiles were also obligated to give is addressed. The simple and straightforward conclusion was that if the Gentiles have been partakers of spiritual things, it is their "duty" to minister to them in material things (or contribute money as the case may be).

So the question has been answered. Jews and Gentiles alike have an obligation to give of their material means (money) if they have been partakers of the gospel (spiritual things). There is no mention of any one person or group of people being given a "free ride" or a "free pass" on the issue of giving. If you name yourself as a follower of Christ (partaker of the spiritual things), then you are indeed "obligated" to give of your material means. This instruction is clear; it is concise; it is unquestionable!

Reflections...

MARCH 25

Proverbs 19:17 *He who has pity on the poor lends to the Lord, And He will pay back what he has given.*

Where do you lend your money? If you have money deposited in the bank, then you have lent that money to the bank and in return, they pay you interest (though small it is). If you have money invested in stocks, then you have lent them the money and when they make money, they pay you dividends in return. If you have your money in automobiles, then the value of your money is going away rapidly, as boiling water evaporates to nothing.

You can park money in many different and varied investment vehicles (not cars, but investment ventures). In our current economy, it is easy for one to become bewildered with the minuscule returns from investments. Many of us are gullible when it comes to investing money and will fall for almost anything that offers an attractive return. Then again, it may not be gullibility at all; it may be greed within our nature that drives us to ignore common sense and make stupid investment choices that promise unbelievable returns. At any rate, we are always on the lookout for a good investment opportunity.

Well, if any of the above describes you, then pay close attention. No doubt, you probably are of the opinion that the Bible is a fairly reliable source of information that would not lead you astray, right? Well, straight from the pages of the Bible, this verse in Proverbs gives some really, really, outstanding investment advice. When you show mercy to the poor, when you show kindness to the poor, when you come to the aid of the poor, you are effectively "lending" to the Lord. WOW!!! Think about that for a moment; you are lending to the Lord! Surely you would never question His credit worthiness. I mean, He owns the cattle on a thousand hills (**Psalms 50:10**); He even owns the earth and everything that is upon the earth (**Psalms 24:1**). I don't think He would have any problems paying back anything that you or I may lend to Him, do you?

168

The last part of this verse gives us God's promissory note of repayment. It simply states that He (God) will pay back what you and I have given. That is an ironclad contract. We can take that one to the bank (pun intended)!

If you are looking for an investment with a sure-fire, guaranteed return, this is it. Help the poor. The return on investment is guaranteed by God!

Reflections...

☐

MARCH 26

Mark 10:28-30 *Then Peter began to say to Him, "See, we have left all and followed You." (29) So Jesus answered and said, "Assuredly, I say to you, there is no one who has left house or brothers or sisters or father or mother or wife or children or lands, for My sake and the gospel's, (30) who shall not receive a hundredfold now in this time - houses and brothers and sisters and mothers and children and lands, with persecutions - and in the age to come, eternal life."*

We have all heard and read (probably many times) the story of the rich young man coming to Jesus and asking what he must do to have eternal life. Commonly referred to as the "parable of the rich young ruler", the story ends on a very sad note. Apparently this young man was very sincere in his approach to Jesus. He had lived a moral life and had in fact, kept the commandments as much as was within his power to do so. Jesus startled not only the young man, but also those standing around when he told him to sell all that he possessed, give to the poor, and come, take up the cross and follow Him.

There have been numerous arguments as to whether Jesus was speaking figuratively or literally. However, as much as we would like to rationalize the words of Jesus and justify our own position, it is apparent that Jesus meant exactly what he said. The young man's security and hope rested in the possessions. Jesus requires us to trust in Him alone, not 51% or even 99%, but totally Him. Now let us pause for some time of personal reflective evaluation...

Quick-to-speak Peter did not fail to fulfill the normal expectancy of those who knew him. *"See, we have left all and followed You"* he quipped. Jesus responded with a promise that leaves all our excuses and rationalizations settling in the dust when we try to make arguments for NOT giving our monetary means and NOT sacrificing for the gospel. He basically said that everyone who has given up their home, family and lands for the sake of following Him in ministry of the gospel would be nicely reimbursed, in this life as well as the life to come.

So, if you have not relinquished everything to Him, what's your excuse? Do you think you put up a more convincing argument than that of the rich young ruler? Before you jump to the "but I'm not rich" cliché, remember that if you live in America, by the world's standard, you ARE rich. We all need to take another look at the promise with which Jesus responded: *"Assuredly, I say to you, there is no one who has left house or brothers or sisters or father or mother or wife or children or lands, for My sake and the gospel's, who shall not receive a hundredfold now in this time - houses and brothers and sisters and mothers and children and lands, with persecutions - and in the age to come, eternal life."* It kinda leaves us without an argument, doesn't it?

Reflections...

MARCH 27

2 Corinthians 9:8, 12 *And God is able to make all grace abound to you, so that in all things at all times, having all that you need, you will abound in every good work. ... (12) This service that you perform is not only supplying the needs of God's people but is also overflowing in many expressions of thanks to God.* (NIV)

God has a plan of economy that will transform our lives if we can ever catch a glimpse of it and then activate it in our day-to-day living. Read carefully **2 Corinthians 9:8-15**. Now go back and read it again and then again. Within these few verses is a plan that God designed for man; it is His plan of economy for us to live by.

Let me invite you to take a pencil and paper and use your instinctive drawing talents. Draw a large circle on the piece of paper. At the top of the circle, write "GOD." This is the starting point from which we will go around the circle. Subsequently, it is the ending point also. God is the point of commencement of all that we think, say and do, and He is the consummation point of all that we think, say and do. As these verses are written in the context of finances, God is the beginning of our money. He is the beginning of man's economy. It is He who gives us power to get wealth (**Deuteronomy 8:18**). Lest there be any doubts about the ability of God to provide, consider the opening phrase of verse 8: God is able! No matter what the need that you face, here is your answer: God is able! When you are facing impossible circumstances, here is your solution: God is able!

Track counterclockwise downward on the circle to the 9:00 o'clock position. Here, write in "All Grace Abounds." His grace is unlimited; it is sufficient for any need that we have and it is available in any hour we need it. It is there as a provision to us "in all things, at all times, and providing for all needs."

Now that the unlimited source has been established, continue to trace the perimeter in a counterclockwise direction to the 6:00 o'clock position of the circle, which is the bottom point, and write in "Man."

172

We now have a half circle with man located at the lowest point. However, we know that above us is God with unlimited resources and a willing Grace to provide for our needs. As we continue counterclockwise on the perimeter to the 3 o'clock position, write in "Every Good Work." Good works that are begun by God, lead people to God, and honor God, are works that merit God's favor and resources. As we are involved in such activities (good works), God's plan of economy is there to supply the needs encountered.

The final leg of this circular representation of God's plan of economy is found in verse 12: *"This service that you perform is not only supplying the needs of God's people but is also overflowing in many expressions of thanks to God."* While meeting the needs of people, the final result of God's plan of economy brings glory and honor to Him. He only is to receive honor, not us. He is the one to be praised, not us.

Again, God has designed a plan of economy by which man is to live. That plan begins with God and it ends with God. He is the source and He is the One to be honored. Get in on God's plan of economy today!

Reflections...

□

MARCH 28

John 6:9 *There is a lad here who has five barley loaves and two small fish, but what are they among so many?*

There are many things to be learned from the story in John 6, commonly referred to as "Jesus Feeding the 5000." This miracle is recorded in all four Gospels with only minor variations of rendering. In Biblical times, only men were counted when numbering the size of crowds. Given the fact that 5000 men were fed, the actual number that was fed conceivably could have been as high as 15,000 - 20,000 when women and children were counted. It really makes no difference whether there were 5,000 or 20,000 considering there were only two fish and five barley loaves. The bottom line is simple: feeding such a large number with so little food was an impossibility.

This is where things begin to get interesting and we can see miraculous feats take place. First, God "gave" the lad the fish and bread. God gives everyone of us all that we have. He owns everything and therefore He gives us all that we have. Secondly, the lad "gave" the fish and loaves to Jesus. Next Jesus blessed the food and then He "gave" it to the disciples. Think about what must have been going through the disciples' minds as they saw the food multiply before their very eyes when Jesus broke it and handed it to each of them.

Have you ever considered that the disciples were probably hungry also? They may have been tempted to just turn their backs and enjoy the fish sandwich they held in their hands. Well, thank God, they did not use the opportunity to appease their own appetites. Instead, they "gave" to the thousands who ate and were "filled." This may have been the first "All-You-Can-Eat Buffet" recorded in history. They ate all they wanted and when the leftovers were gathered, there were 12 baskets full. Being one to always ask questions of possibility, I wondered where the baskets came from ...I don't doubt, I just wonder.

Okay now, let's put this together in order to glean the impetus of what took place. Let's take it one step at a time:

- God **gave** the lad two fish and five loaves.
- The lad **gave** all he had to Jesus.
- Jesus blessed the food and **gave** it to the disciples.
- The disciples **gave** food to the thousands to meet their needs.
- The disciples gathered the leftovers and **gave** them to the lad.

Do you see the common threads here? Do you see the end results? Let's list a few:

- There is the common theme of giving. The failure of any one person to **give** would have thwarted God's miraculous plan.
- Another commonality in this is the involvement of humanity. God chose to use the act of giving from the hands of **people** in order to accomplish His plan.
- When people followed God's plan of **giving**, everyone's needs were met.
- The lad had to solicit help to carry home all the miracle food that he ended up with (I don't know that, but I can imagine it to be true. How else can he carry 12 baskets full of food?).

Let's all learn God's plan of giving and meeting needs. You are the key! When you do not give, there will always be those downstream from you who will have needs that will not be met. YOU ARE THE KEY TO GOD'S MIRACULOUS PLAN OF GIVING AND SUPPLYING NEEDS!

Reflections...

MARCH 29

Malachi 3:7 *"Yet from the days of your fathers You have gone away from My ordinances And have not kept them. Return to Me, and I will return to you," Says the Lord of hosts. "But you said, 'In what way shall we return?'"*

The last book of the Old Testament, Malachi, bears a message to which our country needs to sit up and give attention. Israel had been released from Babylonian bondage only a few short years before. Yet, they had returned to their old ways of greed, adultery and idolatry. They basically lost their fear of God. God sent His messenger Malachi to deliver an ultimatum to Israel.

We know that Israel had departed from God in many areas too numerous to mention. God beckoned to Israel to *"return to Me and I will return to you."* This is a standing invitation of God through the ages when His people had departed down their own paths and ignored Him. A very familiar example of this is: *"if My people who are called by My name will humble themselves, and pray and seek My face, and turn from their wicked ways, then I will hear from heaven, and will forgive their sin and heal their land."* ...**2 Chronicles 7:14**.

As Malachi delivered God's message, the question arose, *"In what way shall we return?"* Here is an unchanging principle: The point of return is the same as the point of departure. If one veers from God's path, the way back is to return to the point of departure. This is exactly where Malachi directed Israel in their return to God.

They had been robbing God. Consequently, Malachi sent them back to that place as a point of returning to God. What a novel idea! Even though these people were guilty of the commission of many different kinds of sins, the point of giving was at the heart of their problems. There is a striking resemblance of this story and the current moral and economic condition of our country today. As a nation, we are on the brink of economic disaster. Morally, our country as a whole has abandoned every ounce of moral fiber by which we were once guided. Christianity is under attack from every direction. God's standing invitation of returning to Him is as pertinent to America today as it was to Israel when Malachi issued this proclamation.

God says to America, *"Return to Me and I will return to you."* And we say, *"In what way shall we return?"* We can return to God by simply going back to the point of our departure. God's judgment upon Israel was that they were cursed because they stopped their giving of tithes and offerings; in essence, they were robbing God. Almost 50% of the members of all evangelical churches in America today give nothing (that is "$00.00") to God's ministry. Do we hold any privileges over the Israelites to whom Malachi preached? To the churches in America, return to God; stop robbing Him!

Reflections...

_____

_____

_____

_____

_____

_____

_____

_____

_____

_____

_____

_____

_____

_____

MARCH 30

2 Kings 4:7 *Then she came and told the man of God. And he said, "Go, sell the oil and pay your debt; and you and your sons live on the rest."*

How big is your bucket? When you go to God and ask Him to supply a particular need in your life, how much are you prepared to receive? We may need to further qualify this in consideration of the state of many of our churches today and those members within the confines of the churches. Maybe the first qualifying question should be, "When you have a genuine need, do you even pray for God's provision?" Many of us methodically go about the business of exhausting all possible secular solutions and never turn our dependence to God. But for the sake of discussion, let's assume that we do call upon the name of the Lord with our need. What do we expect to receive?

In this story in **2 Kings 4**, this widow was in the midst of turmoil. Her husband had died and left her and her two sons in debt with no means of payment. The creditor was threatening to take the sons into slavery to satisfy payment. The man of God, Elisha, came upon the scene and asked, *"What shall I do for you?"* Think on this for a moment. When we go to the Lord in petition for a need, He is standing by saying to us, "What shall I do for you?" Do we hear His question to our prayer? Maybe we are too busy continuing to "beg" God for an answer and we never stop long enough to listen. Or, maybe we are giving God directions on how we want Him to provide the answer to our prayer. Or, maybe we are just going through the prayer motion aimlessly and not expecting anything from God. The list of possibilities is probably too lengthy to list here. The ultimate question is, "What is our expectancy when we bring our needs to God?"

This widow was experiencing a dire need for money to pay the creditors. In our vernacular, we could say that she was between a rock and a hard place. Thankfully, she did hear Elisha. Then, she had enough faith to step out and do what he told her. Listen to his instructions: *"Go, borrow vessels from everywhere, from all your neighbors - empty vessels; do not gather just a few. And when you have come in, you shall shut the door behind you and your sons; then pour it into all those vessels, and set aside the full ones."*

Note that Elisha told her to borrow vessels from all the neighbors. How many was she supposed to get? ..."NOT A FEW!" Once the sons brought the containers, she was instructed to start pouring oil from her bottle. This she did and the oil continued until the last borrowed vessel was filled. At that exact point, the flow of oil ceased. What would have happened if she had 97 tankers that carry 6,500 gallons each? All would have been filled! The limit of her blessing was her preparation to receive. She was told by Elisha to sell the oil, pay her debts and live on the rest.

When we have needs and pray for God to supply those needs, we should prepare to receive. There should be expectancy. There should be excitement. How about you? When you pray, do you prepare to receive? HOW BIG IS YOUR BUCKET?

Reflections...

□

MARCH 31

Deuteronomy 15:5-6 *only if you carefully obey the voice of the Lord your God, to observe with care all these commandments which I command you today. (6) For the Lord your God will bless you just as He promised you; you shall lend to many nations, but you shall not borrow; you shall reign over many nations, but they shall not reign over you.*

In chapters 14 and 15 of the Book of Deuteronomy, God speaks to the people, giving them specific laws by which they are to abide. If we take a look at these laws and compare them to the rule of law of our current society, they certainly would indeed seem very odd. One of the most important aspects that we observe from these passages is not the laws themselves since they pertained to a certain group of people in a certain time in history, but the promise that God made to the people in rewarding them for their obedience. Many of these laws dealt with the management of money and debt and the interaction of those people involved. While God gave specific laws on these subjects to people of a certain historical period, He has likewise given many directives for us in our historical time frame to manage money. God's attitude and promises concerning faithfulness and obedience are the same (**Hebrews 6:17**). God has not changed.

God promises that if we will obey the voice of the Lord and observe with care His commandments, then He will bless us. How? "We will lend to many nations and not borrow; we will reign over many nations, but they shall not reign over us." I challenge you to consider the economic position of our nation, the United States of America. One will quickly conclude that our country certainly does not fall into line with God's promise concerning "lending and not borrowing." We are a debtor nation meaning that we borrow more than we produce. As a debtor nation, our subsequent position is simply one of a servant or slave. As a borrower, we must answer to the nation(s) from whom we borrow. Draw the conclusion for yourself. In effect, those nations to whom we are indebted literally reign over us. This is not a discussion

180

that is popular. One seldom hears our political leaders discuss truthfully the nature of our position. It is politically incorrect to admit that other nations reign over us.

If we do not return to God and His principles, the future of our country is rather bleak. It is not a pretty picture, especially for those of us who are old-school patriots in our fundamental beliefs. America, it is time to turn back to God, to carefully obey the voice of the Lord, to observe with care all His commandments! Although one seldom hears this proclamation, it is nonetheless true. Day by day, America is writing its own destiny. The church should lead the way. Beginning with the church, it is time that, as a nation, we obey the voice of the Lord and observe His commandments!

Reflections...

APRIL 1

John 12:24 *Most assuredly, I say to you, unless a grain of wheat falls into the ground and dies, it remains alone; but if it dies, it produces much grain.*

A seed, be it corn, wheat or whatever, is truly amazing. It holds tightly the secret of life that no man has been able to figure out or understand. It is indeed a mystery that what appears to be a lifeless, dried mass is so powerful. When this dried mass, called a seed, is buried in soil in favorable conditions, it literally decays. Then miraculously, life shoots forth in the form of a minuscule sprout and begins to grow. While in the darkness of earth, it contains unexplainable power. A sprout from a single seed has been known to lift a thick concrete slab, a feat that requires thousands of pounds of force. As a seed germinates and grows into a plant, it has the ability to reproduce itself many times over. For instance, one kernel of corn can routinely produce 1600 kernels.

The context of this verse from the Gospel of John is Jesus telling that the time had come for His life on earth to end. He used the analogy of a seed being planted in the ground to relate the impending event of His death, burial and resurrection. Of course, we know that His life did not stop with the resurrection. Through His death and resurrection, millions have sprouted into eternal life.

Being an agrarian culture that depended upon agriculture, the people could readily relate to this explanation given by Jesus. Paul also used the analogy of a seed in explaining money given in offerings. He related money given to a seed. He further detailed that there is money that is designated to be given (or planted) as seed and there is other that is given to provide for food and sustenance. Paul prayed for God to bless the seed given for sowing and that used as bread for food. He prayed that the seed sown (money given in offerings) would be multiplied and there would be an increase of the fruits of righteousness and that all would bring honor to God (**2 Corinthians 9:10-11**).

182

When you give money in offerings, it is like seed planted in the ground. You literally give up possession in faith believing that God is going to cause it to multiply and accomplish what you could not do if you chose to keep it in your hand. If you were to choose to consume that seed, it would benefit you very little and for sure, it would be temporary. Yet if you sow the seed, God will cause it to reproduce itself many times over, meeting many needs in the process while bringing honor to Him. As the planting of a seed and the subsequent harvest that follows cannot be explained by man, neither can the results of offerings given to God be explained or understood. Our lack of understanding the process of God's miraculous principle of "sowing and reaping" does not inhibit the reality that it works. It never has and it never will. It is not ours to understand and explain; it is ours to obey and do!

Reflections...

APRIL 2

Luke 12:13 *Then one from the crowd said to Him, "Teacher, tell my brother to divide the inheritance with me."*

Although we do not know all the circumstances surrounding this request for Jesus to fulfill the role of arbitrator, one thing we do know; people react today the same as they did then. How many times have you known of this scenario playing out where children get into squabbles over inheritances? While specific circumstances vary from incident to incident, there are usually several aspects that are similar in nature.

First, there is usually the failure on the part of the parent(s) to properly and legally prepare for the transfer of an inheritance to their children. We all have this "thing" of not talking about the disposition of money and property at the end of our lives when it is time to check out. There is an uncomfortable silence that prevails in almost every case. Author and financial advisor, Ron Blue, strongly advises that parents talk to their children about their plans concerning the details of transferring of inheritance. In many cases, it is financially wise to actually perform the transfer before death occurs. If all the children know the inheritance plan of the parents, there are no surprises and the likelihood of an ensuing argument is diminished greatly.

If you have not already done so, get your will done! Dave Ramsey says it is "rude" to die without a will. Even though practically everyone knows that getting a will done is the right thing to do, they avoid it like the plague. Some say that they do not like to think about dying and find it overtly difficult to deal with the subject. Well, here is one for the record: getting one's will done does not make one die sooner! If you haven't already done so, GET YOUR WILL DONE!!!

The root cause of the family feud over inheritances among heirs is usually greed. Greed will drive good people to do things they normally would never dream of doing. Greed, when not checked, has destroyed family relationships in the process of "fighting over Daddy's two toothpicks." God knew the covetous nature of mankind and thus He

184

cautioned against it early on: *"You shall not covet your neighbor's house; you shall not covet your neighbor's wife, nor his male servant, nor his female servant, nor his ox, nor his donkey, nor anything that is your neighbor's."* ... **Exodus 20:17**.

In His reply to the request of this man, Jesus told the story of the foolish rich farmer who was concerned only with his own greedy desires. He then ended with this statement: *"So is he who lays up treasure for himself, and is not rich toward God."* ... **Luke 12:21**. Greed causes one's heart to stray from God. Man's greedy efforts to gain treasure will drive a wedge between him and God. Just as that inheritance leaves the ownership of the parent and moves to the children-heirs, they too will give it up soon. Earthly treasure is temporary. Don't allow greed to control you; instead, seek to be rich toward God!

Reflections...

185

APRIL 3

Proverbs 18:9 *He also who is slack in his work is brother to him who destroys.* (NASB)

Do you work when you are at work? You may be surprised to learn that many people do not work when they are at work. They have the job, but the only part they really want is the "pay" part. Many years ago when I was in college, I worked at a nearby agency of a division of the government. You have no doubt heard the stories of people sitting around and not working on the government jobs. Well, I got to see this first-hand. One of the men came into the shop after returning from the Thanksgiving holiday break. He announced to his co-workers that he had done all the work he was going to do for the balance of the year. Beginning that very day, he found his comfortable place and perched upon a piece of shop equipment. He prepared his spot with a 6-inch thick foam cushion on which he reclined and propped up his feet. Day after day through the end of the year his daily routine consisted of clocking in, taking his "recliner" position and sitting until morning break time. After the break, he resumed his position until lunch time. After lunch, he found his way back to his recliner until afternoon break and, you guessed it, was back reclining until time to clock out at the end of a tiring day! The one thing that can be said about him was that he absolutely fulfilled his promise. He did not lift a finger to perform any task during that month-long period.

Maybe you have seen a similar situation. Hopefully, you were not the one assuming the recliner position. This scenario is seemingly becoming more and more popular. Many do what we call "come to work," but have no desire to work. Work ethic suffers greatly in the workplace today.

This verse in Proverbs is somewhat sobering. Most of those who resort to an attitude of work slothfulness probably would never take a bush ax and destroy the jobsite. Most would not consider driving a machine through a neighborhood and destroy everything with which he comes into contact. Yet this verse proclaims that when one is slack in his work ethic, he is like one who goes about to destroy. At best, he is stealing from his employer. Even worse than his personal non-productivity, he very well may be impeding the production of many of his co-workers. He is destroying production and destroying progress.

Colossians 3:23 gives us a model to follow in our work ethic: *"And whatever you do, do it heartily, as to the Lord and not to men."* When we work "heartily, as to the Lord," our work ethic changes drastically. Our production goes up, lost time goes down, and quality increases significantly. Don't become slack in your work; rather, work heartily as to the Lord!

Reflections...

APRIL 4

1 Chronicles 29:14 *But who am I, and who are my people, that we could give anything to you? Everything we have has come from you, and we give you only what you first gave us!* (NLT)

As King David encouraged the people to give for the purpose of building the Temple, the response was literally overwhelming. A part of his encouragement was that he led by example. He gave liberally himself. You probably know the story of how the people really got involved in giving to the point that it could be termed miraculous. It would be great to see God's people come together with an attitude of giving such as this.

While the motivation of David and, subsequently, the response of the people were tremendous events, there is another aspect of this incident that stands out even more vividly. While it is true that this was one of the great outpourings of liberal giving when considering the amount, there is still another point that is more important. What could be more important than the involvement of all the people and the abundant bounty that they gave? The outstanding aspect is simply what David prayed here in verse 14. The recognition of the SYSTEM by which the people gave is the pinnacle of the event.

Look closely again to uncover this magnanimous "giving system." *"Everything we have has come from you, and we give you only what you first gave us!"* What did the people give that actually belonged to them? The answer of course is that they gave nothing that they owned. Why? Because everything they gave came from God. So, in essence, they gave back to God what He had given to them. They had no problem giving because they recognized that they were not the owners ...God was the owner!

Centuries have come and gone, but that truth has not changed: God owns everything (**Psalms 24:1**). If we can get into our spirit the fact that we are not owners, then it is easy to give. Why? It is easy to give away things which belong to someone else. That is the most

188

outstanding part of this episode of giving about which David was giving thanks. I, along with others, call it the conduit principle found in the New Testament in **Luke 6:38:** *"Give and it will be given to you: good measure, pressed down, shaken together, and running over will be put into your bosom. For with the same measure that you use, it will be measured back to you."* As a friend of mine so amply states it, "If God can get it THROUGH YOU, He'll get it TO YOU!"

Reflections...

▢

APRIL 5

1 Kings 17:13-16 *Then Elijah said to her, "Do not fear; go, do as you have said, but make me a little bread cake from it first and bring it out to me, and afterward you may make one for yourself and for your son. For thus says the Lord God of Israel, 'The bowl of flour shall not be exhausted, nor shall the jar of oil be empty, until the day that the Lord sends rain on the face of the earth.'" So she went and did according to the word of Elijah, and she and he and her household ate for many days. The bowl of flour was not exhausted nor did the jar of oil become empty, according to the word of the Lord which He spoke through Elijah.* (NASB)

The story of Elijah's encounter with the starving widow and her son is probably one with which you are at least somewhat familiar. But, have you stopped to consider just how illogical and how unlikely the subsequent events really were? Let's take a brief look at a few of these "unusual" happenings.

There was a famine in the land to the point that people were literally starving to death. We probably cannot fully relate to this situation; but, try with your might anyway. As the custom was, upon meeting this widow, the tired and thirsty prophet, Elijah, asked the woman for a drink of water to which she responded. Next this "preacher man" fully knowing the food shortages that were being experienced in the area and especially by a widow without means of provision, asked the widow to prepare him a morsel to eat. The widow related her bewildering story of having only a "handful" of flour and a little oil in a jar and that she was gathering wood for a fire with which she was preparing to bake the last meal for her and her son. This last meal was her preparation for them to die from starvation since they had no more food. Then, this preacher had the audacity to direct her to go ahead and make the meal, but to give it to him first. If we consider the logic in this, we would probably draw the conclusion that this was one arrogant and self-centered man who was thinking only of himself.

However, that certainly was not the case. God had directed this entire scene.

Amazingly, the widow recognized the message from God and followed by stepping out on faith. In the face of starvation, she gave all she had based solely upon the word of the Lord. Her giving opened the door for God to give back to her. I have often wondered what my response would have been in this situation. How would you have responded?

We read further in the story how God honored the action of this widow who gave all she had, even the very sustenance that could keep her and her son alive a little longer. God came to her rescue and gave her unending provision of food until the country was relieved from the famine. Yes, God honored the widow's faith by showing His faithfulness.

You will note that God does not give any exclusion to His instructions to "give." Regardless of one's wealth or one's poverty, God has instructed us to give. In the time of abundance and in the time of starvation, God says "GIVE." As we contemplate what our response would have been given the same situation, let's bring this home to where we live right now. God has told us in His Word that we are to give. Are you following God's instruction? In **Luke 6:38**, we are told to "give and it will be given to us..." The first step of action falls squarely upon us...we are to give before anything happens. This is exactly what happened in this story of Elijah and the widow.

How is your faithfulness in giving? Are you opening the door for God to give to you?

Reflections...

□

APRIL 6

1 Corinthians 9:10-*11* ... *Yes, for our sake it was written, because the plowman ought to plow in hope, and the thresher to thresh in hope of sharing the crops. If we sowed spiritual things in you, is it too much if we reap material things from you?* (NASB)

It has often been said that farmers possess the greatest faith of any group of people on the face of the earth. Perhaps you have had the privilege of association with farmers in your past. Farmers are forever optimistic. They spend countless man-hours plowing and preparing the soil in which they will plant seed, thoroughly and absolutely expecting a crop and subsequent harvest to come forth. Each and every year they literally bury a fortune in the ground in the form of seed, fertilizer and herbicides. From that point, they are completely dependent upon God to provide favorable weather conditions that will cause the crops to flourish. They plow with an expectancy that the harvest will follow; most of the time it does, but sometimes it does not. Even in the time when crop failure is the outcome of much hard work and expense, hope is not diminished. There is always a faithful looking forward to the next year.

Paul used an analogy of the farmer (plowman) to that of the minister of the gospel. With the same expectancy, a true minister called of God should faithfully expend the duties to which he has been called closely followed by the expectancy that his material needs will be taken care of by those to whom he has ministered.

In consideration of the giving statistics of evangelical Christians, this discussion is sure to rub some the wrong way. Almost half of confessing evangelical Christians give nothing (zero - notta - $0.00) to the ministry of the gospel. It is difficult at best and impossible in practicality to reconcile these two: a professing Christian who does not give!

Giving and Christianity are synonymous. There should not even be a question as to whether or not shepherds of flocks should be cared for by those to whom they minister. As the Apostle Paul puts it, this is to be expected. Think about this one seriously, because if you are not a giver, you are going to need a rehearsed explanation when you stand before God and give account: *"If we sowed spiritual things in you, is it too much if we reap material things from you?"*

Reflections...

☐

APRIL 7

Acts 20:35 *I have shown you in every way, by laboring like this, that you must support the weak. And remember the words of the Lord Jesus, that He said, "It is more blessed to give than to receive."*

Giving and receiving...a topic that catches our attention, especially the receiving part. However, the giving part is the one that Jesus encouraged us to concentrate upon. It was He who made the rash statement that it is more blessed to give than to receive. This sounds good, but do we really believe this statement of Jesus? Recently, I was thinking about the way we train our children in this particular area.

There is no doubt that child rearing has undergone some drastic changes over the past couple decades. Call it "old school" or whatever, but when I was a child, there was only one occasion where the average child received gifts; that was Christmas. Even then, gifts were very few in number and certainly were not expensive. Today, parents seemingly look for yet another holiday as an excuse to shower gifts upon their kids or manipulate circumstances to encourage others to heap gifts upon their children. In addition to Christmas, gift-receiving occasions nowadays are likely to include birthdays, engagements, Easter, Halloween, graduations, proms and probably many others with which I am not (nor do I want to be) familiar. I am wondering if Groundhog Day is going to qualify next year!

While much to-do is made over receiving gifts, very little effort, if any, is invested in teaching children the virtues of giving to others. Constantly receiving gifts is the breeding ground of an entitlement mentality. Constantly receiving gifts creates an attitude of self-centeredness and literally thwarts humility and servant-spirit. Constantly receiving gifts creates an air of arrogance. Constantly receiving gifts creates a superiority complex since the recipient is always the center of attention and placed upon a pedestal.

Jesus taught by example (His life) the spirit of servitude. He assumed a lowly position in order to minister to the needs of others always preferring their needs over his own. We would do well to live by this teaching of Jesus, especially during the Christmas season where commercialization has become rampant. We would do well to teach our children the virtues of giving rather than the self-centeredness of constantly receiving. Life holds a richer meaning for us when we learn that *"It is more blessed to give than to receive."*

Reflections...

☐

APRIL 8

Deuteronomy 24:19 *When you reap your harvest in your field and have forgotten a sheaf in the field, you shall not go back to get it; it shall be for the alien, for the orphan, and for the widow, in order that the Lord your God may bless you in all the work of your hands.* (NASB)

O ur government has created a welfare system to aid those who are among the less fortunate. Certainly, there exists the need of many who do not have the ability to generate income sufficient to sustain themselves and in some cases, their families. However, in the midst of bureaucracy, good intentions have turned into a vicious process that turns good-willed people into dependent, helpless individuals with an entitlement mentality. The system of rewarding individuals for doing nothing reduces those who once had entrepreneurial motivation to individuals standing in line awaiting the next free handout.

Were you aware that God had His own welfare system? It is right here in this verse. Keep in mind that this was written to an agrarian society, one that depended primarily upon agriculture as its main industry. The farmers were instructed to leave a small portion of grain around the perimeter of fields. This was done purposefully in order that widows, orphans and strangers (aliens) could glean and have enough food to sustain themselves. Someone may be asking what is so unique about such a system and what makes it so different from our current welfare system. In God's welfare system, there were no handouts. Those in need were required to go into the fields and harvest for themselves. They were not rewarded to sit home and do nothing. Even though extreme poverty existed, there was still dignity in the fact that in order to receive benefits, individuals were expected to gather for themselves, unlike our government welfare system.

The uniqueness of receiving assistance and yet maintaining dignity and hope to provide for oneself is something of which our politicians should take note. As we have seen our government assistance programs expanding at an alarming rate, there has been a corresponding degradation of work ethic. Many openly say, "Why work when you can sit home and receive a check?" While it is not wrong to assist the needy, it is wrong to destroy dignity and work ethic.

There is no doubt that God's welfare system is superior!

Reflections...

☐

APRIL 9

Matthew 6:12 *And forgive us our debts, As we forgive our debtors.*

<u>Forgive</u>: To pardon; to remit, as an offense or debt; to overlook an offense; to treat the offender as not guilty (Webster's Dictionary).

It is interesting that in Matthew's account of the model prayer that Jesus used in teaching the disciples to pray, he used the term debt. Certainly this word (debt) has many interpretations, one of which would indeed include a debt of money. Paul used similar verbiage in his letter to the Romans: *"Let no debt remain outstanding, except the continuing debt to love one another, for he who loves his fellowman has fulfilled the law."* ... **Romans 13:8 (NIV)** . Yes, Jesus no doubt was referring to a multiplicity of items, but rest assured, money certainly is one of those.

Jesus taught about forgiveness of debt by using the parable of the steward who was forgiven and then went out and found those who owed him money. He grabbed them around the neck and threatened them because they were unable to pay him. He had been forgiven much, but did not forgive those who owed him little.

There are times when we should recognize that some debt needs to be forgiven and it is within our power to do so. From time to time, God may indeed lead us to forgive debt. To refuse to do so in those situations is to repudiate the spirit of forgiveness. God has forgiven us much in a variety of situations. Note that our forgiveness of others is linked directly to God's forgiveness to us. When we seriously consider this, it can be somewhat scary.

As Jesus taught in the model prayer, we need to be constantly conscious of the fact that our ability to forgive others is a serious spiritual matter. God's forgiveness to us hinges on our forgiveness of others (including money debts).

198

Reflections...

◻

APRIL 10

Deuteronomy 26:13 *then you shall say before the Lord your God: 'I have removed the holy tithe from my house, and also have given them to the Levite, the stranger, the fatherless, and the widow, according to all Your commandments which You have commanded me; I have not transgressed Your commandments, nor have I forgotten them.*

The Bible tells us in several places that the tithe is the Lord's. Malachi discusses in detail the fact that we "rob" God when we do not pay the tithe and give offerings. I used the term "pay tithes" purposefully; since it belongs to the Lord, it is not ours. In fact, we owe that portion to the Lord. Technically, the tithe is the starting point, but certainly not the ending place. We are instructed to give beyond the tithe. The tithe, or tenth, is given first and is in actuality one-tenth of our increase. Beyond the tithe, we give "offerings" from our surplus.

The present-day church is the counterpart of the Old Testament "storehouse." It is noteworthy that in the Old Testament, the tithe was used to care for the Levites (ministers), strangers (homeless), fatherless (orphans), and the widows (today should include single and military moms). Sadly the church has withdrawn its caring hand from much of the biblical ministries of both the Old Testament and the New Testament early church. The caring arms to the homeless, widows and orphans have been relegated to government agencies and by doing so, the church has forfeited many opportunities of ministering the love and compassion of God.

Maybe it is time that the church refocuses itself upon the "calling to which it was called." In order to do so, the laity must step up to the responsibility to which we have been called ...the "paying of the tithe." The implication in this verse is clear beyond any doubt. The tithe is the Lord's. It was literally a relief when it was removed from the house and placed in its rightful place ...the ministry of caring for the ministers, homeless, orphans and widows.

Reflections...

☐

APRIL 11

Ezra 1:4 *And whoever is left in any place where he dwells, let the men of his place help him with silver and gold, with goods and livestock, besides the freewill offerings for the house of God which is in Jerusalem.*

The Book of Ezra in the Old Testament gives the account of the Lord speaking through His prophet Jeremiah with a call of His people to return to Jerusalem and build Him a house. It is always interesting to see the pieces fall into place when the Lord sets His plan into motion. The Lord moved upon the heart of King Cyrus who was instrumental in this project to the extent that he not only gave his permission for the people to go to Jerusalem, but he highly encouraged them to go.

There is a great lesson in this overall project that we as present-day Christians can draw. That is the example of a tremendously successful mission trip, maybe the greatest mission trip of all times. First and foremost, the project was God's plan, not that of a self-seeking prophet, king or any other person. God was the one who started the project and He was the one who received the honor of the project.

Of particular interest is the fact that while all men were encouraged to go on this mission, none were required to go. They were given free will to choose. However, those who chose not to make this journey to work building the temple were given a strict responsibility that they were expected to fulfill. All who remained were instructed to support the mission with their monetary means. They were to help with silver, gold, goods (supplies), livestock (food), plus freewill offerings.

Jeremiah proclaimed this great mission and everyone without exception was a part of that mission project. Those who chose to make the journey chose direct involvement; those who chose not to go chose indirect involvement in their material and monetary support. We, as a part of the church, are under a similar proclamation. As the earthly ministry of Jesus came to an end, the Holy Spirit was sent to dwell "in" followers of Christ. Along with the indwelling was the proclamation: *"But you shall receive power when the Holy Spirit has come upon you;*

and you shall be witnesses to Me in Jerusalem, and in all Judea and Samaria, and to the end of the earth." ... **Acts 1:8**. Everyone, without exception, who is a follower of Christ, is included in this call. There are some who will make the choice to take the gospel to the ends of the earth. The burden of provision for them to go falls directly upon those who choose not to go, as was the case in Ezra 1.

Those of us who choose the comforts of our modern society in lieu of taking the gospel to the ends of the earth, surely have an obligation to support those willing to sacrifice those same comforts for the sake of answering the call to carry the gospel. How can we support these sacrificing missionaries? Simple ..."*with silver and gold, with goods and livestock, besides the freewill offerings."*

Reflections...

☐

APRIL 12

Psalms 140:12 *I know that the Lord will maintain The cause of the afflicted, And justice for the poor.*

For most of us in America, we are "bothered" when we are confronted with those who are less fortunate than we. Now, there are always exceptions, but the majority does not want to be confronted with the issue of giving assistance to those in third-world countries who may be starving. I have personally had the comments thrown my way that go something like this: "I think those people need to take care of their own and let us take care of ours." Statements like this make me want to rave back, "Great, tell me about how 'you' are helping to alleviate poverty and helping the homeless in your city." I am still awaiting a comeback to that statement. Why? ...because most of us in this country have become calloused to the point that we do not want to think about lending a helping hand to those who have fallen upon hard times. We prefer instead to focus our attention and resources on our own wants and desires in our self-centered state of being. Self gratification is all that matters.

All through the Bible, God's attention is directed to the poor. Jesus spent most of His earthly ministry focusing on the poor. We are instructed many times in the Bible to help the poor and afflicted. In this particular verse, there is an interesting and even convicting nugget that we most likely have not considered. Note, the Lord will "maintain" the cause of the afflicted and justice for the poor. These terms have the connotation of an attorney making an argument against those who do not participate in helping the afflicted and the poor. In essence, the cause (concern) for the afflicted and the justice (fair treatment) for the poor will be maintained by God. There will be accountability for the failure to give appropriate assistance by all who are able to render such. God is not going to forget, but He will "maintain." The issue will not just dry up and blow away. We will each be required to give account of how we have reacted when confronted with the issue of ministering to the poor and needy.

204

This is no small matter even though many turn a deaf ear and look the other way. We in America are blessed beyond measure. However, we prefer not to be disturbed by issues like ministering to the afflicted and the poor. If you happen to be feeling a little guilty and convicted, just think how you are going to feel when you stand before God and make your argument to Him!

Reflections...

APRIL 13

Deuteronomy 24:17 *You shall not pervert justice due the stranger or the fatherless, nor take a widow's garment as a pledge.*

Yet again, our attention is directed towards those in society who are the underprivileged. The strangers, orphans and the widows constitute a group that our current culture would term "undesirable." As followers of Christ, we need to carefully re-evaluate our attitudes concerning the "undesirables."

Numerous times throughout the Bible, we are instructed to care for the strangers, orphans and widows. We are directed to be defenders of widows (**Psalms 68:5**). We are told not to exploit the widow's wage (**Malachi 3:5**). We are instructed not to devour the widow's house (**Matthew 23:14**). We are told to not neglect daily distribution to the widows (**Acts 6:1**). We are to honor the widows (**1 Timothy 5:3**). We are told not to afflict the orphans and widows (**Exodus 22:22**). We are to love the strangers, fatherless and widows (**Deuteronomy 10:18**).

The list could go on and on. Jesus chose to spend most of His time while on earth with these "undesirables" that we tend to shun. These people held a special place in the heart of our Savior. Have you ever stopped to consider that, but for the grace of God, you could be one of these "undesirables?"

I am convinced that each time our path crosses the path of an undesirable, it is a test that God has allowed to take place to see how we will react. If that is in fact true, I am afraid that most of us have failed this test repeatedly. May I issue a challenge to you? The next time one of these incidents occurs, immediately stop for a few seconds and ask God to guide your response. I have a hunch that if you do this, then your attitude and your actions will begin to take on a completely different flavor.

Again, but for the grace of God, we would be the "undesirable" that others avoid. Allow the Holy Spirit to purge your heart and your attitude.   This is no small matter.   Consider the words of James: *"Religion that God our Father accepts as pure and faultless is this: to look after orphans and widows in their distress and to keep oneself from being polluted by the world." ...* **James 1:27 (NIV)**

Reflections...

☐

APRIL 14

1 John 3:17 *But whoever has this world's goods, and sees his brother in need, and shuts up his heart from him, how does the love of God abide in him?*

John, in his writings, plays hard ball. He does not beat around the bush, mince words or hold back. He just opens up and lets it fly. A lot of what John writes catches us right between the eyes. In fact, John speaks to Christians in much the same manner as Jesus spoke to the Pharisees. Maybe there is a correlation there.

Notice John's direct approach in this verse: "whoever has this world's goods." He is talking to those of us who have more materials and sustenance than we need to make it through this day and into tomorrow. In America, we fail to realize that we are rich by the world's standard. Consider the following:

- If you have food in your fridge, clothes on your back, a roof over your head and a place to sleep you are richer than 75% of the world.
- If you have money in the bank, your wallet, and some spare change you are among the top 8% of the world's wealthy.
- If you woke up this morning with more health than illness you are more blessed than the million people who will not survive this week.
- If you have never experienced the danger of battle, the agony of imprisonment or torture, or the horrible pangs of starvation, you are luckier than 500 million people around the world who are alive and suffering.
- If you can read this message you are more fortunate than 3 billion people in the world who cannot read it at all.

So who was John talking to in this verse? For certain, he was talking to Americans since we possess a major portion of the wealth of the entire world. Yet, if you ask the average person on the street why does he think he is blessed to live in America and experience the opportunities and prosperity of this society, his reply will probably be to enjoy success and the comforts that money can buy. We have become a society of hyper-consumers.

John poses a legitimate question to us. If we see those in need and shut up our hearts, then how can we claim to be Christian? How can we say that we have the love of God abiding in us and not reach out to those who are in need? How can we say that we are Christian and not act like Christ? There is a one-word answer to these questions ...HYPOCRITE!

Reflections...

☐

APRIL 15

Luke 20:22 *Is it lawful for us to pay taxes to Caesar or not?*

O h no, it's that time again!!! Tax reconciliation day - the day we all love to hate! In the midst of turmoil of partisan politics, hassling, bickering and arguing, it is very easy for us to become so discouraged and distraught that we question whether or not we, as Bible-believing Christians, should pay taxes. As more disclosure reveals that portions of our tax dollars go for biblically immoral purposes such as funding abortions and alternative lifestyles, it is difficult for a Christian to feel good about the way his tax money is being used.

With all that being said, we can resort to the Bible for our answer to the question of whether or not we should pay taxes. This same question was asked to Jesus. Of course, the question was asked by a group who were attempting to trick Jesus into saying something that could be used against Him. Nevertheless, the truth that He spoke stands even today and is applicable to the question of our day about paying taxes. His answer was unequivocal and unquestionable: *"And He said to them, 'Render therefore to Caesar the things that are Caesar's, and to God the things that are God's.'"* ...**Luke 20:25**.

The problem present-day Christians have with the answer given by Jesus may surprise you. It is not the part about giving taxes to the government; it is the part about giving the part to God. Most of us readily pay our taxes, albeit not joyfully. However, most of us DO NOT give God the portion that He has directed us in scripture to give. Yes, we render to Caesar the things that are Caesar's, but we fail miserably when giving to God the things that are God's!

210

Reflections...

☐

APRIL 16

Job 34:19 *Yet He is not partial to princes, Nor does He regard the rich more than the poor; For they are all the work of His hands.*

Our human nature seems to favor the lifestyles of the rich and famous. We are mesmerized when we are in the presence of someone of prominent stature. We are sometimes boastful if we make the acquaintance of a wealthy person. The downfall of many people in our country has been the rat race of trying to "keep up with the Joneses." In many cases, the upscale home in an elite area that beckoned with our name seemingly written on it, led straight to financial demise. Why? We were driven in an effort to attain the prestige of our friends and win their approval. Many families have lost their homes under just such circumstances.

This same attitude has spilled over into our spiritual lives. In too many cases we do not want to associate with those who are not "like" us. We have developed an attitude wherein we only desire to worship with our "chosen" friends. Furthermore, we sometimes act as though we have God's special favor showering down on us and us alone. Sadly, almost all of our prayer time is spent asking God to "bless us", to keep us from suffering, to make us "feel good", to keep us from all disappointment, and give us everything that we ask in order that we can be happy.

I challenge you to stop and listen to your own prayers; I challenge you to listen to the prayers of others. We are reminded numerous times in the Bible that God does not show partiality to anyone. Consider these scriptures: **Galatians 2:6; Acts 10:34; 2 Chronicles 19:7; Romans 2:11; Ephesians 6:9; Colossians 3:25; James 2:1; James 2:3; James 2:9; Leviticus 19:15; Deuteronomy 1:17; Deuteronomy 16:19**. God does not regard the rich more than the poor. God does not bless the elite more than the downtrodden. God does not favor the well-dressed, uptown American church attendees more than the destitute orphans and widows in dark Africa. God does not show partiality to us because we have money; neither does He show partiality to us because we do not have money.

God, let us see through Your eyes; let us hear with Your ears; let us love with Your compassion. Let us see ourselves as You see us!

Reflections...

□

APRIL 17

John 21:6 *And He said to them, "Cast the net on the right side of the boat, and you will find some." So they cast, and now they were not able to draw it in because of the multitude of fish.*

I don't like someone telling me what to do and how to do it. You are probably the same. Most of the time, it is our human nature to think that we know the best way to do things. Many times, even in the face of failure, we maintain our stance with the stubbornness of a mule. All too often absolute failure has to be experienced before we admit that there may be a better way to do things.

A couple of years back, my wife's car developed an electrical problem that periodically drained the battery. The problem was intermittent and unpredictable. Needless to say, going out in the mornings to go to work and discovering the car's battery was dead did not set well with her, or me for that matter, since I had to take her to work and pick her up in the afternoon. I took the car to the dealer's service department on two occasions. They had no clue as to what was causing the problem, albeit, they still gave me a quote of $2,000 to replace some parts. Over a period of weeks, by a process of elimination, I finally diagnosed the problem. I went back to the dealer and discussed my discovery with the service manager and his "factory trained" technician. They both did everything just short of telling me not only was I wrong but there was no way that my diagnosis could cause the problem. In their presence, I replaced the defective relay that was the culprit and bingo – problem solved. Their only reply was, "Well, maybe...?" My $6.95 part corrected the problem for which they had given a repair quote of $2,000. They were not happy that I had proved them wrong.

Most of us have made some horrific mistakes in managing money. With the average family in America basically insolvent in their personal finances, one might say that as a society, we have blown it. Our federal government is even worse. On this very day, each household's portion

214

of the national debt of our country is more than $150,000 compared to the average family's accumulated savings of a measly $6,042!

The men named in this chapter were professional fishermen. They knew how to catch fish, yet after fishing all night, they had caught nothing. Then came the instructions from Jesus which, for some reason, they followed. He simply told them to cast their net on the "right" side of the boat. Their catch was more than they could pull into the boat. It was abundance galore! ...more than enough! Their problem was that they had been casting on the "wrong" side of the boat. Following the Lord's instructions is always best, even when we think we know best.

We should learn a lesson in managing our personal finances from this account. Following biblical principles in managing money, the Lord's instructions, is casting on the "right" side of the boat. Following the principles of our current culture is casting on the "wrong" side of the boat!

Reflections...

APRIL 18

James 5:3 *Your gold and silver are corroded, and their corrosion will be a witness against you and will eat your flesh like fire. You have heaped up treasure in the last days.*

If one is not careful and diligent in study, he may conclude that the Bible is paradoxical with respect to its instruction of giving and saving money. In one place we find that we should be saving for the future for we do not know what a day may bring. On the other hand, we are told repeatedly that we have responsibilities in caring for the widows, orphans and poor. So, which is right?

The answer is "yes." We are, in fact, to do both! We are to provide for our household or we are worse than unbelievers. We are to store a reserve and make provision for the future; we do not know how the future events of this fallen world are going to unfold. On the other hand, we also have the responsibility of giving, and that is a big responsibility!

James points out in the context of these few verses that if we become possessed with only saving and piling up treasure, then that very treasure will become cankered. Heaping up treasure for the sake of possession is just a form of covetousness. It is greed in action. In addition, it is idolatry since money becomes the object to which we look for all provision. We do not see God if we allow money to blind our vision. In this scenario, the very treasure that has become the focus of our endeavors will eventually and inevitably witness against us.

God shares His material treasure with us for a purpose. First, money is a test. Since God has given explicit instructions to us about its management (which, by the way, includes giving), we are experiencing a test each and every time we get additional money. To put it plainly, each of us is challenged with the question, "What are you doing with what you have right now?" What happens afterwards is dependent upon how we score on the test. We are told to "Give and it will be given to us." (**Luke 6:38**). Here, James tells us that if we ignore the poor and choose rather to greedily pile up treasure, that very treasure will be a testimony against us later. Again, the somber question that we all face constantly is, "What are you doing with what you have right now?"

Reflections...

□

APRIL 19

Proverbs 12:14 *A man will be satisfied with good by the fruit of his mouth, And the recompense of a man's hands will be rendered to him.*

Every once in a while you run across a "really" good person. By that, I mean someone who is consistent day after day, regardless of what may be going on around him. I was just thinking about such a person with whom I became acquainted several years ago. Billy was his name, "Mr. Billy" as I always called him. Mr. Billy made a positive impression on everyone he met. I named him the "Southern Gentleman." In the face of irate customers who were experiencing problems with their equipment, Mr. Billy had a special finesse of settling the customers down in what seemed an almost magical manner. I had a factory engineer from up North with me on one occasion and we observed Billy's ability to bring calm to a situation that seemed impossible. Needless to say, the engineer was impressed beyond words.

Mr. Billy had not always eaten from the trough of luxury. In fact, he had travelled the hard road. Mr. Billy loved the Lord and was always able to speak a "good" word in any situation. Although death had claimed his wife of many years, he was not detoured from his gentle mannerism punctuated with a word of wisdom in every situation. Mr. Billy was blessed to enjoy good from the fruit of his mouth. He was very successful simply because he could say the right thing at the right time in the right way.

We could all learn a lesson from Mr. Billy. Regardless of the situation, most of us have room for improvement in our communication skills. Honest work was another attribute of Mr. Billy. If he was supposed to do something, you never wondered if he did it. You KNEW he did! Dependability and thoroughness were parts of his work ethic. On a daily basis, it was evident that Mr. Billy worked "as unto the Lord."

The next time you are having a bad hair day and things are not going well, maybe you will give thought to Mr. Billy's philosophy. Always speak a good word from your mouth while doing honest, dependable and thorough work with your hands. *"A man will be satisfied with good by the fruit of his mouth, And the recompense of a man's hands will be rendered to him."*

Reflections...

APRIL 20

Matthew 6:31 *Therefore do not worry, saying, 'What shall we eat?' or 'What shall we drink?' or 'What shall we wear?'*

Have you ever gone on a diet? You are probably in the select group of approximately 99.99% of Americans whose answer is 'yes.' If you happen to be one of these not so unique dieters, then you may have come to the same conclusion as me. In America, we don't have a problem with food; we have a problem with the obsession of eating! We do not necessarily eat when we need food or when we are hungry. We eat by the clock.

It has been said that the Unites States of America feeds the world. Yet in all the abundance of food, many of us still worry about *'what shall we eat?'* In a country where everyone has good water to drink, we worry about *'what shall we drink?'* With our closets overrunning with clothes to the point that we are "forced" to rent additional storage in which to keep the extras, we worry about *'what shall we wear?'* Are you beginning to see a pattern here? We live in abundance and still ask the same questions. Now, if we were in a third-world country that had a lack of all of these, maybe we might be justified in asking these questions...maybe?

'What shall we eat?' has nothing to do with concern as to whether or not there is nourishment in the house. In our society, it most likely is a question of whether we are going out to Logan's or Outback. *'What shall we drink?'* has nothing to do with the supply of clean water. *'What shall we wear?'* is code for I'm going shopping to buy something new.

While there are people in the world who are asking these same questions out of legitimate concern of lack, we in America are certainly not among them. Yes, there are millions and even hundreds of millions of people who are genuinely concerned about their next meal, a glass of clean water, and clothes for warmth from the cold. But, rest assured, most of us who live in the land of plenty need to re-establish our real needs.

In this verse in Matthew, Jesus was addressing those who suffered from lack of the essentials. His message to them was simply not to worry about these needs knowing that the heavenly Father was well aware of all their needs. If Jesus told those who had the "real" needs not to be overly concerned, then where does that leave those of us who do not suffer from lack and still concern ourselves with trivial matters instead of being concerned about our relationship with Him? ...something to think about!!!

Reflections...

□

APRIL 21

Luke 12:42 *And the Lord said, "Who then is that faithful and wise steward, whom his master will make ruler over his household, to give them their portion of food in due season?"*

Times have changed tremendously over the past 50 years or so. Almost daily, the news is blasting forth with another student that has been arrested with a gun at school. Rewind time about five decades and you never heard such. It was not because students did not carry guns to school then because many of the boys had their hunting rifles in their vehicles. Practically every boy carried a weapon to school every day in the form of a pocket knife. This was standard procedure, but again, times have changed.

I attended a country elementary school in grades 1 – 8. Being an eighth grader in those days was the equivalent of being king of the castle. It was the goal to which everyone strived. Our eighth grade teacher was also the principal of the school. In addition, he was a farmer. There were occasions when he needed to leave school to attend to other things of which we dared not ask. Before leaving, he would assign enough work to keep every studious person busy until he returned, sometimes one or two hours later. Again, there was enough work to keep the "studious" individuals busy; as a side note, everyone was not "studious." But as he left, he would tell us that the ones who did their work and were well behaved would be rewarded with greater privileges and responsibilities. This worked for some; for others, it did not. As I reminisce on the events of those bygone days, it makes me a little nervous in comparison with today's world. However, there was much expected in those days and likewise, there were rewards for good performance.

This is similar to the teaching of Jesus in this portion of the 12th Chapter of Luke. In this passage, He taught the ethic of commitment to doing what was right even though the master was not constantly looking over his shoulder. I would call it 'doing what is right because doing right is the right thing to do.' Jesus said that this work ethic

222

would be blessed. At that, Peter asked if this only applied to those present to whom Jesus was speaking. Jesus, in summary, related that it applies to everyone. A faithful and wise steward is one who does the right things when the master is present and likewise, when the master is not present. He does the right thing because doing the right thing is the right thing to do!   Faithfulness will be rewarded by the Father. *"And the Lord said, 'Who then is that faithful and wise steward, whom his master will make ruler over his household, to give them their portion of food in due season?'"*

Reflections...

_____

_____

_____

_____

_____

_____

_____

_____

_____

_____

_____

_____

_____

_____

_____

☐

APRIL 22

James 1:10 *But the rich should take pride in their humiliation--since they will pass away like a wild flower.*
(NIV)

How much of your time is spent on matters that pertain only to you and your particular interests? That question could be expanded and asked how much time do you spend preparing for and accumulating material possessions? How does the equation balance out between "getting" and "giving?" If I am honest with myself, then I would have to admit that in consideration of my entire life, I have spent an awful lot of my time trying to accumulate "stuff." And, I'll bet if you are really honest, you probably will admit that you are not much different than me. The question begs to be asked, what is the purpose of it all?

Now, don't misunderstand, everyone is not piling up wealth these days. They are, however, working feverishly to buy all kinds of stuff, much of which is not needed. It matters not whether one is working to buy stuff or working to pile up wealth. The preoccupation of working to accumulate is the same. Again, the question ...for what? A quick response might be in order to have a better quality of life. Oh, really? Our society floods our children with all kinds of entertainment and gadgets; but, are their lives really better? With suicide the second leading cause of death among teenagers in America, the argument that their quality of life is better does not hold water. Marriages are breaking down at an unprecedented rate today. Apparently, this pursuit of a better quality of life is not working for the adults either.

Man's life is made up of a series of cycles. In fact, according to this verse, the entire life of man is a cycle; he is here for a season and then he will pass like a wild flower. The wise man Solomon alluded to the seasons in Ecclesiastes 3. There was even a #1 hit song about this in 1965 by the popular pop group, *The Byrds*. Author and pastor, John Ortberg, wrote a popular book a couple of years back titled, *When the Game is Over, It All Goes Back Into the Box.* We live...we die...and then someone else takes all our stuff; it's a cycle.

224

The bottom line is that none of us is going to get out of this world alive. It is also important to note that none of us will take any of our "stuff" with us when life's final day dawns. With that being reality, maybe we should spend more of our time following the example set by Jesus. Maybe we should spend more of our time "giving" and less time "getting."

Reflections...

APRIL 23

James 2:5 *Listen, my beloved brethren: Has God not chosen the poor of this world to be rich in faith and heirs of the kingdom which He promised to those who love Him?*

Can one have wealth and still be an heir to the kingdom? Some would argue no. Based solely on this one verse, we might get the idea that the kingdom is comprised of only the poor. However, when we consider the context of scripture as a whole, we quickly reach the conclusion that this theory would not be accurate. That does not mean that there are contradictions in the Bible concerning the issue. This verse in no way states that the rich are excluded from the kingdom. It simply states that God has chosen the poor of this world to be rich in faith and heirs of the kingdom. But notice, it does not stop there. James continues in stating that the kingdom is promised to those who love Him.

There are a few points of logic that should be iterated on this issue. First, it is more common that the poor look to God as their source to supply whatever need they may be facing. Where else can they turn? That within itself is not necessarily a bad thing. Secondly, the poor have fewer distractions to take their attention from God. The absence of all the latest technological toys, the expensive automobiles, the large homes plus the vacation homes, the country club membership, and the list goes on (until the money runs out), leaves time and space for the poor to seek God. Thirdly, due to the lack of resources, I am convinced that it is easier for the poor to exercise faith in God. Exercising faith simply means the launch of action based on God's Word when one does not know what the outcome is going to be. It means to start walking when God says 'walk' even though you do not know where you are going.

Unfortunately, many people with wealth look to their money as their source. God will not play second fiddle to anyone or anything. Jesus taught that it is impossible to serve God and money (**Matthew 6:24**). Those who possess great wealth have greater pressures coming against them in an effort to effect the dissipation of their possessions. Every possession that a person has requires a portion of that person's life. That is not to say that every possession is bad; that is far from the truth. However, every single thing requires some portion of your life regardless of its usefulness or its uselessness. For instance, a car requires a certain amount of maintenance. The fact that one owns a car also requires the "time" it takes to drive the car. There goes a portion of your life. The requirement of a lawnmower is similar. In fact, when it will not start and run, I am convinced it burns time at an exponential rate. The TV, the stereo, the iPad, iPod and certainly the Smartphone, the laptop, the Game Boy and X-box, the vacation home, the golf cart, the bicycle and the 4-wheeler each require a portion of the life of the owner. You begin to get the picture that the people with wealth have more distractions simply because of their "stuff."

It may be time to have a garage sale and apply a good "selling" to a lot of stuff. Decrease "stuff" and increase your life. Take the money from the sale and use it to minister to the poor; now, that would be a good and noble gesture! God does not show partiality to the poor; they just show more honor and obedience to Him!

Reflections...

APRIL 24

2 Thessalonians 3:10-11 *For even when we were with you, we commanded you this: If anyone will not work, neither shall he eat. (11) For we hear that there are some who walk among you in a disorderly manner, not working at all, but are busybodies.*

Work ethic in our country is a major concern these days. The recent "Occupy" movement and subsequent demonstrations that have, on numerous occasions, escalated into nothing short of destructive riots should cause uneasiness in all true-blooded Americans. There are many in our country today who openly promote their entitlement agendas. Strong work ethic and entitlement occupy opposite ends of the spectrum. Our country was built upon sound ideals of which a strong work ethic was one. Yet today, almost half of the population of our country is drawing government financial aid in some form.

Who comes to your mind when you read this scripture penned by the Apostle Paul to the Thessalonians? Without question, this is a strong statement. If you don't work, you don't eat! Maybe your thoughts go to some able-bodied individual who sits at home awaiting the mailman to bring the next welfare check. Or maybe it is the hobo sitting at a busy intersection holding a sign which reads, "Need Food." Maybe it is a family member who is always mooching off other family members, but never looking for a job. In my mind, I immediately go back to the 1957 movie *Old Yeller.* The neighbor who did not go with all the other men on the cattle drive but chose to stay around "just in case the women-folk needed something" was a man by the name of Bud Searcy. Mr. Searcy was quick to the table, but slow to do anything that resembled work. He was a busybody whose only apparent purpose was to find the next free meal. I am sure you know the kind.

I grew up in a world that was quite different from that of Mr. Searcy. I recall when I was a young teenager one of my friend's family was going through some difficulty. He asked if he could come and live with us. There were five of us kids living at home at the time. I will always remember what my dad told him: "You are welcome to come live with us – when we eat, you eat and when we work, you work." And that is the way it was. There were never any questions, no grumbling and no complaining. We all did work and we all did eat. Little did I realize it at the time, but we were living by the scriptures!

Our country is in need of a work ethic revival. We need to re-learn the lesson penned centuries ago by the Apostle Paul: *"If anyone will not work, neither shall he eat."*

Reflections...

_____

_____

_____

_____

_____

_____

_____

_____

_____

_____

_____

_____

_____

☐

APRIL 25

2 Corinthians 9:6 *But this I say: He who sows sparingly will also reap sparingly, and he who sows bountifully will also reap bountifully.*

This is one of the most direct and relevant scriptures that affects Christians on a daily basis, but also one to which we pay the least attention. It is God's principle of sowing and reaping. Everyone has probably heard the joke about the person who had opened a checking account for the very first time and within just a few days had written checks and overdrew the account. When informed that the account was overdrawn, the reply was, "There is no way I'm overdrawn, I still have checks left." Unfortunately, that is the way many believers approach their spiritual lives; they are forever making withdrawals but never stop to consider that there must also be some deposits. We live in an age where Christians have a strong desire to set up camp directly beneath the spout of God's blessings and soak everything that comes out like a giant sponge. Many have no desire to go out and sow; they are there only for the harvest. The sidelines are full of benchwarmers, but there is not a large number who want to get into the game.

Our churches are full of grumblers and complainers. One of the most prevalent complaints is that they are not getting "fed" at church. This may be a good time to re-assess in view of this verse. The first question should be, "What have you sown?" If you have sown sparingly (or in many cases, not at all), then you can expect to reap sparingly. This is not complicated; it is not sophisticated; it is just the truth. And, by the way, where did we get the idea that we are supposed to be "fed" at church anyway? Babies require feeding; mature individuals feed themselves. We should come to church to worship God and be equipped to serve Him. It is not about us; it is about Him! Too many church members come to church to be entertained and get that "feel good" feeling. Again, church is not about you or me; it is about GOD!

Meditate on this verse and ask God to allow the Holy Spirit to reveal its truth. If you need a blessing, then sow ...go out and "be" a blessing to someone. If you need a friend, then sow ...go out and be a friend to

230

someone. If you need someone to help you, then sow ...go out and help someone. If your finances need a boost, then sow ...go out and give to someone in need. You will notice that the harvest (receiving) comes only after sowing. Additionally, the size of the harvest is proportional to the sowing: sow a little, reap a little – sow a lot, reap a lot.

As we examine our spiritual lives, let us determine just how much we are sowing before we complain about the harvest. As we sit under the spout of the blessings of God just soaking up His goodness like a satiated sponge, maybe it is time to ask Him to reach down, pick us up and wring us out. Maybe it is time that we go out and sow those soaked up blessings into the lives of others. *"But this I say: He who sows sparingly will also reap sparingly, and he who sows bountifully will also reap bountifully."*

Reflections...

APRIL 26

1 Timothy 6:7 *For we brought nothing into this world, and it is certain we can carry nothing out.*

A new bank opens just down the street in your town. Now, we all know that a bank is a bank is a bank, right? But curiosity gets the best of you, so you mosey on down to check them out. You want to know what makes this bank different from the others, or in fact, is there any difference? As you inquire of the customer service rep, she begins to explain this new bank to you. You discover, to your dismay, this bank really is different; in fact, it is drastically different! You open an account in this bank, make deposits and start the accumulation process. Along the way, you write a few checks, but the main objective here is accumulation to the maximum. In fact, you are even encouraged to sacrifice in order to maximize your constantly increasing bank balance. Sometimes, the kids may not even have everything they need, because the main objective is accumulation. Whatever you do, accumulation pre-empts everything else. When the explanation about the bank began, you were a little skeptical. However, you got over it and really began to buy in on this accumulation thing. And then, the bank rep drops the bomb on you; you see, we saved the best to last.

After you spend years depositing your hard-earned money into our bank, sacrificing as it were along the way, when you begin to age, you are required to give up all that you have saved. At this point, you go ballistic demanding to know why you must give up the fortune that you have built up. The only explanation you get is that you are not allowed to carry anything out.

This is the way that most people approach and live their lives. We start with nothing, we accumulate some stuff, and then we die and someone else gets it all. The ironic thing about all this is that Christians know what is going to happen in the end, and yet they continue down the same path as those who are uninformed. As followers of Christ, we have been instructed differently: *"Do not lay up for yourselves treasures on earth, where moth and rust destroy and where thieves break in and steal; but lay up for yourselves treasures in heaven, where neither moth nor rust destroys and where thieves do not break in and steal."* ... **Matthew 6:19-20.** None of us are going to take any of our accumulated wealth with us when we die. When we consider the totality of this situation, we come up looking ridiculous. First of all, we act as though we are going to defy the laws of nature and that we are going to actually be the first to live forever. Then, we build on that stupidity and act as though we are going to take our "treasure" with us if we do, in fact, succumb.

Well, the Bible has news for us. *"For we brought nothing into this world, and it is certain we can carry nothing out."*

Jim Elliot, the martyred missionary to the country of Ecuador, left us this philosophy concerning wealth: "He is no fool who gives what he cannot keep to gain what he cannot lose."

Reflections...

APRIL 27

1 Timothy 6:9 *People who want to get rich fall into temptation and a trap and into many foolish and harmful desires that plunge men into ruin and destruction.* (NIV)

Unfortunately, many people miss the point of this verse. On numerous occasions, I have heard ministers draw from this verse and expound the evils of money and riches. Its dangers are to be feared, they say, and ruin belies the one who falls into its grasp! Wow! What a revelation!

Actually, this verse is not at all about the evils of money. What it addresses is people with a misdirected focus of life. It is about people who place the value of money above the value of relationships and most of all, their relationship with God. It is about people who place a greater value on money than they do on the goals that they can accomplish with money. Isn't it ironic that we can so easily place the emphasis on the wrong thing?

It has been stated many times, money is not bad and money is not good. Money does not have morals; it is amoral. Money can be used for many evil purposes; conversely, money can be used for many good purposes. The money itself has no vote on how it gets used. The person in whose hand money is found makes that decision. Let's take this pursuit one step further. Money does not cause a person to change for the worse; money does not cause a person to change for the better. Again, money is neutral; it is an innate object, similar to a rock (we just put more value on money that we do rocks). Money is like a magnifying glass. It only brings out of a person what is already there. So, if a person has a well covered, deep rooted evil nature, money is likely to bring it to the surface in an enlarged proportion. If a person has a deep desire to do good, money will bring that to the surface in greater proportions.

When man sets his will to obtain riches, he opens himself to all types of temptation and traps, not because money is evil, but because he has re-defined his focus. The very goal for which he labors becomes a trap of his own making. It is not the fault of money; rather, it is the fault of man. It is not money that sets the trap; it is man who "wills" to be rich at any price. It is the foolish and harmful desires of men that plunge them into ruin and destruction. Let's put the blame where blame belongs!

Reflections...

□

APRIL 28

1 Timothy 5:8 *But if anyone does not provide for his own, and especially for those of his household, he has denied the faith and is worse than an unbeliever.*

One of the questions that I am frequently asked when I am doing financial counseling concerns giving. In the majority of cases (not all, but most), the counselees are in financial counseling because they are experiencing financial difficulties, so it is no secret that money is in short supply. Most are experiencing too much month at the end of the money. Seeking to do the right thing, they inquire as to what level they should be giving and balance, at the same time, their responsibilities of providing for their families. From the viewpoint of a Christ follower, this is a fair, but very difficult, question.

From the onset, let me make this disclaimer. In most cases, people get themselves into financial difficulties because of one primary reason ...they did not follow God's principles of managing money in the first place. Having said that, it closely follows that once a person(s) is/are in this difficult position, some sacrifices have to be made to correct the situation. Thus we arrive at the point of this discussion – where is the balance? What gets paid and what gets left unpaid when it is impossible to stretch the money to cover everything? Not to evade these questions, but there is no hard, firm rule that covers every situation.

There are, however, two things that are emphatic in the Bible that should apply in these dire circumstances. First, throughout the Bible, the instruction of giving (or paying as I like to say) the tithe is consistent. Simply put, we should give God the first fruits of our increase – 10%. Any giving in excess of 10% is referred to as offerings. The second emphatic teaching is to provide for our household. Offerings are given from surplus; tithes are given as the first 10% of our increase. One should not be giving in offerings until the obligations of providing the essentials for the family are met, as this verse instructs. Nowhere (other than TV evangelists) are we instructed to give in offerings before the essentials of our families are met.

I have counseled with couples who were behind on their house payment, but current on a pledge they made to a TV evangelist. This is not biblical. If you happen to fall into this category, you have priorities out of order. I am not necessarily down on TV evangelists; let's just say that I am up on what the Bible teaches. I hope that you are able to give in offerings. In fact, I hope you are able to give a lot in offerings. However, it must be done in God's order. If you do not take care of your household, you are worse than an unbeliever!

Reflections...

APRIL 29

Zechariah 7:9-10 *Thus says the Lord of hosts: 'Execute true justice, Show mercy and compassion Everyone to his brother. Do not oppress the widow or the fatherless, The alien or the poor. Let none of you plan evil in his heart against his brother.'*

Christians today do not like to be disturbed. They do not want to be reminded that there are some responsibilities that go along with the "ride to glory." There is one camp that says it does not matter what you do after you are saved; the only thing that matters is that you are saved. Another camp maintains that anything you "do" is in fact an attempt on your part to earn salvation or work your way to heaven. And then there are those who are just plain apathetic. They are not moved or feel any responsibility to do anything.

There are many who fall into the latter category. Their attitude is, "leave me alone and don't bother me with what the Bible says." I am reminded of an incident that happened recently in a Christian small group discussion. When one lady made a certain generalization about what was right, the group leader asked for Bible references to back up her position. Of course she could not give any and the group leader went on to give scripture references which in fact refuted her claims. Her emphatic reply was, "I don't care what the Bible says; I still believe my way is right." Sadly, there are many in churches today who would echo this same message if they were honest. They really have no inclination to investigate the scriptures to see what the Bible says about their self-concocted theology. They just believe what they want to believe in spite of what the Bible says. Likewise, they could not care less about direct principles given by the Bible that are foundational to Christian beliefs.

The prophet, Zechariah, gave a word from the Lord concerning God's attitude toward some of the less fortunate in society: the widows, the fatherless (orphans), the aliens and the poor. We may be apathetic and show no reaction to the instructions that the Bible gives with respect to these people. However, the Bible repeatedly gives a consistent message to us about our responsibilities of caring for these special people (yes, these are special people). In America in particular, we are so preoccupied with our own self-centered activities and self-gratification that we have no time to get involved with these whom God has placed in our paths.

Every time we are faced with an opportunity to minister to the underprivileged, we are literally undergoing a test that God has placed upon us. We will have to give an account of our negligence and failure to follow God's word. We will have to try to explain why we spend extravagantly upon ourselves while saying we cannot afford to minister to widows, orphans, and those who have been abandoned by society. We may go through our lives turning our heads and looking the other way, but we will be held accountable for our actions.

Again, look closely at the word of the Lord that was spoken through Zechariah: *'Execute true justice, Show mercy and compassion Everyone to his brother. Do not oppress the widow or the fatherless, The alien or the poor. Let none of you plan evil in his heart against his brother.'*

Reflections...

APRIL 30

1 Chronicles 29:28 *So he died in a good old age, full of days and riches and honor; and Solomon his son reigned in his place.*

The life of David is one of the most interesting in the Bible. David was almost everything you can think of: good – bad, rich – poor, weak – strong. At some point in his life, David lived all of these.

A dissertation could be written about each of these qualities in David's life. From the lowly beginning as a shepherd boy to the most powerful king of the known world, David's life spans over every conceivable stretch. He was one of God's most valiant warriors in battle. He won battles when the possibility of victory was only a prayer. On the one hand, he was an adulterer and murderer and on the other, he was a powerful king who set all the groundwork in order for the building of God's Temple. At times, he was conniving, yet he is remembered as being a man after God's heart. He was a friend like no other to Jonathan, yet he had many enemies. As a shepherd, he knew the depths of poverty, yet God raised him up to be a man of riches.

Many today consider money to be evil. Some even consider poverty to be "godly." Yet, God blessed David with great riches. Riches and money are not measures of spirituality. The manner in which one handles money is, however, a reflection of one's spiritual life. David recognized that God was the essence of the supply of riches as well as everything in life (**1 Chronicles 29:11-12**). That is a point that most of us miss. We say we believe God is the source of everything and that He owns everything; our words say one thing but our actions say something completely different. David was commissioned by God to raise the resources with which to build the Temple of God. He proved the epitome of leadership in this task by stepping forth and giving from his personal wealth and not just from that of the office he held. He was not "required" to do so; however, he chose to be a giver. David's attitude and testimony was "everything that I give comes from your hand, oh God."

At the time of David's death, he had everything he ever wanted:
- he had lived to an old age and enjoyed good health;
- his days were full in that he had lived to see practically everything accomplished or moving forward toward completeness that he had lived for;
- he was rich making it possible to not only give to God during his life but also leave a great fortune at his death for completion of the building of the Temple;
- he was a man of honor even though he had experienced low points during his life.

David acknowledged that all his riches came from the hand of God. He used those riches to bless the work of God both during his life and at his death. How about you? Can you say that you are using the money with which you have been blessed for the work of God while you are living? Do you have a plan in place to honor God with your riches at the time of your death? In life and death, David honored God with his riches!

Reflections...

☐

MAY 1

Job 21:13-14 *They spend their days in wealth, And in a moment go down to the grave. Yet they say to God, 'Depart from us, For we do not desire the knowledge of Your ways.*

In the Old Testament, Job was an upright man who feared God. He was blessed and was one of the richest of his day. Although he was a man of God, he endured the loss of all his possessions, bore unimaginable pain and suffering, and was ridiculed by his friends. You probably are very familiar with Job's story. Basically, he lost everything (except a nagging wife and we will leave that one right there).

All of Job's so-called friends instantly became therapists and began to tell him why he was experiencing so much misfortune. Just when he needed solace and encouragement, they lowered the boom citing their assessment of the causes of his adversity. With friends like that, Job did not need enemies!

Amazingly, through all his losses, Job was still able to spiritually discern more accurately than all his friends what he was enduring. Unlike most of us when we face calamity, Job kept unwavering faith that God was in control and was aware of what was going on in his life. Too many times when we face loss and adversity, our eyes immediately catch a glimpse of an unrighteous person who is prospering and we question why it is that they are doing well and we are fairing so horribly. Job addresses that very issue in the entire 21st chapter. More specifically, he iterates in these two verses an observation that most of us have made at some point in our lives. Paraphrasing, he is basically saying that these heathen are living it up with their wealth, enjoying the moment all the way to the grave, all the while saying that they do not want to know anything about God or have anything to do with Him. And in the midst of this irreverent lifestyle, they still prosper. How can this be?

Job raises many interesting issues in this chapter. You probably can relate to most of what he asserts. The bottom line is that when we

242

suffer loss, feel pain, or when we are rejected by so-called friends, we tend to feel sorry for ourselves. If I am experiencing financial difficulty, my natural tendency is to focus in on some vile person who is making money hand-over-fist and question "why is this happening?" In Job's case, his friends were literally helping him along.

In reality, we see only our immediate situation. Many times, we have our eyes as well as our hearts fixated on our own situation as if it were all eternity. It is NOT! This life with all it experiences, both good and bad (as we would define them), is but a rehearsal for the real thing – eternity! Don't become so focused upon the things of this life that you lose sight of the GOAL. So what if we get a bum rap in this life? It is only a test that God has placed before us that will help us to achieve the real goal. Therefore, when things are going well for the unrighteous and rotten for you, thank the Lord for the opportunity of preparing for the real thing ...ETERNAL LIFE!

Reflections...

□

MAY 2

Proverbs 19:22 *What is desired in a man is kindness, And a poor man is better than a liar.*

There is within the heart of most men the desire to do good and show kindness toward his neighbors. It makes one feel good to be able to reach out and help someone in need. You might already be asking the question, if this is so, then why don't we see more kind expression taking place around us? Good question.

The reason people do not follow this innate desire is that something gets in the way. There is something that comes between the heart's desire and the motivational performance of the good deed. This "something" is found in practically every one of us. In fact, this "something" becomes evident at an early age. From time to time, we are literally in battle to squelch that "something" so that it does not interfere with doing the good deeds. At times, we have a strong desire to completely eliminate this "something" from our lives, but find that it is impossible. What in the world is this "something" that prohibits us from doing the good that we want to do and that we should do? It is called "SELF."

I have discovered that "self" is selfish and self-centered. "Self" thinks only of me. "Self" is covetous and stingy. "Self" can cause me to be arrogant and rude when it does not get its way. "Self" can cause me to say hurtful things when it has its way and goes unchecked. "Self" can cause me to hoard and not give, even though I have a surplus and can well afford to give. "Self" can distort my life and turn me away from the plan that God has for my life.

This verse directly addresses the poor man. He cannot give to effect acts of kindness since he does not have anything to give. The verse, by implication, addresses the man who does have sufficiency to give, but because of his selfishness, he chooses to lie and say that he does not have anything to give. Thus, the conclusion is drawn that it is better to be a poor man than a liar. The commentaries of both Barnes and Matthew Henry are in harmony with this interpretation.

244

Selfishness will cause one to hoard and not fulfill God's plan in life. With the percentage of givers in the church at the low ebb where it has hovered for years, it is evident that "self" has probably run interference on a continuing basis. Have you allowed "self" to interfere with God's plan for your giving? Look to God, pray, and consider: *"What is desired in a man is kindness, and a poor man is better than a liar."*

Reflections...

MAY 3

Jeremiah 22:3 *This is what the LORD says: Do what is just and right. Rescue from the hand of his oppressor the one who has been robbed. Do no wrong or violence to the alien, the fatherless or the widow, and do not shed innocent blood in this place.* (NIV)

It sounds as though this verse could have been directed straight to those of us living in the USA in this very year. Of course we know that the prophet Jeremiah was not on the TV evening news; however, one mystical attribute of the Word of God is that it is "living" and many times can apply to situations other than the specific one to which it was directed.

In our current society, there are many situations in which justice is not served and righteousness is not even a remote consideration. Even within our judicial system, justice is sacrificed frequently on the grounds of political correctness or some flimsy technicality. This verse specifically instructs us to rescue from the hand of the oppressor the one who has been robbed; yet, in our legal system, the victim is often treated as the criminal under the guise of protecting the rights of the perpetrator.

God apparently has a special concern for the underprivileged. And yes, that goes for the underprivileged in the USA as well as third world countries and all around the world. The vulnerable (aliens, orphans and widows) are easy prey for those who have no conscience or scruples but do have an overwhelming desire for the almighty dollar. Orphans frequently become victims of human trafficking rings. Widows who are hard-pressed to make ends meet are prime suspects to someone looking to turn a quick buck. I recently was privy to one such situation in which a single mom, whose electrical power had been turned off, was taken advantage of by a scam artist "helping" her get a car. What he, in fact, was doing was "helping" himself to her scarce food money. I often wonder if God will provide a special punishment to robbers who so haughtily take advantage of those whom God has specifically called out - the aliens, the orphans and the widows.

Those of us who identify ourselves as Christians would do well to heed these words of wisdom: *"Do what is just and right. Rescue from the hand of his oppressor the one who has been robbed. Do no wrong or violence to the alien, the fatherless or the widow."*

Reflections...

MAY 4

Mark 4:24-25 *"Consider carefully what you hear,"* he continued. *"With the measure you use, it will be measured to you--and even more. Whoever has will be given more; whoever does not have, even what he has will be taken from him."* (NIV)

In the beginning of Chapter 4, Mark gives the account of Jesus expounding the Parable of the Sower. As a culmination to a tremendous amount of material that He had presented, he summarized in these two verses. In the parable, Jesus talked about the gospel being distributed to various groups of people. There were some who never paid any attention; some listened, but then went on their way; some stopped long enough to take in what was being said, but then became overcrowded by all the things in their lives. Then, of course, there were some who comprised the "good ground." In these, the gospel took root and grew.

What is so interesting about this entire account is the fact that Jesus used an illustration about money to pull it all together in a way that those hearing (including us) could understand the truth concerning the gospel and spiritual walk. Again, the scripture bears out that the way we handle finances is reflective of our spiritual walk: *"with the measure you use, it will be measured to you – and even more."*

The bottom line is that as a follower of Christ, each of us is called to be a good steward. (**1 Corinthians 4:2** *"Moreover it is required in stewards that one be found faithful."*) When we are good stewards of God's money, He will repay. With the same measure that we use, He will replenish and even more.

Of course, the real stinger comes in v. 25: *"Whoever has will be given more; whoever does not have, even what he has will be taken from him."* Many people have a problem with this. It is not uncommon to hear complaints that this is not fair. Consider this: God has set the rule and by His rule, it is fair! ...end of discussion!

This is really not a complicated mathematical exercise. Of course, Jesus was not talking about money only. He was talking about the entirety of the gospel. But, there is no getting around it; He used the example of money to drive the point home. To the point that Mark used in the beginning of v. 24: *"Consider carefully what you hear ..."*

$Reflections...$

☐

MAY 5

Luke 19:15 *And so it was that when he returned, having received the kingdom, he then commanded these servants, to whom he had given the money, to be called to him, that he might know how much every man had gained by trading.*

On many occasions, Jesus used parables when He was teaching. This verse is a part of the Parable of the Minas. The master called ten servants and distributed ten minas among them. His instruction to them was plain and simple: "Do business until I come." The money distributed to the servants was not given to them for personal consumption. There was a specific purpose; they were to do business for their master. Subsequently, they were required to give a report of their activity. They were held responsible for their decisions and actions concerning the master's money.

Of course, you probably are familiar with the story. The first he called had done a good job and his minas had multiplied to ten. Likewise, the second reported that his minas had increased to five. But then came the third servant who had no increase at all. This servant was scolded for his lack of prudent action. Not only was he scolded, the one mina in his possession was taken and given to the servant who had the ten. While the first two servants were verbally commended for their faithfulness in watching over and carrying out the interests of the master, they were openly rewarded by the master for a job well done. Conversely, the unfaithful servant was scolded and that which he had was taken from him.

We are instructed to be good stewards over God's money and property. What does that include? It includes everything because God owns everything (**Psalms 24:1**). Some of us have not followed the instructions of our Master; we have not been doing business till He comes. In fact, we need to drill down one level on this subject.

The unfaithful servant in this parable wrapped the mina in a handkerchief and kept it until the master returned. Many of us have not managed as well as this servant since we have not kept what the

Master has entrusted to us. To be perfectly honest, many of us have taken what the Master has entrusted into our care and instead of "doing business till He comes" we have spent His money for our personal use! We have used God's money (tithes and offerings – **Malachi 3:10**) to buy "stuff" for ourselves, things like new cars, 4-wheelers, 4-wheel drive pickup trucks, bigger houses, country club memberships, and on, and on, and on...

Let's try to draw a conclusion from this: if this unfaithful servant was in hot water and without excuse for his slothfulness, where do you think we will appear when we stand to give account? If we do not even have what God gave us in the beginning because we have CONSUMED it, do you think there may be a problem??? This is not going to be a pretty picture!

Reflections...

□

MAY 6

Luke 7:41-42 *There was a certain creditor who had two debtors. One owed five hundred denarii, and the other fifty. And when they had nothing with which to repay, he freely forgave them both. Tell Me, therefore, which of them will love him more?*

This devotional could start out with, "How many debts have you forgiven lately?" But, I will spare you the gut-wrenching escapade of reliving long-forgotten regret and move on to hopefully more productive thoughts.

Yet again, we find Jesus teaching by utilizing stories to which those who made up His audience could relate. Jesus apparently was a pro when it came to storytelling. He knew exactly which story would bring to light the truth that He wanted to teach. In this particular setting, His audience was one of those self-righteous people, you know the type. Jesus was in the home of a Pharisee, the religious sect of the day. A "sinner" woman, who was most likely a woman from the "red light district," heard that Jesus was dining in the home of this Pharisee, so she found her way into the presence of Jesus, albeit, she came up to His back. She stood behind Him weeping because she recognized something that the Pharisee apparently did not know: she was in the presence of God. As she wept, she washed his feet with her tears and dried them with the hair of her head and anointed them with oil. Consider for a moment the boldness of this woman to seek out Jesus in the home of a Pharisee. Consider the risk she was taking by coming into this place. Consider the tremendous motivation and commitment that she exhibited.

I am sometimes baffled when a minister, in giving an invitation to come to repentance and accept Jesus Christ as Lord, diminishes the committal experience by saying if you are too embarrassed to walk to the front of the church just pray silently where you are. Now, let it be known that I am not shallow enough to believe that walking to the front of a church has any saving power attached. There is, however, a certain degree of commitment that is required to make Jesus Christ

252

Lord of one's life. My argument is simply that the commitment to walk forward during an invitation pales in comparison to the commitment required to make Christ Lord of one's life. If one does not have enough fortitude to make a public confession before a group made up primarily of followers of Christ, then how is he going to muster the commitment to make a public statement of his experience of transformation by living that commitment before unbelievers?

In his mind, the Pharisee condemned this woman because she had many sins. Jesus acknowledged the sin of the woman but looked past her sin to see her "faith" in seeking Him. Jesus hit the nail on the head when he told the story of two people owing debts to a creditor; one owed a very small amount and the other a very large amount. Of course, the creditor forgave the total debts of both. Jesus then asked the question: *"...which of them will love him more?"* Note also that yet again, Jesus used the subject of money in teaching a spiritual lesson. Why? Because we can all relate to the money issue. Some will say that the way we manage money has a spiritual connotation; I say that the way we handle money is a reflection of our spiritual walk. Jesus concluded that the one whom is forgiven more, loves more! The final word to the woman from Jesus should motivate us: *"Your faith has saved you. Go in peace."*

Reflections...

□

MAY 7

Exodus 18:21 *But select capable men from all the people - men who fear God, trustworthy men who hate dishonest gain - and appoint them as officials over thousands, hundreds, fifties and tens.* (NIV)

What to you look for in a leader? In all honesty, do you look for the qualities given in this verse: capable men, men who fear God, trustworthy men who hate dishonest gain? Or, do you look for someone who will cater to your personal desires? Do you look for someone who will show partiality to your way of thinking and pander to your pork barrel projects? Do you want a leader who does the "right" things or do you want someone who does what you want him to do?

Sadly, we cannot say (with honesty) that we want leaders with these attributes. How can I say that? Stop and take a look at the political leaders in our nation. These men and women were elected by majority vote to be our leaders. Therefore, a strong argument can be made that they are exactly what the majority of our nation wants (as a whole). You will see that in almost all cases, the leaders filling the political positions in our government do not possess these qualities. Unfortunately some do not possess ANY of these qualities! Quite a few of them are indeed capable, just not motivated in the right direction. Precious few literally fear God. One has to look long and hard to find those who can be deemed trustworthy. Almost none hate dishonest gain! Most live by the philosophy of "Get all you can and can all you get." You probably have read some of the reports comparing our political leaders' financial net worth when assuming office to their net worth after being in office for a few years. Our national politicians set separate rules for themselves as compared to their constituents.

In this story in Exodus, Moses' job as leader of the Israelites had become too large for one person to handle effectively. Moses' father-in-law, Jethro, exercised great wisdom in advising Moses to delegate leadership responsibilities to selected individuals. Moses accepted the advice from Jethro; in observance of our current government leaders, one could very well draw the conclusion that they too have received advice from Jethro, Bodine that is, from the Beverly Hillbillies, black gold, Texas tea! Far too many of our leaders have personal financial gain as their primary motive. In no way would they qualify as "hating dishonest gain."

America needs to repent and ask God to send us real leaders. We need leaders that fit the bill given to Moses: *"capable men from all the people--men who fear God, trustworthy men who hate dishonest gain."*

Reflections...

☐

MAY 8

Isaiah 33:15 *He who walks righteously and speaks uprightly, He who despises the gain of oppressions, Who gestures with his hands, refusing bribes, Who stops his ears from hearing of bloodshed, And shuts his eyes from seeing evil:*

Isaiah gives some of the attributes of those who walk and live uprightly before God. In this verse, he touches on several guidelines to which a follower of God should adhere. Specifically, he speaks about ill gotten gain and bribery.

I am reminded of a number of occasions from the past where people were caught with their hands in the cookie jar, the cookie jar of ill gotten gain and the jar of bribery. Have you ever noticed that many times when someone is caught in such violations, their first step is to instantaneously become religious? They make sure the TV cameras catch them in either coming from or going to church. Their conversations suddenly are not about materialistic agendas, but about God. Now, I don't mean to be judgmental, but as one of my college professors used to say, "The proof of the pudding is in the eating thereof."

These same violators were not displaying these "religious" behavioral patterns prior to their being caught. They were not the goody-goody do-gooders until it was in their own interest. And, after the heat cooled, they inevitably returned to their previous self-gratifying ways of life.

Isaiah's exposition of the upright followers of God does not fall into sync with those described above. Isaiah speaks of those who live uprightly day in and day out, in the good times and the bad. They are consistent lovers of God, not just when it is to their own selfish advantage. Too often, there are those who despise ill-gotten gains only when they find themselves on the losing end; likewise, bribery is wrong only if you get caught. Integrity has become a rare commodity in our modern society.

How is your attitude concerning money that may come from questionable activities? Are all of your daily dealings fair and equitable to all involved or does money sometimes get passed under the table in order to make a deal? As you examine your personal integrity, look again at how Isaiah describes a person of God: *"He who walks righteously and speaks uprightly, He who despises the gain of oppressions, Who gestures with his hands, refusing bribes, Who stops his ears from hearing of bloodshed, And shuts his eyes from seeing evil:"*

Reflections...

MAY 9

Matthew 12:35 *A good man out of the good treasure of his heart brings forth good things, and an evil man out of the evil treasure brings forth evil things.*

There is much ongoing and opinionated discussion about the evils of money. Many believe that money has detrimental effects upon people. Some think that money itself is evil, albeit, I have never met anyone who removed the evil tempter of money from himself. It is difficult to understand those of this mindset. They usually think that a small amount of money is okay and in fact, desirable because it is required to exist. However, a large amount of money somehow falls across the undefined line of evil. The questions begs, how much can one acquire before he crosses the "evil" line?

As has been maintained by this writer in the past, money is amoral. It does not have morals. It is neither good nor bad. Money can be used to accomplish good and conversely, money can be used for evil purposes. Money has no say on how it gets used. That decision is made by the one in whose hand money is held.

This verse, yet again, bears out this truth. Money in the possession of a good person with good intentions is referred to as "good" treasure and is used to bring about good things. Money in the possession of an evil person with evil intentions is called "evil" treasure and is used to bring about evil things. It does not take a rocket scientist to conclude that the morals of money are not in question here. Money assumes the nature imposed upon it by the person in whose hand it rests.

In some ways, money is analogous to water. Water is one of the necessities of life and more specifically, human life. Water quenches the thirst of man. Without water, we die. Yet that same water can consume the very life that it saves. If it is inhaled into the lungs, a person can drown; it destroys life. If it is swallowed by a thirsty person, it saves life. It is not the water that determines whether it will save life or destroy life. The way it is used makes that determination.

A good person, a follower of Christ, uses good treasure to bring about good things; an evil person uses his evil treasure to bring about evil things. It is the heart of the person holding the treasure who determines the destiny of its use. **Jeremiah 17:9** *"The heart is deceitful above all things, And desperately wicked; Who can know it?"* If you have a heart to follow Christ, let Him direct you to use your treasure to bring about good things!

Reflections...

☐

MAY 10

Luke 3:12-13 *Then tax collectors also came to be baptized, and said to him, "Teacher, what shall we do?" And he said to them, "Collect no more than what is appointed for you."*

If you are at all a student of Bible history, then you are aware that the tax collectors at the time Jesus was on the earth had a reputation that left a lot to be desired; in fact, they were low-down scoundrels. If you think you have it bad having to pay taxes today, just remember that in comparison to the taxes imposed by the tax collectors in biblical times, you've got it made! These tax collectors levied against the people far more than the law required. The ironic thing is that the law allowed this practice to continue. The tax collectors literally extorted money from all whom they found could pay. Like I said, they were conniving scoundrels.

As John the Baptist was making his debut into ministry, he preached and then held baptismal services. Crowds gathered for the baptisms as it was a popular thing to do. Many in fact came forward to be baptized. John spoke rather harshly to the crowds telling them to show themselves worthy prior to requesting baptism. It was in this context when the tax collectors asked what they had to do to show themselves worthy of baptism. John's reply to them was to collect taxes only to the extent the law required. That meant they had to stop their cheating and extortion. In essence, they had to show evidence of changed lives.

When we turn our lives to God, there should be a change of attitude concerning the way we view money, just as John's requirement of the tax collectors. Instead of cheating and conniving, we should have no desire for ill-gotten gain, especially by taking advantage of the vulnerable. In the previous verse, John stated that "giving" to those in need was one way to show oneself worthy of repentance and subsequently baptism.

As followers of Christ, we should constantly ask ourselves if we are showing ourselves worthy of repentance in the way we handle money. Are we good stewards for God or are we low-down, conniving scoundrels? If that was an appropriate question for John the Baptist to ask the tax collectors who desired to be baptized, certainly it is one that we should ask ourselves.

Reflections...

MAY 11

1 Timothy 3:8 *Likewise deacons must be reverent, not double-tongued, not given to much wine, not greedy for money,*

I f you have ever been under consideration for the position of deacon, you are aware of some of the scrutiny to which one is subjected. In most cases, it is not unlike the FBI coming to town to see what kind of dirt can be turned up or what dirty laundry you may be hiding in your closet.

This close examination is well-founded. In fact, it is the scriptural thing to do. The Bible lays out guidelines that are appropriate for the office of deacon. A deacon must be reputed to be of good character in the community as well as in the church by maintaining an attitude of reverence. He must not be double-tongued or, as we would say, swayed by the direction that the wind is blowing. His opinions and beliefs must be biblically founded. He should not be given to wine and strong drink (...enough said about that one). And then, here comes the one that is never discussed and seldom investigated; he must not be greedy for money.

Maybe each candidate for deacon should be asked to produce his checkbook so that the pattern of his financial affairs can be properly evaluated. Certainly, a credit check should be run to ensure that his dealings in business and community affairs are clean and above board. Maybe a few who have done business with the candidate should be called for personal interviews in order to determine first-hand the financial character with which this person under consideration has dealt with the public.

By now you are, no doubt, saying that this whole discussion has become facetious. You are probably saying that no one in his right mind would ever consent to such harassment, and you are probably correct. However, in view of the seriousness of the position, would this really be asking too much? The very next verse reveals the magnitude of the task: *"holding the mystery of the faith with a pure conscience."* In this dog-eat-dog culture in which we live, the financial aspect of the character of candidates for deacon is certainly at risk. Likewise, according to scripture, it should be reviewed diligently when considering one to assume the responsibility of maintaining the mystery of the faith with a pure conscience!

Reflections...

□

MAY 12

Titus 2:9-10 *Exhort bondservants to be obedient to their own masters, to be well pleasing in all things, not answering back, not pilfering, but showing all good fidelity, that they may adorn the doctrine of God our Savior in all things.*

We no longer have slaves in our country, and for that we should all be thankful. Most of us probably have a problem coming to the true realization of the importance of these verses since we cannot fully appreciate the position of a slave or bondservant. These verses, however, still hold truth from which we all can benefit. The same guidelines that are given here for the relationship between the bondservants (slaves) and their masters can be applied to the employee/employer relationship as well.

The story is told of a factory worker who caught the eyes of the company security guards as he would leave work each day. The guards suspected the worker was pilfering company tools; yet, as they stopped him daily and inspected him, they could never find anything that the worker was taking. Daily as he left work pushing his wheelbarrow, the guards pulled him over to the side for thorough inspection. All they ever found in the wheelbarrow was the worker's lunchbox, his jacket, and a few personal effects. After a couple of months of daily searches and inspections, the guards finally, in disgust, threw up their hands and told the worker, "Alright, we give up! We know you have been stealing something, but we cannot catch you. If you will just tell us, we promise to forget about the whole deal. We just have to know what you have been stealing." Calmly, the man replied, "Wheelbarrows..." Sometimes the obvious overshadows the evident.

First, let it be stated that there are many hard-working employees who are dedicated and as honest as the day is long. In fact, I certainly hope that a large majority of employees in our country fall into this category. With that being said, let's move on to those who maybe are not so dedicated and who are not so honest. These verses certainly apply. You probably have known someone who identified themselves as Christian and yet they exhibited questionable discipline when it came to honest work. Maybe they had sticky fingers (no, not the food chain restaurant) and were in the habit of taking company tools home and never bringing them back. Maybe they continuously had bad attitudes, with a constant display of arrogance and independence rather than doing their jobs as instructed. Maybe they had a habit of petty theft, stealing from fellow workers. Whatever the situation, these verses set the expectation for the way a follower of Christ should conduct himself with respect to his employer. Anything less is dishonoring to the One who is really our Master!

Reflections...

MAY 13

Psalms 37:11 *But the meek shall inherit the earth, And shall delight themselves in the abundance of peace.*

Some people live their lives hoping that they will one day discover that they had a rich uncle, of which they were unaware, that died and left them a huge fortune. It, at least, makes a good plot for a movie, doesn't it? However, the reality of life is that few of us are in line to receive a fortune by way of inheritance. I did have a great uncle who left me a ring once upon a time, but that's about it.

When we set our eyes upon the material value of this world, we will probably end up in a state of depression if our desire is to inherit a fortune. As already stated, it probably is not going to happen. However, if you are a follower of Christ, there is a promise on which you can place your hope and trust. As this verse states, the meek shall inherit the earth, so go about your life making sure that you qualify to be an heir. How? Delight yourself in being a peacemaker. This same promise is given by **Matthew 5:5** – *"Blessed are the meek, for they shall inherit the earth."*

What will be the value of this inheritance? What is the value of the earth? If you are wondering, it is more than our minds can comprehend. Consider **1 Corinthians 2:9**: *'But as it is written: "Eye has not seen, nor ear heard, nor have entered into the heart of man the things which God has prepared for those who love Him."'*

I have always heard that if you are going to dream, then dream big; it doesn't cost any more. However, you don't have to just dream about a huge inheritance. You can prepare for it with confidence. If your objective is to inherit something of great value, why not prepare for the really big inheritance. Our Father, God, owns everything. If you are a child of God, then you are an heir: **Romans 8:17** *"and if children, then heirs--heirs of God and joint heirs with Christ, if indeed we suffer with Him, that we may also be glorified together."*

Reflections...

□

MAY 14

Psalms 62:10 (a) *Do not trust in oppression, Nor vainly hope in robbery...*

There are many business transactions that occur on a daily basis that ethically fall into the "questionable" category. Sometimes those who may otherwise be considered upstanding citizens of the community as well as the church become involved in some of these less than ethical activities. You are probably curious and are beginning to wonder where this is going to lead. Well, before we dive in, let's investigate and determine who might be on the short end of some of these questionable business deals.

There are a number of groups of people that may fall into a category we call vulnerable. Older people are prime suspects for scam artists. You have, no doubt, seen many news reports of scams that take advantage of the elderly. Sometimes the elderly may not be the most informed. In addition, they are usually more trusting of individuals who represent themselves to be acting in their best interest. Single moms make up another group that fall prey many times to someone who may be less than honest. Military families, as a general rule, operate households on small budgets. They too are vulnerable and often fall into traps set by the greedy. You probably are acquainted with someone who has been taken advantage of in the past.

Sherwood Baptist Church in Albany, Georgia, has produced several very popular movies over the course of the past few years. These include *Facing the Giants*, *Fire Proof*, and the most recent, *Courageous*. All of these are excellent. However, many are not familiar with the first movie from Sherwood entitled *Flywheel*. Of all the movies from Sherwood, *Flywheel* is my favorite. If you have seen *Flywheel*, you know that the used car salesman, Jay Austin (Alex Kendrick) is representative of a professing Christian (of sorts) who was in the business of taking advantage of others for self profit. In the movie, Jay Austin took advantage of everyone from students to single moms to his own pastor.

Sometimes professing Christians align themselves in business activities that are literally designed to take advantage of some of those mentioned above. A business transaction within itself may not be dishonest or deceptive; however, if there is not full disclosure to the point that all parties concerned fully understand the ramifications of that deal, then it is being represented in a deceptive manner. Some sales people will say whatever the customer wants to hear in order to generate a sale. Misrepresentation is not a problem to a sales person with low ethical values. Although not directly involved, sometimes there are well-meaning Christian people who are part owners of companies who employ such sales people.

This verse is a wake-up call to all of us. It is an invitation for us to do an evaluation of all our business activities, those in which we are directly involved and those in which we are indirectly involved. Without calling out specific businesses, let each of us make sure that we *"Do not trust in oppression, Nor vainly hope in robbery..."*!

Reflections...

MAY 15

Luke 16:13 *No servant can serve two masters. Either he will hate the one and love the other, or he will be devoted to the one and despise the other. You cannot serve both God and Money.* (NLT)

I have often heard it said that we humans can learn a lot from our dogs if we will but pay attention. If you have ever owned a dog, you probably would agree. Here are a few things we can learn from our dogs:

- Always run and greet loved ones when they come home
- Take naps
- Stretch before rising
- Avoid biting when a simple growl will do
- Be loyal
- Never pretend to be something you're not
- If what you want is buried, dig deep until you find it
- When someone is having a bad day, be silent, sit close, and nuzzle them gently

There are several other things that could be added to the list. You probably could think of one yourself, especially if you have a dog. There is one in this verse that captured my thoughts. A watchdog is trained to listen to the commands of his master – one person and no more. A seeing-eye dog is trained to listen to the commands of one person – only his master and no more. A trained dog is faithful to his master.

Once in a church small group, we had a blind person who was led around by her seeing-eye dog. We met in the same classroom for several weeks. It was quite amazing when the dog and his master entered the room one night and found someone sitting in the chair where this blind person sat each prior week. The dog went straight to the chair and stopped immediately in front of the person who was sitting in the "wrong" seat. Even though the dog did not talk, his actions screamed out, "You're in the wrong chair Buddy!" It was

270

evident that this dog was focused upon making sure that his master was taken care of and knew that someone else was occupying her seat. Needless to say, the seated person immediately found another seat and the dog and the master sat in their usual places. The moral of this story is pretty simple. The dog was trained to serve one master. He did his job well. Oh, that we humans could learn that lesson as well as the dogs can.

Jesus knew the dangers of man allowing money to become an idol and to come between man and God. Money is a great tool when used properly. Money is a great servant but a very bad master. We humans, however, are susceptible to allowing money to become our master instead of our servant. We cannot serve God and money; it is one or the other. What is money to you ...servant or master?

Reflections...

☐

MAY 16

Luke 12:33 *Sell what you have and give alms; provide yourselves money bags which do not grow old, a treasure in the heavens that does not fail, where no thief approaches nor moth destroys.*

People in our society love to collect things. What do we collect? You name it, we collect it! One ironic aspect about collecting is that the collectibles do not have to possess value to draw our attention. Some things have value and meaning while others have none. To illustrate the contrast, some people collect rocks; some collect arrowheads. One has value and meaning, the other does not. Some people collect baseball cards. Some collect antique cars. Some collect stamps. Of course, we all collect money!

If you happen to be a fan of the early '60s *Andy Griffith Show*, you may remember the episode in which Mayberry goes bankrupt. An old miser named Frank Meyers lived on the north edge of Mayberry. His house was a junk pile and an unsightly representation of what the townspeople wanted travelers to see as they came through their fair town. Frank Meyers collected odd things like a medallion from the 1906 St. Louis World's Fair and a spoon that was in the shape of the skyline of Milwaukee, Wisconsin. Of course Frank had other valuable collectibles like a genuine whale bone napkin ring and a red, white and blue sleeve band to wear on July 4th. The ultimate collectible was the $100 bond issued to Frank's grandfather in 1861 at an interest rate of 8 ½% compounded annually. The payout required for cashing the bond would bankrupt the town since its value was more than $300,000. Well into the episode, the banker finally came to the realization that the bond was issued with Confederate money which rendered it worthless following the Civil War. All of Frank Meyer's collectibles were just like yours and mine; they were worthless!

When it's all said and done, all our collectibles have no value at all. They are all worthless, even our money and wealth. All the "stuff" we collect is just that – stuff. The only things that have real value are those with eternal value. That brings up another subject completely, and one, I might add, that you seldom, if ever, hear defined. What exactly has eternal value? The Bible gives only two things that have eternal value; that is, value that will last throughout eternity. We are directed on a number of occasions in the Bible to invest in things that have eternal value. So what are those things?

Specifically, the Bible tells us that heaven and earth will pass away, but the words spoken by Christ will not pass away; that value is eternal value (**Matthew 24:35**). Secondly, the souls of men will live eternally. These are the things in which we can invest and consequently reap eternal rewards. The benefits from these "collectibles" will pay dividends through eternity.

Therefore, Jesus tells us in this verse to wise up. He instructs us to sell some of our earthly collectibles and give (invest in eternal things) alms. Too often we hear people say they do not have anything to give. Maybe it is time to sell some "stuff" so you will be able to follow the directions given by Jesus. Reposition your valuables in moneybags that do not grow old, in the treasury of heaven that will never fail and where you don't have to worry about moths corrupting or thieves stealing. In short, sell some "stuff" and GIVE!

Reflections...

Luke 12:34 *For where your treasure is, there your heart will be also.*

God gave each of us the privilege of choosing where we spend money. This is not as simple as it may appear. There are far reaching ramifications to each and every transaction into which we choose to enter. In fact, the effects are far greater than initially meet the eye.

Have you ever noticed the behavior of someone immediately after he bought a new car? All he wants to talk about is his new car. He wants you to know every detail of every feature of his new purchase. Why? The answer lies directly in this verse. His heart has shifted to where he has recently committed his treasure. What a revelation this is! And, you, by the way, are no exception; we all do the exact same thing. Where we choose to place our treasure is exactly where our heart finds residence. It is as if there is a string attached to our treasures on one end and our hearts on the other end. This is an unchanging financial principle of God's way of handling money. The principle can be readily found in our own lives as well as the lives of others. It is demonstrated by the middle-aged couple who has worked hard to be successful. They make the decision that they "deserve" a beach condo. Even though they have been committed Christians actively involved in ministry, their new investment has a direct effect upon their personal values. Their ministerial activities begin to fade because they now spend all their non-working time at the condo. Their rationale is that they now have to take advantage of the condo in order to make the value of their investment worthwhile. In truth, the heart has shifted to where the treasure is.

It does not have to be a beach condo to reposition one's heart. The location of one's treasure does not affect the principle. The principle works in the opposite direction also. We have recently been involved in a project of finding and enrolling sponsors for orphans in Africa. Suddenly, those who have committed to sponsor orphans are inquiring about the orphans and talking about them repeatedly. Why? The heart has shifted to where the treasure is.

The challenge in this verse is to consider where you place your treasure. Do a personal inventory. Take a close look at your checkbook and financial statement. It is guaranteed to reveal exactly the current position of your heart. Warning! When you perform this personal spending audit, you may not like what you find. You may come to the realization that you are placing your treasure in the wrong places. Don't despair! You can change that. You may have to sell some "stuff" and reposition some assets. Don't hesitate to take corrective actions if you find that your heart has been drawn to the wrong position because of misplaced treasure. Fix it!

Reflections...

☐

MAY 18

Luke 9:13 *But He said to them, "You give them something to eat." And they said, "We have no more than five loaves and two fish, unless we go and buy food for all these people."*

Get this picture...you are at a large gathering (...and I mean large, like 10,000 - 15,000 people) and lunch is catered in to them. As the caterer is coming in to settle the bill, the leader of this great meeting points in your direction while telling the caterer, "Pete is picking up the tab today." Now, that is all right ...unless your name is Pete! If you are Pete, you have big-time problems right about now!

The incident in this passage did not occur quite in that progression, but no doubt, there are some striking similarities. Jesus had been teaching this huge crowd for quite some time when the disciples came to Jesus and urged him to disband the meeting. The crowd had not eaten and was in need of food. I can imagine "quick-to-speak" Peter was the spokesman for the disciples. I have always thought that Jesus must have spoken somewhat forcibly to the disciples when He told them, *"YOU give them something to eat!"* He did not instruct them to appoint a committee to discuss the problem and come up with a 3-step solution. He did not sanction them to place an order with the local caterer and have sack lunches delivered to the hill. No, Jesus placed the responsibility squarely upon the shoulders of the disciples in telling them it was their responsibility to feed this crowd.

As I have reflected back through numerous events over the course of my life, there have been many times when I would feel there was a specific need for which someone should step forward and accept responsibility. Many of those times, that someone wound up being "me." In fact, more times than not, that has been the case. If you hear God detailing a need which requires attention and maybe some "elbow grease," He is probably calling you to task. If you see a financial need that requires someone come forward with an open pocketbook, God is probably calling "YOU." That is exactly what happened to the disciples in this particular situation.

You are probably already thinking of a time when you felt God revealed a need to you that far exceeded your means to meet. Can I tell you that God very well may have been calling you to task? If you think the call is bigger than you, good! That means you will have to depend upon God to help you accomplish the task. Think about the disciples; what means did they have to feed these thousands of people on the spur of the moment? They had to depend upon Jesus. Once the disciples followed in obedience, the need was met. The same will be true in our lives if we will but heed the call and then depend upon Him.

The next time you see a need and think, "Somebody needs to _____," listen very closely. You very well may hear God say, "YOU do it!"

Reflections...

MAY 19

Luke 12:42-43 *And the Lord said, "Who then is that faithful and wise steward, whom his master will make ruler over his household, to give them their portion of food in due season? Blessed is that servant whom his master will find so doing when he comes."*

We sometimes hear the question asked, "How good is good enough?" Many times the question is inappropriate because it is asked out of context. More times than not, it is asked with respect to the acquisition of eternal life which we receive only as a gift, not any works we do. However, when it comes to rewards and pleasing our Father, we are held accountable for our works, or lack thereof. If we drill down and ask more specifically, "How can I please my Father?" then we have a legitimate question and of course the answer is "by doing the will of the Father." Being a good steward and doing the will of the Father was a concern of Jesus when He lived on the earth: *"I can do nothing on My own initiative. As I hear, I judge; and My judgment is just, because I do not seek My own will, but the will of Him who sent Me."* ...**John 5:30**.

Even though we cannot do work to earn salvation, good works after conversion are outward evidences of the inward conversion that has occurred. In other words, after we become new creatures through conversion, the old has passed away, we become new beings (**1 Corinthians 5:17**) and we should have a desire to be faithful and wise stewards by doing the will of our Father. Our good works of being faithful and wise stewards should be outward evidence of an inward work that was performed by the Holy Spirit in us.

We can have the assurance that we are being faithful and wise stewards when we are following the principles of God as He has declared in the Bible. Conversely, we can know that we are not pleasing God when we knowingly violate His principles. There are always consequences to pay when we violate Gods laws; though sometimes delayed, we will be held accountable if we are not faithful and wise stewards. It is comforting to know, however, that when we do His will by being faithful and wise stewards, God is very much aware and He promises *"Blessed is that servant whom his master will find so doing when he comes."*

Reflections...

MAY 20

Romans 13:9 *For the commandments, "You shall not commit adultery," "You shall not murder," "You shall not steal," "You shall not bear false witness," "You shall not covet," and if there is any other commandment, are all summed up in this saying, namely, "You shall love your neighbor as yourself."*

Paul uses this verse in the context of the point that he is making that we are no longer bound by laws and rule keeping. That is not to say that the content of these rules is invalid or not pertinent. As you recognize, Paul is quoting five of the Ten Commandments. Those commandments have residual value and we should adhere to them. However, as Paul accurately points out, we are bound by a much broader commandment; if we keep this commandment, love our neighbor as ourselves, then we automatically kept the ones that he specifically enumerated.

It is interesting, however, to take note of the commandments that he selected in this illustration. Two of the five are associated with money and/or material wealth. Stealing and coveting deal directly with money or materialism. Again, we see that the man is susceptible to the financial part of life and that affects his spiritual life. There is no separation of the two. Let it be clear: it is not the money in question. It is the person (the human being) into whose hand the money rests that is susceptible to corruption.

Paul gives the cure for the weakness of the human will. Love your neighbor as yourself and you will not be tempted to steal from your neighbor. Love your neighbor as yourself and you will not have a problem with the things your neighbor owns (covetousness).

When approached by a group of Pharisees who had ulterior motives in asking Jesus about the greatest commandment, Jesus replied, *"Love the Lord your God with all your heart and with all your soul and with all your mind and your neighbor as yourself"* (**Luke 10:27** NIV). He went on to say that the second *(love your neighbor as yourself)* was like unto the first and the Law and the Prophets hang on these. So, what is the bottom line? Basically, these two commandments cover the whole gospel. These two commandments are to be our guide through life. If we can get these right, the money, the adultery, the lying and cheating and all other "bad" plagues of the human spirit will come into alignment. Maybe it is time to get our attention off ourselves and focus on God and our neighbor!

Reflections...

□

MAY 21

Luke 12:22-23 *Then He said to His disciples, "Therefore I say to you, do not worry about your life, what you will eat; nor about the body, what you will put on. Life is more than food, and the body is more than clothing."*

D o you get overly concerned about trivial matters in life? If you are normal, your answer is probably yes. Most of us get freaked out at times about things that will have no meaning at all 100 years from now. ...just joking. Honestly, we do get stressed at times by some very small matters.

Several years ago, we were hosting a get-together in our home for our Sunday school small group. One couple who was relatively new to the group was bringing a cake to the occasion. Granted, her day had not gone well to the point that she was extremely stressed. As she was getting out of the car, holding the cake of course, her hand slipped and the cake tumbled to the ground. Now if that had happened to most of us on a normal day, we would have made light of the disaster with some frivolous joke like, we need some grit to go with the icing. But that did not happen on this particular day. The young lady was so flustered that she almost went into convulsions. She burst into tears, started shaking uncontrollably resulting in her husband immediately taking her home. I guess you could say that she had a bad-cake day.

This example is probably extreme, but when we consider the stress that we put upon ourselves over things that we cannot control, the end results are similar. With our economy currently in the gutter, many Christians are stressed almost to their breaking points. We all need to make sure that we are good stewards of God's "stuff" whether it is money or relationships or our families. Will we make some bad choices in the process? Yes, we absolutely will! But don't let your mistakes demobilize you. Make amends, make adjustments, give apologies where necessary and do whatever you have to do, but move on in life. Life is more than the food we eat and the clothes we wear. Do the best you can and then trust God, but don't get bogged down with the things over which you have no control. This may be God's way of giving you the opportunity to really place your trust in Him. Listen closely, " *Then He said to His disciples, "Therefore I say to you, do not worry about your life, what you will eat; nor about the body, what you will put on. Life is more than food, and the body is more than clothing."*

Reflections...

☐

MAY 22

Romans 13:7 *Render therefore to all their due: taxes to whom taxes are due, customs to whom customs, fear to whom fear, honor to whom honor.*

It is especially hard at times to abide by biblical instruction. When we see tax money wasted on frivolous activities and projects, our better judgment kicks into gear and we try to find some way we can express our disapproval. When politicians make vain promises, we do not want to continue our support by way of tax dollars. When we see able-bodied men and women munching off the government with hands extended awaiting more handouts, our emotions want to slap those hands and tell freeloaders to get to work. Now, let it be known that I am not condemning those who have legitimate needs, those who have been dealt a raw hand by life. I am referring to those who are able to do work, but don't want to work; they are content to receive government support rather than looking for a job. There are many of those today.

The number of people receiving government support in the United States is increasing at an alarming rate. A large number of these have stopped looking for work altogether. Yet, even in the state of condition that we find ourselves today, we still have to go to the scriptures to determine exactly how we as followers of Christ are supposed to deal with the situation of taxes with which we do not agree.

Even though we have to swallow hard, grit our teeth (and possibly bite our tongues), we are instructed to be faithful to honor those who rule over us. We are specifically instructed to pay taxes that are due. We are commanded specifically to honor those to whom honor is due. That means that even though we do not always agree with the status quo, we still have to abide by the rules of our government.

In our country, we are given a tremendous privilege that most of us take for granted. That is the right to vote. We have a voice in the selection process of determining who will occupy the offices of rule over us. We have the right of freedom of speech, so we can voice our opposition without fear of reprisal when we disagree with what is required of us. Our problem is not necessarily the levy against us in the form of taxes and inept leadership; our problem is that we (Christians) have become lackadaisical and just plain lazy. In a recent national election, 63% of evangelical Christians stayed home rather than entering their voice in the selection process. It is irresponsible for a professing Christian to fail to vote!

In America, we have tremendous rights for which we have lost appreciation. When we fail to live up to our responsibility of voting and expressing our opinions, then we see our rights begin to diminish. Remember, our vote of silence (failure to vote) is a vote to relinquish our freedoms with which we have been so blessed. So, when you have an urge to complain about taxes and an even greater urge to not pay taxes, consider the scripture: *"Render therefore to all their due: taxes to whom taxes are due, customs to whom customs, fear to whom fear, honor to whom honor."* Also, remember that YOU have a voice in the future. Our rights and freedoms are sustained only when we assume and execute our responsibilities!

Reflections...

☐

MAY 23

Proverbs 2:4-5 *If you seek her as silver, And search for her as for hidden treasures; then you will understand the fear of the Lord, And find the knowledge of God.*

Our society expends much effort for the purpose of gaining knowledge. Our current education system concentrates practically all efforts solely upon the acquisition of knowledge, but little emphasis on the application of knowledge. We have more highly educated people in our country today than at any time in history. However, in the midst of so much knowledge, we have what some refer to as a "bunch of educated fools. "

In my own simplistic way of thinking, knowledge is of little value unless it can be applied. The first definition of wisdom by Webster is the "right use or exercise of knowledge." It is ironic that in a culture with highly educated mathematical geniuses, it is hard to find someone who can count out change for a dollar! There are people who have knowledge but do not know how to put it to use.

Here is a little food for thought, thrown in as an extra. The Old Testament prophet Daniel wrote in chapter 12 about the "end times." Here is what he had to say about the increase of knowledge: *"But you, Daniel, shut up the words, and seal the book until the time of the end; many shall run to and fro, and knowledge shall increase."* ... **Daniel 12:4**. You can draw your own conclusions about the end times. But, suffice it to say that we have seen, and continue to see, a tremendous increase of knowledge.

Let's turn this discussion back to what the wise man Solomon wrote in these verses here in Proverbs 2. The context of his words is summarized by saying that we desperately need to seek wisdom, understanding and discernment. He emphasizes that we should seek discernment as we seek silver (money). That means we should be diligent and put forth deliberate efforts to gain the trio of wisdom, understanding and discernment. We should place great value upon these and hold them up as priorities in life. If we placed as much value upon wisdom, understanding and discernment as we do upon the acquisition of knowledge, the world would be a different place. If we sought after wisdom, understanding and discernment as we do wealth, WE would be different individuals!

Reflections...

MAY 24

Luke 16:19 *There was a certain rich man who was clothed in purple and fine linen and fared sumptuously every day.*

Let's start this discussion out by first saying that it is indeed an honor and a privilege to have been born an American and to live in the USA. There is no disputing this fact. However, one thing is always true. Honor and privilege carries a price tag; the price tag is called "responsibility." Honor and privilege without responsibility leaves one vulnerable to shocking disappointment. Taking honor and privilege for granted will inevitably lead to downfall.

This verse is an example of a man who had everything, yet took it all for granted. My fear is that our American culture has fallen into the same path as this rich man described in this verse. The American culture has become very irresponsible. We have forgotten the price our forefathers paid for our freedom. We have forgotten the sacrifices our grandparents made for our lives of ease. We are prone to complain at the drop of a hat, and most of us carry the hat ready to drop it in a moment's notice. We become very impatient with any interruption of our conveniences. If the temperature is warm, it's too hot; if it is cool, then it's too cold. We use bad weather as an excuse to miss church, yet we drive through blizzards to go on vacation.

We read this passage and see the ultimate disastrous end to which this rich man came. Yet we still go out and sacrifice our lives, families and many times our relationship with God attempting to gain wealth. As has been discussed previously, wealth is not bad. There are many examples in the Bible of people who were very godly and wealthy at the same time. However, this rich man was not one of them. He was only concerned with himself. He had no compassion on the poor. As we like to say, he enjoyed the "finer things of life."

Our American culture has seemingly gone the way of this rich man. We are a society that is carried away with entertainment, self-fulfillment and doing whatever it takes in the pursuit of happiness. In our pursuit, let us awaken to the demise of this rich man. God, grant that our pursuit will be focused not upon riches, entertainment and the pursuit of happiness, but upon an intimate, daily relationship with YOU!

Reflections...

MAY 25

Luke 16:1-2 *He also said to His disciples: "There was a certain rich man who had a steward, and an accusation was brought to him that this man was wasting his goods. (2) So he called him and said to him, 'What is this I hear about you? Give an account of your stewardship, for you can no longer be steward.'"*

In the past few years, we have witnessed fraud and corruption in the economic sector of our country on a scale that one would not have thought possible. The Enron scandal rocked the entire financial world, indirectly if not directly. The Bernie Madoff pyramid scheme redefined the known concept of pyramid design. The fall of the giants in the Wall Street marketplace to include the likes of AIG, Lehman Brothers, Fannie Mae, Freddy Mac, Wachovia, Bear Sterns, National City (...and the list goes on and on) have left us all wondering if there are any honest people in the financial business.

Two common threads were woven through all the above mentioned firms as well as many that are still operational today. The first thread is "self deception." Those in leadership of each of these institutions deceived themselves into thinking that they had it all figured out; their schemes, in their minds, were flawless and would work to their benefit. They were going to become prosperous and never get caught with their hands in the proverbial cookie jar. All of these were stewards of public trust who violated their fiduciary responsibilities in lieu of personal gain and yet, they all deceived themselves into believing a lie.

The second thread in all these firms is simply the fact that reality caught up with them. None of the schemes worked; they never do! Unfaithful stewardship is not rewarded in this life or the life to come. Some connivers may continue for a period of time without being caught, but sooner or later, they will be called upon to do exactly what the wicked steward in these verses had to do: *"Give an account of your stewardship, for you can no longer be steward."*

290

We are all stewards – some good, and some not so good. God has entrusted to each of us some of His valuables and thus, we have a fiduciary responsibility to manage them in a way that pleases the owner – God! Each of us has a mandate about the task of managing God's stuff: *"Moreover it is required in stewards that one be found faithful."* **...1 Corinthians 4:2**

How is your performance as one of God's stewards? Are you conscientious and faithful? Do you follow God's plan of managing money? Remember, it is required that we do our jobs faithfully. How will you react when you hear, *"Give an account of your stewardship"*?

Reflections...

MAY 26

Luke 18:22 *When Jesus heard his answer, he said, "There is still one thing you haven't done. Sell all your possessions and give the money to the poor, and you will have treasure in heaven. Then come, follow me."* **(NLT)**

Reality shows us that the more wealth a person has, the harder it is to hold on to it. The wise man Solomon told us basically the same (**Ecclesiastes 5:11**). As goods increase, so do those (friends and enemies) who come along to consume them. An increase in wealth requires a corresponding increase in the amount of time required to hold that wealth. This time requirement can consume a person if his priorities are misplaced. He may become so involved that he has no time for the really important things in life.

I am reminded of a story that illustrates the point. If you have a 5 gallon bucket with only a pint of water in it, you have no problem carrying it. In fact, you can probably carry the bucket with its light load with a single finger for an extended period of time. As the volume of water is increased in the bucket, you have to exert more 'grip' in order to carry the bucket with its load. If the bucket is filled to the top, 5 gallons weighing 8.34 lbs per gallon or a total of 41.7 lbs, you now have to hold very tightly in order to carry the load. Not only do you have to hold on tighter, you will grow weary in a short period of time. With only a pint of water in the bucket, you could carry it with ease, probably indefinitely. With the bucket full, you have a new job – trying to hold on to what you have!

Regardless of the amount of wealth one has, it can always be lost. In fact, it WILL be lost after only a brief period of time. Solomon questioned the benefit of wealth since there will always be someone close by to take what we have. That "someone" may be a thief, robber or swindler. It might be our own salacious appetite of consumerism or entertainment. It might be death's calling card with your name engraved upon it. Regardless of the "consumer," we will all give up the material wealth of this life upon which we have laid claim. So the question begs, as Solomon asked, "What is the benefit?" The only real benefit is that we can lay our eyes upon it. That's it! We can look at the new car, the large home, the increasing investment portfolio, but shortly, time will be called and all our wealth will be taken by someone else.

Jesus related to the rich ruler that he could not maintain his wealth and follow Him (**Mark 10:17-31**). He had to make a choice. If you, like the rich ruler, are building your hope upon your wealth, you can know with certainty that you will be able to view it for only a short period of time. Build your hope on things eternal through Christ. Money "will" leave you; Christ will not!

Reflections...

◻

MAY 27

Ezekiel 44:30 *The first of all the first fruits of every kind and every contribution of every kind, from all your contributions, shall be for the priests; you shall also give to the priest the first of your dough to cause a blessing to rest on your house.* (NASB)

If you are a business owner, you know the importance of having a business plan. If you work for a large company, you no doubt have heard about and probably been involved in discussions concerning the budget for your department. Your family should be giving consistent consideration to a managed spending plan for the household finances (also known as a budget). Practically all entities exist with a plan of operation. That plan may take on the various identities or be called by any number of names.

Early on, God established a plan of economy by which His ministry to mankind would be funded financially. His plan is simple; in fact, it is so simple that many of us miss its significance. His plan is fair to all. His plan is very straightforward. His plan is non-negotiable. His plan is longstanding; it has been around for most, if not all, of the existence of humanity. His plan "requires" our obedience; no one gets a free ride or a ticket of exception.

Ezekiel states God's plan of economy in this verse. His plan is that ministry is supported by tithes (first fruits) and offerings. That is God's plan throughout the Bible. He does not force us to support His plan, but He does promise, on several occasions, blessings for our obedience to His plan. Our participation in God's plan proves the interaction and working of God's plan (**2 Corinthians 9:13**). While we can make all kinds of excuses for not participating in and supporting God's plan, we cannot change the fact that it is God's plan. We can explain why we may disagree, but we cannot dispute the fact that God has reiterated His plan many times throughout the Bible. When we are long gone from the scene, God's plan will still be in effect.

Malachi challenged us to test God's plan (**Malachi 3:10**). If you are not a plan participant, why not take that challenge and prove God. Remember, it is His plan, not the plan of man!

Reflections...

MAY 28

Exodus 22:25 *If you lend money to any of My people who are poor among you, you shall not be like a moneylender to him; you shall not charge him interest.*

If you are 50 years old, you remember a time in our economy when borrowing money was a process involving applying for a loan. The process was governed by one's credit worthiness, not a credit score. One had to show not only that he had a good credit history but also that he had sufficient financial means with which to repay the amount borrowed.

In our recent past, practically all sensible measures of repayment ability were overlooked since that dictated certain guidelines must be met and thus "discriminated" against those who could not meet those prescribed guidelines ...d-u-u-h-h!!! Thus most practical repayment guidelines were laid on the sidelines and everybody was able to borrow more money than they could pay back. Enter ...economic downturn and home mortgage debacle.

We have seen this pattern of loaning money turn somewhat to a more common sense process, albeit, there are still some large gaps in the system. The end result of this economic circus is tremendous financial pain and suffering with record home mortgage foreclosures and business failures. Most of this could have been averted simply by following common sense guidelines, namely, if you don't have the means to pay back, then you don't get to borrow.

The Bible poses an interesting concept of lending money that we seldom see in our society. This verse in Exodus instructs God's people to lend money to their fellow followers of God in a manner different from the moneylenders (the equivalent of our banks) of that day. Money was lent as a ministry among God's people and no interest was charged. Now there is an intriguing concept and one that would make for an interesting ministry in the modern church.

If a church has a surplus, think what a difference they could potentially make within the lives of some believers. Suppose there are members who are blessed with surpluses who could minister to fellow believers by making no-interest loans. Granted, such an endeavor would have to be scrutinized closely, but it certainly would make for an interesting ministry in the modern church.

If you happened to have been blessed generously and have surplus funds, why not consider a really unique ministry: *"If you lend money to any of My people who are poor among you, you shall not be like a moneylender to him; you shall not charge him interest."*

Reflections...

MAY 29

3 John 1:2 *Beloved, I pray that you may prosper in all things and be in health, just as your soul prospers.*

For eons, this verse has been used to propagate the message that God wants you to prosper financially. Note however that finances are not specifically used in the verse. Rather, he uses the term "in all things." Certainly, money is one of those things, but in no way is this verse limited to money. If we are not careful, we can easily fall over the edge into a "prosperity gospel" wherein we defy all principles and laws of God and nature for the sake of justifying the one belief that God intends financial prosperity for me regardless of _____. Regardless of what, you may ask? Regardless of any and everything! TV evangelists are notorious for pushing this doctrine. Isn't it ironic however, that they always, always, always instruct you to send your money to them. I have never heard one tell you to send it to someone else. For the record, the Bible instructs us where to send our tithes and offerings (**Malachi 3:10-12**) and it is not to the TV evangelists!

Before we jump onboard the prosperity gospel train, like a largemouth bass onto a shining minnow in early spring, let us consider one aspect of this verse that is overlooked almost all the time. Read the verse again, very carefully: *"Beloved, I pray that you may prosper in all things and be in health, just as your soul prospers."* Does anything jump out at you?

Note the standard by which the writer, John, is praying for prosperity. The standard to which his prayer is directed is the "prosperity of one's soul." That brings about a whole new issue. Statistics concerning today's church (several Barna Group surveys) reveal an apathetic body with little interest in spiritual matters. Considering that the church is made up of individuals, the same attributes that apply to the church also apply to the individual members at large. In short, we can easily draw the conclusion that the soul of the church, i.e. souls of the church members, is not faring too scrumptiously. In fact, the church today is rather anemic with very little effectiveness.

So, before you jump on board with the populace praying for God to send materialistic prosperity to match up with the prosperity of your soul, you may want to take inventory of how well your soul is prospering. For some of us, if God answers our prayer of prosperity in wealth to match our soul's prosperity, He will plunge us headlong into financial bankruptcy.

It is probably a good idea for all of us to spend more of our prayer time asking God to prosper our souls; the natural overflow of our prospering souls will lead us into the other areas where God can also cause prosperity to flow.

Reflections...

MAY 30

1 Thessalonians 2:9 *For you remember, brethren, our labor and toil; for laboring night and day, that we might not be a burden to any of you, we preached to you the gospel of God.*

Followers of Christ sometimes do not conduct themselves in a manner that is worthy of the name "Christian." Our conduct betrays our words and leaves a void in the understanding of those around us. If we say one thing and do another, we lose credibility in the eyes of the very ones to whom we are sent to be a witness. A Christian's testimony is his life preserver in the sea of life. Without a credible testimony, one sinks from sight and cannot carry out the Great Commission.

Although I certainly did not originate it, I have often said that I had rather see a sermon any day than hear one. This is probably a modern-day paraphrase of the 12th century Catholic friar and preacher, Saint Francis of Assisi (1181-1226) who stated: "Preach the Gospel at all times and when necessary use words." Research has revealed that adults learn much more visually than audibly. As much as 80% of communication is accomplished through body language and the balance of 20% through the words we speak. Our behavior (actions) is a major part of who we are.

The Apostle Paul was very much aware of these facts. In this chapter in 1 Thessalonians, he is reflecting upon his behavioral patterns that had been exhibited in the past. Of particular interest is this 9th verse wherein he recounts the fact that he worked and provided for himself all the time he was preaching the gospel and ministering to this church. In fact, he did not just do little "keep me busy" jobs. He "labored" night and day! In other words, he earned his living by the sweat of his brow.

Paul did not impose his convictions upon those who followed. He was simply stating facts, and important facts they were. He went out of his way to make sure his personal testimony was not tarnished with accusations dealing with money and personal support. Maybe some of the high-flying nationally known preachers of our day should take note of Paul's conduct. He did not live the lifestyles of the rich and famous. He was not chauffeured around in a limo or a Rolls Royce. He did not have his own personal jet plane using the excuse that the airlines just did not fly his schedule. No, Paul went to the extreme in the other direction because he knew his testimony had to be spotless and untarnished.

We are all ministers. We all should have the mindset of Paul when it comes to money and our testimony. Remember, what you do speaks much louder than what you say!

Reflections...

_____

_____

_____

_____

_____

_____

_____

_____

_____

_____

_____

_____

_____

_____

MAY 31

Ecclesiastes 5:13 *There is a severe evil which I have seen under the sun: Riches kept for their owner to his hurt.*

Money can cause hurt if used in the wrong way. It doesn't have to be that way, but it can happen. The ways in which money can be the cause of hurt and pain are too numerous to list, but here are a few. Money can be the object of hurt if it is used to the detriment of one's health. Drugs, alcohol, smoking, fast cars all put the owner at great risk and can be the source of tremendous pain. One with money may become the victim of a robber and suffer as a result. Money may be used in a business venture that fails resulting in great distress. One may leave money to his children without teaching and preparing the children how to manage money. That is a great disservice to the child and great pain to the families.

Money and riches can be used to do good deeds and relieve suffering. Conversely, money used improperly causes great suffering. While that may sound a bit paradoxical, it really is not. The end result of the use of money is determined not by the money, but by the one who holds it.

You may recall the Oklahoma bomber, Timothy McVeigh, from April 1995. McVeigh used a rented U-Haul truck to transport explosives to the Federal Building in Oklahoma City and parked the truck at a strategic location to effect the greatest destruction possible. The U-Haul truck was a tool used to perpetrate a great travesty against human life. The question begs, "Was the U-Haul truck evil?" Of course, the answer is a resounding no. U-Haul trucks have been used for decades by millions of American citizens to accomplish much good. But in the hands of one person with evil intent, this U-Haul truck became a weapon of mass destruction.

The intent and actions of the one holding money determines its destiny. Be careful how you choose to use money. It can be a tool that can bring about good and relief from suffering. Or, if used incorrectly, it can bring the owner great hurt!

Reflections...

JUNE 1

Hebrews 7:4 *Now consider how great this man was, to whom even the patriarch Abraham gave a tenth of the spoils.*

It truly would be interesting to be able to fully understand the motivation behind Abraham as he gave a tithe to Melchizedek, the Priest of Salem. These verses in Hebrews depict Melchizedek as being the priest of priests. Even though we know little about Melchizedek, we do know that he was a great man.

Today, in churches across America, congregants are hard-pressed to give a tithe of their increase. In Jesus Christ, we have a high priest much greater than Melchizedek. Pastors are faced with the task of leading churches that experience shortfalls in budgets because the congregants are not giving. Depending upon the source, as there are varying results from different polls, only about 3% of evangelical Christians give 10% of their income. The Bible has many scriptures of instruction concerning our giving. We Christians apparently have a problem in transforming that instruction into inspiration.

Abraham did not have a heritage of giving handed down from his forefathers. He did not have the scriptures of instruction about giving. He did not have ministers delivering the inspired messages of encouragement to trust God and give. No, Abraham did not have all the advantages that we have today. He just had to listen to God.

God revealed to Abraham what He wanted him to do. Abraham exercised faith and did it! If Abraham heard from God and was inspired to give a tenth of his possessions to the priest Melchizedek, surely we should have no problem in believing God and giving at least a tenth to our high priest Jesus Christ! It all boils down to whether or not we trust Christ. Do we trust Him to be who He claimed to be? Do we trust Him to be faithful in supplying our needs? Do we trust His Word that He has given us? If we do, then it is time to exercise our faith and do what His Word tells us over and over again. The tithe, one tenth of our income, is a great place to start!

Biblical Guidance in Daily Doses . . .

Reflections...

☐

JUNE 2

James 2:15-16 *If a brother or sister is naked and destitute of daily food, and one of you says to them, "Depart in peace, be warmed and filled," but you do not give them the things which are needed for the body, what does it profit?*

James has a way of confronting issues head-on. He does not dilly-dally around or beat around the bush. His approach is usually full steam ahead and let the chips fall where they may. In view of our current society wherein political correctness is the norm, James' approach is like a breath of fresh air. You don't have to wonder what he is saying. One does not have to comb through with a fine-tooth comb to determine the issue that he is addressing. He is "to-the-point."

Through the years that I have been a Christian, too numerous are the times when attention was drawn to a particular need of someone or some family in the community and the response of the church was exactly as James writes. "We will pray for them" is the usual response. Most of the time, this is only a flippant response since few actually do follow through with prayer. I have seen occasions when someone would make known a specific need and the response of the church would be to gather around and pray for that individual, sometimes by the laying on of hands, but never offer any fulfillment to the need. Now, let it be known that I am in full agreement of praying for the needs of fellow believers as well as non-believers. Also, let it be known that I stood just as guilty as everyone else by not reaching out and allowing God to use me to meet some of those needs (ouch!).

James drills down to a different level. He goes directly to the level of personal involvement by letting us know that prayer alone is not always all that God has in mind. He reminds us that there are times when we just need to suck it up, step up to the plate and become the bearer of God's blessing to the one in need. When someone has no food to eat, prayer will not satisfy their gut-wrenching hunger pains. They need a bag of groceries! We can pray for them, and we should; but, we also should give them food!

This instruction from James sounds resoundingly similar to the response of Jesus when His disciples reminded Him that the huge crowd, who had gathered to hear Jesus teach, was hungry and in need of food. When they told Jesus to send the crowd away so they could get food, listen to the reply of Jesus: *"But Jesus said to them, 'They do not need to go away. YOU give them something to eat.'"* ... **Matthew 14:16** (emphasis added).

Do not fail to pray for those who have needs. More importantly, do not fail to step up and bless those who have needs by providing for them. God uses us to bless others. In so doing, we likewise are blessed. Don't miss your blessing by failing to bless others!

Reflections...

☐

JUNE 3

James 2:2-4 *For if there should come into your assembly a man with gold rings, in fine apparel, and there should also come in a poor man in filthy clothes, (3) and you pay attention to the one wearing the fine clothes and say to him, "You sit here in a good place," and say to the poor man, "You stand there," or, "Sit here at my footstool," (4) have you not shown partiality among yourselves, and become judges with evil thoughts?*

From 1984 through 1995, one of the most popular TV programs was *Lifestyles of the Rich and Famous.* Millions of Americans gathered around their TV's "oohing and ahhing" and some even drooling over the rich lifestyles of the world's most wealthy. Even after this show began to subside, numbers of other similar shows depicting the rich lifestyles of the supposed "elite" spun off this popular production. Many are mesmerized by wealth and what they call "living it up."

To my knowledge, there was never a show about the lifestyles of the poor and homeless. Poor people are not magnetic in nature; they do not draw the crowds. No one is interested in the way they live their lives. No one desires to know how they make it from day to day sometimes wanting for the bare necessities of life.

Sadly, this mentality of partiality to the rich is prevalent within the church. Many local churches cater to the elite and show favoritism to those who by definition are the "target groups" for outreach and potential membership. The wealthy are viewed by many as being desirable because of their potential financial advantage and contribution prospective. Conversely, the poor are viewed as liabilities with no financial advantage.

You may be in awe that such prejudice is present in churches. If so, answer this question: When was the last time you offered to come by and pick up a homeless person and "bring" him to church? That's different you say! Oh, is it really?

James talks very directly about showing partiality to the wealthy within the church and showing disrespect to the poor. I challenge you to look over the congregation at your church next Sunday morning. You draw your own conclusion! May God allow us to see as He sees, to love as He loves, and to have compassion as He has compassion!

Reflections...

☐

JUNE 4

Luke 11:11 *If a son asks for bread from any father among you, will he give him a stone? Or if he asks for a fish, will he give him a serpent instead of a fish?*

It is that time of year that we celebrate Father's Day. Father's Day is a time of reflection upon the person who was an important factor in determining who we have become. For some, death has laid claim on that person and as a result, there is probably a feeling of loss that still surfaces, regardless of the number of years that have passed. For those who still have their fathers, it is a time of expression of appreciation for the sacrifices made and the wisdom imparted through the difficult time of growing up.

Being a father is a tough role, especially in today's world. In a time when the family unit is experiencing an unprecedented assault, fatherhood has been the principal target of the enemy. The number of homes in our country with absentee fathers has escalated to epidemic proportions. In our African-American communities, recent statistics reveal that 72% of all children are born into fatherless homes. Deadbeat dads feel no responsibility for children they fathered and brought into this world. They feel absolutely no remorse in abandoning their families, leaving them to fend for themselves. Worse, they feel no responsibility of the father-figure for teaching, training and being a role model for their children.

Statistics reveal some alarming facts about children coming from fatherless homes. Consider the following:
- 63% of youth suicides are from fatherless homes - 5 times the average. (US Dept. Of Health/Census)
- 90% of all homeless and runaway children are from fatherless homes. (*Fatherhood Statistics* by John Knight)
- 85% of all children who show behavior disorders come from fatherless homes - 20 times the average. (Center for Disease Control)

- 80% of rapists with anger problems come from fatherless homes - 14 times the average. (*Justice and Behavior*, Vol 14, p. 403-26)
- 71% of all high school dropouts come from fatherless homes - 9 times the average. (National Principals Association Report)
- 75% of all adolescent patients in chemical abuse centers come from fatherless homes – 10 times the average. (Rainbows for All God's Children)
- 70% of youths in state-operated institutions come from fatherless homes – 9 times the average. (U.S. Dept. of Justice, Sept. 1988)
- 85% of all youths in prison come from fatherless homes - 20 times the average. (Fulton Co. GA Dept. of Correction)

Luke gives us a glimpse of the epitome of a real father. A real father is more than a sperm donor. A real father is more than just a resident where the mother of children lives. A real father is a man of character, someone who has love, a person of integrity. A real father is one who is a provider of the necessities for his wife and children. A real father does not run from his responsibilities. A real father would never give a stone to his child who asked for a piece of bread or a snake instead of a fish.

To the real fathers, we salute and honor you. To those who may have faltered in the past and come up short, we pray for you that the Holy Spirit may reveal the truth of real fatherhood to you.

Reflections...

☐

JUNE 5

Luke 22:35 *And He said to them, "When I sent you without money bag, knapsack, and sandals, did you lack anything?" So they said, "Nothing."*

I sometimes wonder if God created us humans with bad memories, or do we just allow our brains to get lazy due to the lack of mental exercise. Whatever may be the case, it seems that we are prone to forget many of the good events in our lives. Conversely, we usually have no problem remembering the negative events.

It is good for us to look back on occasion and reflect on good things, especially those times when God intervened and provided us an opportunity to experience something beyond the ordinary. If we don't have our spiritual antennas up and tuned in to God, we find it difficult to even recognize God's intervention, thus making it impossible to look back and draw strength. So first, we have to tune in to God!

Such was the case in this scripture in Luke 22. "Quick-to-speak" Peter had just made his infamous speech about his dedication and allegiance to Jesus by saying that he would be with Jesus through the thick and thin. He was ready to go both to prison and to death if necessary. Of course, Jesus knew the true intestinal fortitude within Peter and told him that he would deny even knowing Him within just a few hours.

Jesus continued in asking the disciples to reflect on the past. Jesus had sent them out without money, without supplies and without proper clothing attire to do ministry. On this occasion, He asked them if they had gone lacking for anything. Of course, their answer was no, they lacked nothing. Even without money, God had supplied their needs.

We find it quite easy to complain about not having everything we want. Instead of complaining, we would do well to take heed of this incident with Jesus and the disciples. This was one of the very last times they were all together prior to the crucifixion of Jesus. In a crucial time like this, Jesus placed priority upon the disciples reflecting back upon the provision of God as they were performing His ministry. Even though they did not have money and were lacking in supplies and clothing, God met their needs. If reflection upon the provision of God was so important that Jesus chose to spend some of His last moments with His disciples in this activity, surely we ought to take time in our lives to look back in our own lives and draw strength from the testimony of God's blessings upon us in the past.

Reflections...

JUNE 6

Psalms 105:40 *The people asked, and He brought quail, And satisfied them with the bread of heaven.*

Everyone who has any degree of biblical knowledge is familiar with the account of Moses leading the children of Israel from Egypt into the land that God had promised them. We are usually quick to criticize them for their straying from God's will. We know they were susceptible to falling into idolatry. They were short on faith in God, or so it seems to us. They were quick to starting doing their "own thing" and forgetting God.

There have been innumerable sermons preached and lessons taught about those wretched, short-sighted Israelites. We quickly point out how God's anger was kindled against these people who just would not do right.

Whoa! Stop and reconsider. These people, which could have easily numbered upward of one and a half million, basically had to trust God for everything. Remember, their flight path led them directly toward what most would have called a watery grave. God provided by parting the water for their passage. They were pursued by a mighty army and they had no weapons of which to speak. God delivered them by allowing the pursuant army to drown. They did not have a Walmart or Target to stop by and buy clothes. God provided by allowing their clothes to not wear out. They could not drop in at the local Kroger or Winn Dixie to pick up a few groceries. God provided for their nourishment.

When they tired of eating the same manna day after day, even though God was providing, they asked for meat and God provided them with quail and bread and they were satisfied. God met their needs and also gave them their desire. So, let's not be too quick to criticize these people who literally had to trust God for their existence.

In comparison, take a quick look at yourself. Do you become annoyed when your cell phone drops a call? Yes! How many minutes are you forgiving when your electricity goes off? Probably about 1 minute and 37 seconds!   When your next door neighbor drives home a new car, how long before you decide that you **need** one also? About 3 days, 6 and ½ hours! What if you lose your job, how long before your anxiety drags you into a state of clinical depression because you have no provision? About 13 days. Are you beginning to get the picture? We are quick to judge the children of Israel, but on a comparable scale, we probably pale in comparison to their faith in God.

Maybe we need to spend more of our time (that God gives us, by the way) trusting God and less time complaining and being judgmental. Maybe it is time for us to spend more time working for God and less time working for ourselves. If we did so, that would mean that we would have to trust God more for our provision, somewhat like the Israelites. If we did so, we may get to the point that when we ask God to supply a need, then it would be like the Israelites asking God for meat: *"The people asked, and He brought quail, And satisfied them with the bread of heaven."*

Reflections...

☐

JUNE 7

Psalms 105:44-45 *He gave them the lands of the Gentiles, And they inherited the labor of the nations, (45) That they might observe His statutes And keep His laws. Praise the Lord!*

You have probably seen the bumper sticker that says, "I owe, I owe, so off to work I go!" Sometimes it seems that we get into a vicious cycle: work, get paid, pay bills and then go back to work... Down through the ages, man has asked the question, "What is the meaning of it all?"

One of my very favorite episodes of the *Andy Griffith Show* is entitled, *The Sermon for Today*. A visiting preacher, the Rev. Dr. Everett Breen, delivers the Sunday morning message in a rather monotone, New Yorker discourse. As his soothing voice decreases in volume repeating "slow down, relax, take it easy," both Gomer and Barney are drifting off into z-z-z-z-z land. At just that moment, Dr. Breen thunders out, "What's your hurry?" Of course, this caused Gomer and Barney to jump almost off the pew. The entire context of Dr. Breen's message to the good people of Mayberry centered on the question, "What's the meaning of it all?"

In our present age, it is easy to fall into a routine and lose the meaning of life. We can become so busy living life that we forget the purpose of life. The only purpose some people have in life is to make this life "easy" and, in this world, better for themselves, completely overlooking the eternal. In fact, I am of the opinion that the majority of our society is of this mindset. We are a generation of hyper-consumers looking only for fulfillment of our narcissism.

As Christians, we surely need to be aware that our lives here on earth have more meaning and purpose than the drudgery of being stuck in the routine of this earthly life. God has given America a major portion of the world's wealth. We produce more food than any nation on the face of the earth. This did not occur because we "deserved" it. Just as God gave Abraham the lands of the Gentiles to honor Him, He has given

America wealth for the same purpose. Let us not get stuck on the gerbil wheel of this world's routine; rather, let those who are followers of Christ heed the high calling about which Paul wrote (**Philippians 3:14**). There is a reason God has entrusted His money, food, and all other provision into our care: *"That they might observe His statutes And keep His laws. Praise the Lord!"*

Reflections...

JUNE 8

Genesis 2:15 *Then the Lord God took the man and put him in the garden of Eden to tend and keep it.*

In our society, children are given the privilege to play. They can spend hours just doing what feels good. For the most part, they are not required to face up to the harsh realities of the real, cruel world. Their parents take that responsibility and thus spare the kids the anxiety of the problems facing their young lives.

There is not a problem with this as long as things are kept in perspective. I might interject here however that all societies are not like ours. In some parts of the world, children are required to scrounge for food as a matter of existence at ages as young as 4-6 years. The problem we are now facing in our society in America is that many young people do not want to face reality even after they have a college degree. They still look to their parents to fend for them. Recent research reports that 21 year olds today are at the same maturity level as 16 year olds one generation ago. As a generalization, young people today do not want to be referred to as an adult until they reach the age of 27. We can criticize the younger generation for the way they are, but here is the reality of this situation: they are exactly what they have been trained to be! There comes a time when children grow up, accept their responsibility as adults and assume their responsibility to work. There is a problem with a 53 year old still playing instead of working.

God appointed humans to be the caretakers of His earth. It started in the Garden of Eden and has extended throughout the ages down to us. God has never intervened and told us that we have a reprieve from this appointment. So until He does, we are under the mandate and obligated to assume our appointed responsibility to work. Actually, we honor God when we work because this is what He has appointed us to do. In return, God rewards us with the provisions to sustain life and He even throws in some conveniences and gives us some of our desires. However, it is important that we keep everything in the correct perspective. It all belongs to God; He is the owner, we are His workmen.

There is a spiritual lesson in this. We are not owners. We are stewards. We are appointed to take care of God's stuff. We don't work for ourselves; we work for God. When we get this into our spirit, we can have contentment instead of anxiety.

May He open our eyes and hearts and let us realize that our task is to be faithful stewards: *"Moreover it is required in stewards that one be found faithful."* **...1 Corinthians 4:2**

Reflections...

JUNE 9

Psalms 37:4 *Delight yourself also in the Lord, And He shall give you the desires of your heart.*

This is one of those scriptures that is often used in the "name it and claim it," "blab it and grab it," so-called prosperity gospel. As you might expect, I am not a fan of this flavor of the use of God's Word to facilitate personal financial gain. God gave us literally hundreds of scriptures in the Bible on the subject of money, possessions and wealth. He directs us along His principles of the management of wealth resources. In my humble opinion, God is not going to overlook my mismanagement of all those principles and miraculously grant my every wish for personal gain for my personal, conceited pleasure.

The Gospel is not about me; nor, is it about you. It is about the Good News of God's Son, Jesus Christ. Jesus had a lot to say about the rich people and how easy it becomes to trust in riches rather than in God. He said that no one can serve two masters; he cannot serve God and money. He said that it is easier for a camel to go through the eye of a needle than for a rich man to enter into Heaven. So, in light of the teachings of Jesus, if my primary motivation is to gain the wealth of this world, I have already stepped over the line and am seeking to serve the master of money.

The first part of this verse is never explained by the prosperity preachers. The phrase "delight yourself also in the Lord" is the key to this verse. It is the main part of this verse; however, prosperity preachers only talk about the "desires of your heart" and those desires usually involve money. *The Message* paraphrase says this: *"Keep company with God."* In order to delight oneself in the Lord, he must first get on the same page with God. How does that occur? It occurs by keeping company with God.

James writes that we ask amiss. In other words, we are not in tune with God or, we are not on the same page with God. John wrote: *"And whatever you ask in My name, that I will do, that the Father may be glorified in the Son."* ... **John 14:13**. Note here that whatever is asked for first must be in His name and secondly, the Son must be glorified. You be the judge as to whether or not Christ is honored by expensive cars, several vacation homes at exotic locations and private jets to get there. John gives additional insight about asking and receiving:

- **1 John 3:22** *"And whatever we ask we receive from Him, because we keep His commandments and do those things that are pleasing in His sight."*
- **1 John 5:14** *"Now this is the confidence that we have in Him, that if we ask anything according to His will, He hears us."*

Again, these verses show vividly that God is the center of answered prayers, not us.

So, does God answer prayers? Or course He does! We just need to get on the same page with Him!

Reflections...

JUNE 10

Psalms 41:1 *Blessed is he who considers the poor; The Lord will deliver him in time of trouble.*

Do you want to be blessed? Do you want the favor of God? If your answer to these questions is yes, then here is the recipe to make it happen: do good to the poor.

As you read through the Bible, the issue of treating the poor fairly and with respect appears scores of times. We are instructed over and over again to deal fairly with the poor. We are told to give to the poor. We are told to lend to the poor and not expect repayment. There is no doubt that God's eye watches our actions in dealing with the poor.

In His ministry on the earth, Jesus spent most of His time with the poor. He ministered to them in teaching as well as healing the sick. His personal association was primarily with the poor. It is no surprise that Jesus proclaimed, *"Blessed are you poor, For yours is the kingdom of God."* (**Luke 6:20**)

Let us not forget that but for the grace of God, we could have been born in a third-world country in the depths of poverty. We had nothing to do with our placement on God's earth. How ridiculous we must appear in the sight of God when we show prejudice against the poor, deal unfairly with the poor or shun the poor because they are not like us. Just who do we think we are?

May God forgive us for our prejudice against the poor; may He impress us to reach out and minister to the needs of the poor as Jesus Himself did; may our hearts become burdened with desire to exhibit the heart of Christ toward the poor!

Reflections...

JUNE 11

Genesis 26:12-13 *Then Isaac sowed in that land, and reaped in the same year a hundredfold; and the Lord blessed him. (13) The man began to prosper, and continued prospering until he became very prosperous;*

I saac grew up under the tutelage of his father Abraham. Thus, he was taught to follow the instruction of the Lord. When there was a famine in the land, Isaac was tempted to go down to Egypt, but God directed him differently. Instead, he went to Abimelech, king of the Philistines, as God directed and was told by God to dwell there in Gerar (**Genesis 26:2**). This is important simply because Isaac "followed the directions of God."

What would happen in our lives if we chose to follow the directions of God? What would happen if we went to great lengths to carry out the Great Commission (**Matthew 28:16-20**)? What would happen if we chose to lay up heavenly treasures rather than working feverishly to accumulate the wealth of this world (**Matthew 6:19**)? What would happen if we chose to honor the Great Commandment per the instructions of Jesus (**Matthew 22:37-40**)? We all know that our lives would probably be drastically different if following God was the top priority of our lives.

Isaac followed God. That is a huge statement. Furthermore, because he followed God, God blessed him greatly. Beginning the very first year that he planted, he reaped a bountiful crop, a hundredfold. It didn't stop there. As this scripture states, he began to prosper and he continued to prosper until he became very wealthy.

This question should be asked: what brought about the prosperity of Isaac? It is evident that his primary motive was not to become rich. Rather, his motivation was to FOLLOW GOD. The prosperity was a subsequent byproduct because Isaac followed the instruction of God.

Some would be presumptuous and conclude that God will do exactly the same for each of us if we follow His instruction. God is not obligated to do for me what He does for you. God is sovereign; we have no right or power to hold Him to our frivolous, self-promoting standard. He chooses whom He will bless and in what manner He will bless. We do not tell Him how to do that! However, by following the instruction of God, we do, in fact, place ourselves in a position for God to bless as He so chooses. Whether He blesses us monetarily or in some other manner, so be it. Again, He is sovereign and He will determine to do as He wills. It is not my place to tell God how to bless me; it is my responsibility to follow His instructions and be open to whatever He chooses!

Reflections...

☐

JUNE 12

Luke 11:39 *Then the Lord said to him, "Now you Pharisees make the outside of the cup and dish clean, but your inward part is full of greed and wickedness."*

Most of us possess a special technique of being able to cover up the obvious in order to conceal deficiencies and sometimes just plain misrepresent truth. In almost all situations, the true colors will come out sooner or later. The result of delayed revelation of misrepresented truth is almost never a positive thing.

I remember more than 40 years ago growing up on a small family farm in South Georgia. Many of us "farm boys" raised hogs that we entered in the county swine show as well as some regional shows. If you have never worked around hogs, you probably will not appreciate the sacrifices we made. An important part of raising a show pig was the training and grooming elements. We would wash the pigs down actually scrubbing them with brushes to clean not only the coat of hair, but also the skin. Several of my pigs were the Black Poland China breed which is predominately black with four stocking white feet and a white blaze up its nose and between the eyes. On show day, the pigs received special treatment. We put Vitalis hair tonic on the black coats to make them shine and baby powder on the white feet and blaze nose to make it snow-white. The essence of our task was to try to convince the pig that he really was not a pig. This worked for a short time; however, once the pigs found a mud hole in which to wallow, they always revealed their true nature. There is nothing a pig loves better than to wallow in the mud. It matters not the number of baths he has experienced or how much Vitalis hair tonic and baby powder has been applied. You can cover the outside with all the ancillary items available, but on the inside, he is still a pig.

That's the way Jesus described the Pharisees. On the external, they went to the extreme to attend to the intricate details of outside appearance; however, on the inside, they were full of greed and wickedness. One may cover greed for a period of time. But sooner or later, the true nature will rise to the surface. The love for money always reveals itself in simple daily activities.

Jesus taught that one cannot love money and love God at the same time. Don't let money skew your love for God. Let God clean up the inside and then your true nature will be to love Him!

Reflections...

JUNE 13

Galatians 5:22-23 *But the fruit of the Spirit is love, joy, peace, longsuffering, kindness, goodness, faithfulness, (23) gentleness, self-control. Against such there is no law.*

We can wade through this text and spend a lot of time here since there is so much that could be said. In fact, through my time as a Christian that spans more than four decades, I have heard many sermons preached and lessons taught on the "Fruit of the Spirit." Even so, we probably still come up lacking and have not given just attention to this verse. Its breadth is overwhelming.

The one fruit that strikes me as receiving particularly unjust attention is self-control. As I reflect, all comments that I can remember on this subject have been directed to discipline and behavior, or the lack thereof. Of course, these disciplines do indeed fall into this category. The one subject that I never remember hearing mentioned is self-control in personal finance and managing money. Let's entertain a few thoughts along this line.

It is my opinion that every professing Christian in America should travel abroad to a third-world country at least once in his lifetime, preferably while still a relatively young age. The experience of seeing people live without the conveniences that we daily take for granted will change one's life. To see people who have no running water and in fact, no pure water brings conviction upon the best of us. To see children raiding trash piles in search of a morsel creates a tearful eye. To see the so-called "housing" in which some live, which in many cases is nothing more than a lean-to, will cause one to hang his head almost in shame. We in America are so blessed with abundance that we have literally lost its meaning. It is reported that the average American lives on $90 per day while more than half the population of the entire world lives on less than $2.50 per day.

Yes, we American Christians need a "heads-up" on self-control of money. We need to do a self examination and allow the Holy Spirit to speak to us. I am reminded of Jesus teaching on the parable of the talents (**Matthew 25:14-29**) and cannot but help to wonder if we American Christians with our lack of self-control in the area of money management may be synonymous with the unfaithful servant. In that parable, the master commanded the money be taken from that unfaithful servant and given to one who was faithful. Or maybe we may be synonymous with the rich farmer (**Luke 12:16-21**) who prospered, but only had thoughts of himself and hoarded all with which he was blessed to manage. His life was required when he became so self-contained and self-centered.

May the Holy Spirit teach us to have self-control in managing money and do it in ways that honor God!

Reflections...

JUNE 14

Psalms 37:16 *A little that a righteous man has Is better than the riches of many wicked.*

Money does not make a person. It only reveals or magnifies what that person already is. Unfortunately, when a wicked person acquires money, he becomes highly visible. For some, their wickedness, no doubt, contributes to their ability to gain wealth. Our culture has taught us that regardless of the amount of wealth we possess, we always need a little more. There are few people who consciously quantify how much is enough. May I suggest that each of us would do ourselves a favor by putting a reasonable attainable number to our financial goals in life? Without answering that question, it is difficult to reach a position of contentment financially.

The amount of money a person accumulates has little to do with contentment. The apostle Paul stated: *"I have learned in whatever state I am, to be content..."* ...**Philippians 4:11**. A righteous man's trust is not placed in money; it is in God. **Psalms 84:10** states, *"...I would rather be a doorkeeper in the house of my God Than dwell in the tents of wickedness."* It matters not if the amount of money is great or small. The little of a righteous man is worth more than fortunes of the wicked.

The wicked are not so; they trust in their possessions. They think that if they can acquire enough money, they will find happiness. Again, the problem resurfaces: how much is enough? They search for contentment, but do not find it in riches. The answer concerning how much is enough is simple. No amount of money will bring you peace and contentment. Why? ...because peace and contentment are not found in riches. Peace and contentment come only from God.

We live in a tumultuous world. Regardless of the amount of possessions you have, look to God for peace and contentment. You may never acquire a lot of wealth in this life. That's okay; wealth is not the source of peace and contentment. Always remember, *"A little that a righteous man has Is better than the riches of many wicked."*

330

Reflections...

JUNE 15

Luke 19:45 *Then He went into the temple and began to drive out those who bought and sold in it…*

I can remember as a young person, there was nothing "sold" at church, not in the church anyway. Admittedly, this was probably bordering on legalism, but the older saints of the faith had good intentions. They were on duty at all times to see that the house of God was honored.

Of course, we know from scripture that God is not in the real estate business. The triune God is resident on planet earth today not in a physical temple or man-made building, but in the hearts of men in the person of the Holy Spirit (**1 Corinthians 6:19**). Jesus became angry because the moneychangers were taking advantage of those coming to the temple to worship. They were selling all types of goods and wares. All this commercial activity degraded the temple to the point that it was no more than a common market. Note these verses from *The Message*: *"Going into the Temple he began to throw out everyone who had set up shop, selling everything and anything. (46) He said, "It's written in Scripture, My house is a house of prayer; You have turned it into a religious bazaar."*

To put it mildly, Jesus was not pleased with the commercialized conduct of those in the temple. He literally threw them out – physically! This, no doubt, would have been a sight to see. It makes one wonder what position Jesus may take in the church today with our (sometimes) commercialized activities. What would Jesus think about the way some "prosperity" preachers rake in fortunes at the expense of the gullible and unlearned and then spend it on extravagant lifestyles including multiple vacation homes in exotic locations, luxury automobiles, and even personal jet planes? The famed 18th century preacher, George Whitfield (1714-1770) made the following comments about ministers in his day who took advantage of parishioners: "Our clergy are only seeking after preferment, running up and down, to obtain one benefice after another; and to heap up an estate, either to spend on the pleasures of life, or to gratify their sensual appetites, while the poor of their flock are forgotten."

In consideration of what happened in the temple when Jesus tossed men out by the knap of their necks, the stern words of George Whitfield, and what takes place today in some ministries (in the name of Jesus), we may conclude that some things don't change.

Our prayer is that God will instill within us respect for places of prayer and worship, our bodies which are temples of the Holy Spirit, and our fellow man that we are to love as we love ourselves. May our attitudes and actions never result in bringing about the wrath as Jesus displayed that day in the temple.

Reflections...

_____

_____

_____

_____

_____

_____

_____

_____

_____

_____

_____

_____

_____

☐

JUNE 16

Proverbs 22:6 *Train up a child in the way he should go, And when he is old he will not depart from it.*

This verse has been quoted in many different circumstances. Typically, parents use this verse as a consolation that wayward children who have been taught the ways of the Lord will return to their root teachings.

However, let's back up and take another look at the context in which this verse appears. The first nine verses of this division of the Proverbs deal almost exclusively with money matters. The verse immediately following this admonition to train children correctly is one of the primary principles of financial management: the rich rules over the poor and the borrower is servant to the lender.

While there is no argument that God can always bring a wandering child back into the fold, maybe the primary message in verse 6 is that parents are charged with the responsibility of training their children how to handle money. That certainly is consistent with the context of these verses.

Our current society has a problem here. Parents cannot appear adept in teaching their children how to handle money simply because they, themselves, don't know how. If you doubt this fact, take a look around you. Seven out of ten households live paycheck to paycheck according to USA Today. The average household in America spent more than they brought in last year. We are a generation that lives beyond its means. Parents in these circumstances find it difficult, if not impossible, to be effective in teaching their children to do something that they themselves are not doing. The example they are living overshadows the lessons they attempt to teach.

To those who may be struggling to gain control of finances, this verse should serve as a wake-up call to your responsibility. Get your financial matters in order so you can train your children. If you are doing well financially, by all means train your children godly principles of money management. There may be no greater travesty than a parent who does not train his children how to handle money and then gives a large sum of money to him. Wherever each of us finds ourselves on the financial ladder, this verse is a challenge to us. We absolutely have a responsibility to train our children how to manage money!

Reflections...

JUNE 17

Proverbs 21:26 *Some people are always greedy for more, but the godly love to give!* (NLT)

T he story is told about a large landowner in Texas who was accused of being greedy and wanting all his neighbors' land. "Nonsense," he declared. "I don't want all the land; I just want all that touches mine." One of the problems with greed is that there are no boundaries. Regardless of the acquisition, the desire is to get more.

Noted author, financial planner and financial advisor Ron Blue advises that one of the initial steps in planning for one's future is determining "How Much Is Enough?" It is logical when you stop and think about it. Consider this: if you are going to take a trip, one of the first steps is to define where you are going? If you don't define where you are going, you will never know when you get there (duh!). Yet, most Americans fail to define their financial goals. Most never actually work out a financial plan. In fact, the number one reason for financial failure in our country is failure to plan – not having a plan. Thus, the old caveat, failure to plan is a plan to fail.

A financial plan, with a defined end goal, is an antidote to greed. Sadly, we are a society that is obsessed with the acquisition stage of finances. We never have enough. There is always something else that we want to buy, another trip we want to take, another vehicle we want to purchase, and another... and another... and another... Greed is all about "me" and what "I want." Greed is conceit and self-serving.

The Bible teaches that we are supposed to be givers. Jesus taught, *"Give, and it will be given to you: good measure, pressed down, shaken together, and running over will be put into your bosom. For with the same measure that you use, it will be measured back to you."* ...**Luke 6:38**. Godly people love to give; it is their nature to give because that is the nature of Christ. He was the greatest giver.

So, here is an excellent self examination set forth by the Bible. Are you godly? Do you love to give? Or, are you one of those *"people are always greedy for more?"*

Reflections...

JUNE 18

Ecclesiastes 6:9 *Enjoy what you have rather than desiring what you don't have. Just dreaming about nice things is meaningless—like chasing the wind.* (NLT)

It has been said that the best things in life are free. Bing Crosby even recorded a song by that title. While I cannot prove the validity of that statement, I do know that living a simple life is not altogether bad. Enjoying quality family time rather than "buying" expensive entertainment improves family ties and creates lasting relationships. Reading books from the public library or purchasing used books is an excellent alternative to buying new books that may place a burden upon the family budget. Enjoying what you have is a great way to spend your time instead of constantly wishing you had the things that others enjoy.

Spending your time dreaming about the things that others have is stressful and unproductive; in fact, most of the time it is counterproductive. One of the greatest motivations for people to trade and buy a new car is the fact that their friends have encouraged them to do so. In most cases, the friend has bought a new car and then convinces their friends to do the same. I have been known to offer this solution if you find yourself in this situation: "If your friends are encouraging you to trade in your car and get a new one, you probably ought to trade in your friends and keep your car!"

Enjoying what you have is evidence of peace and contentment. Contentment cannot be purchased with money. As this verse states, just dreaming about nice things is like chasing the wind. Many times, chasing dreams is like chasing the wind; the problem is you never catch it. You spend all your time and effort chasing something that will never materialize and you wind up empty-handed. Life is so much more meaningful when you forget about keeping up with the Joneses; they're probably in debt and facing foreclosure anyway. If your friendships are based upon your attainment of social status, you probably need to find some new friends and enjoy being who you really are.

Father God, may we live our lives not to impress those around us, but to impress You. Allow us to find peace and contentment in the things we have rather than spending our time desiring things we do not have. Let us come to the realization You are our source of peace and contentment and that chasing the wind is futile; let us have a desire to chase You!

Reflections...

JUNE 19

1 Samuel 2:7 *The Lord makes poor and makes rich; He brings low and lifts up.*

Most people work hard throughout their working careers desperately trying to get ahead. Many work long hours sacrificing personal time, sometimes to the detriment of their families. It follows that when one works hard and sacrifices, he develops the attitude that he deserves some rewards. Too often this scenario plays out resulting in him purchasing things that he really cannot afford because he "deserves" the rewards. Thus, a vicious cycle has begun to run rampant that throws many households into a financial frenzy. Simultaneous with the financial frenzy, a relational crisis between spouses starts brewing.

Though sad it is, most of us never learn the paramount lesson taught in this one verse that really has the potential to drastically change our lives in a positive manner. Our society teaches us that if we work hard, we can get ahead. In reality, sometimes that is true, sometimes it is not. The truth of the matter is that the Lord makes the poor and He makes the rich; He lifts us up and He brings us down. As **Deuteronomy 8:18** states, *"remember the Lord your God, for it is He who gives you power to get wealth."*

Remembering that God is in control is the most important career step we can take. Honoring Him in our work will prove rewarding, though not always monetarily. Following his principles in managing money will bring about His favor. Since God is omniscient, He knows what we can handle and also what would bring us to ruin. When our approach to our careers involves our honoring the Lord and knowing He is in control, we will find contentment regardless of whether we are one of the poor or one of the rich. Economic status is not our driving force when we acknowledge God in our work.

By God's principles, when we prove faithful in managing little things, He will give us greater (**Matthew 25:29**). The lesson from this one short verse in 1 Samuel has the power to revolutionize our entire lives.

God is the one in control. He is the one who directs our lives. *"The Lord makes poor and makes rich; He brings low and lifts up."*

Reflections...

☐

JUNE 20

1 Chronicles 16:28-29 *Give to the Lord, O families of the peoples, Give to the Lord glory and strength. (29) Give to the Lord the glory due His name; Bring an offering, and come before Him. Oh, worship the Lord in the beauty of holiness!*

We Christians flippantly use certain terms that have far-reaching impact in their true forms. A couple of these are contained specifically and contextually in this passage. Those two words are "worship" and "holiness." Both of these are the standards by which we are instructed to approach God.

It is noteworthy to look closely at the action in these verses. In coming to God, we are literally "giving it up" for God. As nations, as families, and as individuals, we are directed to give to God. We are to give glory and strength; not only are we to give Him glory, we are more specifically directed to give Him the glory due His name. Note that we are to bring an "offering" when we come before Him. We are to worship Him in the beauty of holiness.

Worship and holiness are closely related. Both include giving the highest and purest recognition and adoration to God. Both include honoring Him with undefiled hands, attitudes and motives. Both include expression of our gratitude out of a heart of love. Holiness has a connation of completeness, whole without any diversion.

Consider the instruction in these verses of coming to God with an offering as an integral part of worship in the beauty of holiness. You are probably asking the same question as me. Is this the way I bring my offerings to God on Sunday mornings? Bringing offerings to God should be as much a part of worship as anything we do. Some would say that God does not need their money, so they don't give in offerings. Their statement of God not needing their offering is correct. God owns everything; He certainly does not need the few, measly dollars that I may bring to Him. He does not need my paltry gifts, BUT I NEED TO GIVE! Giving conditions my heart and checks my attitude lest I forget that all that is in my care is really not mine; I only manage it for God. By giving offerings, I acknowledge God's ownership of everything, not just a portion. Giving builds my faith since it is an expression of my trust in God.

It has been said that one cannot worship without giving. I tend to agree since a lack of giving means that I am holding back and not fully trusting God. A form of worship wherein God is trusted in certain areas of one's life but not in others is not true worship. To worship God in the beauty of holiness, we must worship Him in "wholeness" and without reservation. We must bring an offering when we come before Him!

Reflections...

□

JUNE 21

Job 31:24-25, 28 *If I have made gold my hope, Or said to fine gold, 'You are my confidence'; (25) If I have rejoiced because my wealth was great, And because my hand had gained much; (28) This also would be an iniquity deserving of judgment, For I would have denied God who is above.*

There is no denying that Job was a very unique man. The KJV states that he was perfect; other translations use the term "blameless." Regardless of the vernacular used, in addition to being respected by his fellowman, Job was also recognized by God as being devout.

Job was a man who possessed vast wealth. He was probably the Bill Gates of his day. There may have been none with greater wealth than Job. However, with all the wealth, Job did not lose sight of God. He did not allow money to contaminate his view of the important things in life and more importantly, the Giver of life. In the midst of calamity with his world disintegrating, Job maintained a strong faith in God when all his wealth disappeared.

His hope was not in gold (wealth). He looked beyond the gold and wealth and placed his confidence in God. Apparently, Job was aware of the danger of getting his eye off God and allowing his heart to be drawn astray by wealth (v. 25). He knew that such action on his part would be worthy of God's judgment. Job equated getting caught up with riches and wealth as having denied God who is above. Above what? ...above everything (including the wealth). Job said essentially the same thing that Jesus taught centuries later: you cannot serve God and money.

The highly esteemed Charles Haddon Spurgeon (1834-1892) said it well: "Money is a good servant, but a bad master. If we make money our god, it will rule us like the devil." In addition Spurgeon said, "Many can get money; few can use it well." Job endured hardship and loss of all his possessions, yet he remained faithful to God. Later, God blessed him with even more wealth than before. Job proved to be one of the few who could use money well!

Reflections...

JUNE 22

Jeremiah 22:13 *Woe to him who builds his house without righteousness And his upper rooms without justice, Who uses, his neighbor's services without pay And does not give him his wages.* (NASB)

When one is talking about building a house, there are two avenues of thought that should be considered. Of course, the obvious is the literal sticks, bricks and mortar. The nails must be positioned to secure each member in place. The plumbing must be laid out correctly and the electrical wiring must be sized correctly to carry the demand. In essence, the physical construction of a house involves a great deal of planning, coordination of workmen, and a lot of skill in each and every area. A deficiency in one area will create a problem that affects the entire structure.

Another thought in the building process of a house is expressed more correctly as building a home. A house is a house is a house; but, a house is not necessarily a home. A home is a safe place for all family members. Structurally, it may not be much to gaze upon, but it offers comfort to the occupants as well as escape from the outside world. A real home is built upon righteousness through grace. It is a place to learn about God and it is a place to build a personal relationship with Him. A home is a place where memories are made and lives are formed. A house without righteousness can provide none of these things.

Jeremiah sounded a warning to the man who builds a house without righteousness. One who would do so is apt to place himself in a lofty position rather than living a life of dependence upon God. He is at risk of expressing injustice to those who construct the building as well as its occupants. He may cheat and connive while taking advantage of his neighbors in an effort to fulfill his selfish desires. He may steal from his good-hearted neighbors by not paying them for their labor while in his employment.

Men who conduct themselves in such manner are always of the opinion that they are coming out ahead in the game. In their arrogance, their actions say, "I am better than you!" However, Jeremiah calls this type person to task. He pronounces doom upon a person of such low character. The day will dawn wherein the unrighteous man will give account for all his actions.

Lord, we pray that Your mercies will fall upon us and bring to our attention all of our actions wherein we take advantage of others. Grant us wisdom to deal fairly and justly with neighbors. Let us endeavor to build a "home" and not just a house.

Reflections...

☐

JUNE 23

Luke 6:35 *But love your enemies, do good, and lend, hoping for nothing in return; and your reward will be great, and you will be sons of the Most High. For He is kind to the unthankful and evil.*

One of the landmark phrases used to describe Christianity is found in this verse: love your enemies. We have all heard this phrase and most of us have verbalized it on many occasions, especially if you have been a minister or a small group leader. We have all been taught from early childhood that we are supposed to "do good." Jesus did good during His life upon the earth and we are taught to emulate Him. However, few, if any, of us have ever taught the phrase immediately following: lend hoping for nothing in return.

So what is the big deal here? We teach loving your enemies and doing good, but why do we never teach (or practice) lending with no expectation or anything in return? It certainly is a point to ponder and I am persuaded that it is worthy of our study; otherwise, it would not have been placed in the scriptures. In fact, it is not just included in the scriptures; it is grouped with the two distinguishing landmark phrases used to define Christianity. First of all, lending and not expecting repayment is an awful lot like giving; they may, in fact, be twin brothers. Money is always a volatile subject when considered in the context of giving or using it for ministry. Jesus ran into a like scenario when He and the rich young ruler entered into the discussion about the young man's salvation (**Mark 10:17-31**). In many churches today, members get steaming mad when the minister preaches on the subject of tithing and giving offerings. So, we might conclude that the problem has been around for a long time.

This subject is complex and there is no way we will exhaustively discuss it in a short daily devotion. However, let's consider just a couple of possible factors that contribute to the discomfort of so many. First, we forget who the owner is. Most of us have assumed ownership of something that is not ours – the money that God has given us to manage. When I have a clear understanding that God is the owner and

348

I manage it for Him, I do not have a problem with giving (or lending with no expectation of return) when and where He directs. However, when I get ownership mixed up and think that I am the owner, I find it difficult to give and lend.

Secondly, money is tangible and quantitative. I can see it and touch it; it has physical properties. I can count it and place a definitive value upon it. I know when it increases and I can tell if it decreases. These are qualities that are not present when we are discussing "loving our enemies" and "doing good." When something is tangible and quantitative, it has accountability. I can say that I love my enemies and that I do good, but it is difficult if not impossible to prove. However, there is a paper trail with numbers that reveals my management of money.

Along with our loving our enemies and doing good, we are directed by Jesus to lend with no expectation of repayment. This is where the rubber meets the road. We can make excuses or we can follow the teaching of Jesus; the choice is up to us!

Reflections...

□

JUNE 24

Deuteronomy 14:22 *You shall surely tithe all of the produce from what you sow, which comes out of the field every year.* (NASB)

In the 14th chapter of Deuteronomy, Moses speaks to the people of Israel. The discourse is one of instruction. They were to be a peculiar group of people with customs that set them apart from others in that culture.

Even though some of the details might seem odd to us, the point is that they were to distinguish themselves from their counterparts. Their daily actions were to serve as a testimony to those with whom they associated. Their choice of serving God was to be obvious. Though some of the customs have changed, it is really not that much different in our current culture. We, likewise, are instructed to be different; we are to be a peculiar people (**1 Peter 2:9**). Our lifestyles should identify us as followers of Christ. The things we do as well as the things we do not do should speak our testimony to friends, family and associates.

One of the items of instruction that Moses gave was that of tithing the increase. Giving is one of the things that has not changed through the centuries. Consistently, the Bible teaches that giving is a part of living a life dedicated to God. Tithing is taught extensively throughout the Old Testament and Jesus Himself confirmed it in the New Testament (**Matthew 23:23**).

In our current society, giving is certainly counter to the culture. If you happen to be among those who tithe (give 10% of your increase), you are considered "odd" by the standards of our culture. In consideration of our culture, being labeled "odd" is a good thing! Giving is counter-cultural in this society that runs on the philosophy of "get all you can and can all you get!"

If you are not a tither, dare to be different. Be "odd" for a change. Why not do something that will make your friends consider you weird? Become a tither; consistently give 10% of your increase to God!

Reflections...

JUNE 25

Luke 12:31 *But seek the kingdom of God, and all these things shall be added to you.*

What do you seek in life? We can all come up with answers to that question. However, the answers we give most likely will not coincide with what we are actually doing with our lives. Have we become familiar with all the correct answers to the point that we spout them out without really considering the content of what we say? Have we deceived ourselves?

All of these questions are pertinent since we are talking about the eternal. However, many of us have indeed learned the correct answers. We know that we should seek the kingdom of God first. But, the question that looms over each of us is very simply, "Do we?" The answer is, "Probably not." Most of us become entangled with the cares and concerns of day-to-day living and lose sight of our main objective in life. Oh yeah, we think about it on Sunday morning in church, but we somehow forget it as we walk out the church doors. We fight the constant battle of making money; that touches practically every other phase of our lives. In fact, that has become the preoccupation of most of us in our current culture.

God's Word leads us in a direction that is diametrically opposite to what our culture teaches. Current society teaches us to make all the money we can and when we "get ahead," then we can relax and maybe participate in some charitable giving. However, the Bible teaches us to *"seek the kingdom of God, and all these things shall be added to us."* We have it all backwards!

The immediate question arises in one's mind as to what exactly is the kingdom of God and how can one seek it? The answer is basically the acknowledgment that God is King of Kings and Lord of Lords and that He alone is worthy since He is creator and owner of everything that ever was or ever will be. We come to this knowledge and literally experience it by becoming a part of the kingdom through a personal relationship with Jesus Christ. So in essence, we seek the kingdom by seeking God with child-like faith. Interestingly, Jesus taught, *"Suffer little children to come unto me, and forbid them not: for of such is the kingdom of God."* (**Luke 18:14**; **Matthew 19:14**; **Mark 10:14**)

God grant that we may set aside the teachings of our current culture of materialism and come to you as little children seeking You and Your kingdom.

Reflections...

☐

JUNE 26

Psalms 49:6-7 *Those who trust in their wealth And boast in the multitude of their riches, (7) None of them can by any means redeem his brother, Nor give to God a ransom for him.*

It has been said that money is fun, if you have some! The question follows, what can you buy with money? Many people in our society have sought to discover the answer to that question. No doubt, each of us can make a list that would extend further than the eye can see, but all the "stuff" on our lists will have one thing in common... all are temporary. The problem arises where the writer used the term *"those who trust in their wealth."* Those who trust in wealth or "love money" as stated in **1 Timothy 6:10** find a haunting disappointment. When we "trust" in wealth, we are literally placing our trust in something that is temporary. That is a losing battle!

Regardless of the amount of wealth one has, it will never buy peace and contentment. Money will not buy a wholesome home or a fulfilling marriage. Money will not purchase success for your children, but often does exactly the opposite. Regardless of how much one may boast of his riches, money will not buy health for his family members or friends. One cannot possess enough money to purchase salvation for his son or daughter. In short, trusting in money and wealth as your source of supply will always leave you wanting.

The person who puts his trust in wealth is like an impatient driver on a busy road. He darts in and out of traffic often cutting off drivers, tailgating on the bumpers of others and basically endangering all those around him. However, when the next traffic light turns red, he sits beside those whom he has just endangered and caused extreme anxiety. He has not gained anything with his treacherous driving. At the end of the day, he arrives at the same place about the same time as everyone else. The only way money can be invested to provide eternal returns is to invest it in eternal things, i.e. souls of men, the Word of God, and/or the good works of God (**Matthew 6:19-20**). Wealth can be used to buy "stuff" in this life; however, all that "stuff" is temporary and has no eternal value. Wealthy people are overtaken by the same sting of death as the underprivileged. When that appointed time arrives and the traffic light of life turns red, the wealthy cannot redeem himself nor can he redeem those he loves.

Jesus said, *"I am the way, the truth, and the life. No one comes to the Father except through Me."* We must trust only in Jesus Christ for redemption and eternal life. Lest you are deceived, remember, *"Those who trust in their wealth And boast in the multitude of their riches, None of them can by any means redeem his brother, Nor give to God a ransom for him."*

Reflections...

☐

JUNE 27

Ecclesiastes 5:15 *As he came from his mother's womb, naked shall he return, To go as he came; And he shall take nothing from his labor Which he may carry away in his hand.*

You may have seen the bumper sticker that says, "You will never get out of this world alive!" While it is somewhat comical, I am convinced that many are of the opinion that they are going to be the first to escape the appointment (**Hebrews 9:27**) that has their name etched in the book of the Grim Reaper. To some extent, we all think that we are going to continue to live.

The story is told of three preachers who died and made their way to the Pearly Gate whereupon they met St. Peter. Peter told them that he had a question that he must ask them prior to their entry. He asked, "What do you want people back on planet earth to say about you right now?" The first stated that he wished everyone gathered would say that he was a good husband, father and provider for his family. The second said that he was hoping that everyone would be saying that he was an excellent minister and soul-winner. Peter then asked the third preacher about his wish to which he replied, "I wish that as they are all gathered together someone will say 'Look, he is moving!'" We all hope that we will devise a way to defy our appointed destiny on earth ...death!

Our lifestyles are probably the greatest testimonies to this theory. Day in and day out, we dedicate ourselves to planning, working, earning, sacrificing and even hoarding as if we are going to live eternity right here on earth. Think about it for a moment: if we expended as much of our time and energy on eternal matters as we do on the earthly, our lives would be drastically different.

The wise man Solomon reminds us that we will be taking nothing with us when we leave this world, and yes, we are ALL going to make that appointment. In fact, that is one appointment to which we will not be late. We are going to take the same things with us that we brought when we came into the world. Randy Alcorn notes that there is one way by which we can benefit in eternity from our possessions here on earth. He stated, "You can't take it with you, but you can send it on ahead." By investing our earthly riches and wealth in eternal things (the souls of men, God's Word, and God's good work), we are laying up eternal treasures in heaven (**Matthew 6:20**). Let us all be reminded that we will honor and abide by the wisdom of Solomon: *"As he came from his mother's womb, naked shall he return, To go as he came; And he shall take nothing from his labor Which he may carry away in his hand."*

Reflections...

☐

JUNE 28

Proverbs 28:*25* *Greed causes fighting; trusting the LORD leads to prosperity.* (NLT)

The Bible refers to "greed" or "greedy" some 25 times. Lest there is a misunderstanding, let's look at a definition of the word greed: "**Greed** *is the inordinate desire to possess wealth, goods, or objects of abstract value with the intention to keep it for one's self, far beyond the dictates of basic survival and comfort.*" Greed causes people to forget their morals in lieu of some self-serving purpose. Greed causes harm to one's friends and family. Greed destroys relationships. Greed causes isolation. The list of detriments of greed is almost endless.

There are innumerable accounts of family relationships being torn apart in the pursuit of settlement of wills and estates. Many times loving and well-meaning parents leave an inheritance to their children only to end in disastrous fallout when greed enters the picture. A recently aired news report told the story of a man murdering his friend who refused to share his lottery winnings. Greed makes people do the unimaginable.

The opposite of greed is "trusting in the Lord." Genuinely trusting in the Lord builds character. Good character leads to respect by one's peers and associates. When one trusts in the Lord, he positions himself to win favor with others and consequently places himself in position to prosper. God can pour out His blessing on those who trust Him. This is not the case with the greedy that are always looking for the next opportunity to take advantage of someone.

Are your motives pure or are they fueled by greed? Greed causes fighting and confusion. Trusting in the Lord leads to prosperity!

Reflections...

□

JUNE 29

Proverbs 30:15 *The leech has two suckers that cry out, "More, more!" There are three things that are never satisfied - no, four that never say, "Enough!"* (NLT)

The original word in the Hebrew for leech is actually horseleech. Though there is some disagreement among Bible scholars on the entomology of the creature, all agree on one indisputable truth: the leech has only one objective and that is to literally suck the life out of its prey. Of course, the context of this verse is that the greedy will literally destroy the poor and take advantage of the needy in order to gain more wealth. In fact, it matters not who the victim may be; the greedy will lurch upon the victim for the purpose of self gain and will not give up until everything of value has literally been sucked out.

I recall during the days of my youth, growing up in South Georgia, most of us boys would slip off to the creek to swim (without parental permission of course). The black water of the creeks was the home of leeches in those days. The blood-sucking varmints would on occasion attach themselves on the skin of unsuspecting prey – boys. By the time someone noticed a leech on a comrade, the varmint was securely embedded and could not be removed with anything short of the neighbor's John Deere tractor. The objective of the leech was to suck all the blood out of its victim. He was not content to do otherwise nor would he change his course of action. Once a leech has attached himself to the skin, it is almost impossible to pull him off without the skin coming off also. We did, however, discover that by placing a burning match directly on the leech, he would turn lose. Of course, there was the risk of being burned a little, but the risk of the blood-sucking varmint setting up homestead was much greater.

Greedy people are like leeches. They show no concern for their victims and their objective is to suck away everything the victim has. All they know is more...more! They are never satisfied and they do not know contentment.

Father, we pray that You will remove any spirit of greed that may be in us. If it takes it, allow the Holy Spirit to apply the fire to make us uncomfortable to the point that we turn from life-depleting tactics and look to You for satisfaction and contentment.

Reflections...

JUNE 30

Zephaniah 1:18 *Your silver and gold will not save you on that day of the LORD's anger.* (NLT)

Daily devotions should lift one's spirit ...at least, most of the time that is the case. However, from time to time we need to be challenged by the Word. This is one of those days! I want to challenge you to take 5 minutes and read the first chapter of Zephaniah. Before you begin, I will tell you that this is not going to have you shouting from the rooftops. This is a pronouncement of God's judgment upon God's people (Judah) who had turned their backs on Him.

These people were caught up in worshiping false gods (idolatry). They had turned away from God and had become complacent saying outwardly that God would do no good or evil. In essence, it really makes no difference how we live our lives; God is not going to take action one way or another.

This judgment seems as though it could be applied to our current society in America. It is timely in practically every area of discussion. For instance, look at v. 13 from *The Message*: *"But just wait. They'll lose everything they have, money and house and land. They'll build a house and never move in. They'll plant vineyards and never taste the wine."* ... **Zephaniah 1:13**. This past weekend, I glanced over pages of foreclosures in our local newspaper. The United States economy is troubled. It is on the brink of bankruptcy and legislators show no concern. Their only priority is to get re-elected, not take care of the business at hand that cries out so loudly.

America has turned from God to worshiping our self-created idols ...our jobs, our houses, our automobiles, our vacations, our second homes, sporting events, and the list goes on... The root of this is that we basically worship ourselves and our selfish desires.

Not that I am a prophet of doom, but common sense tells us that our country cannot and will not continue on the same path we are currently traveling. When things begin to crumble, our silver and gold

362

will have no value. Our accomplishments will not save us from God's wrath.

Where is your trust? It is not too late for America to turn back to God. The impending question is, "WILL WE?"

Reflections...

Your thoughts and feedback are desired and welcomed. Send us an email today and let us know what you think:

realfinancialpeaceofmind@gmail.com

WEBSITE:
www.realfinancialpeaceofmind.com

Now that you are at this point of the journey, it is time to continue the challenge by moving on to the next step,

Financial PEACE of MIND from the WORD, Volume II...

FINANCIAL PEACE OF MIND FROM THE WORD

Volume II

(Available soon for online order or from your favorite bookstore.)